D1270123

BEYOND SURVIVAL

BEYOND SURVIVAL

Building on the Hard Times—
A POW's Inspiring Story

Gerald Coffee,
Captain, U.S. Navy [Ret.]

Coffee Enterprises, Inc.

Coffee Enterprises, Inc.
P.O. Box 8
Aiea, HI 96701-0008

Revised Edition 2005

The author gratefully acknowledges permission to quote from:
"Love Letters," by Edward Heyman and Victor Young,
copyright © 1945 Famous Music Corporation,
copyright renewed 1972 Famous Music Corporation,
15 Columbus Circle, New York, NY 10023.
International copyright secured. Made in USA.
All rights reserved. Used by permission.
"High Flight," by John Gillespie McGee.
Used by permission of Ferguson Publishing Company.

Library of Congress Cataloging-in-Publication Data

Coffee, Gerald L.
Beyond survival : building on the hard times—a POW's
inspiring story / by Gerald L. Coffee.
p.   cm.
1. Vietnamese Conflict, 1961–1975—Prisoners and Prisons,
Vietnamese.   2. Vietnamese Conflict, 1961–1975—Personal narratives,
American.   3. Prisoners of war—United States—Psychology—Case
studies.   4. Prisoners of war—Vietnam—Psychology—Case studies.
5. Adjustment (Psychology)—Case studies.   6. Coffee, Gerald L.
I. Title.
DS559.4.C63   1989   89-32916 CIP
959.704'37—dc20

6   7   8   9   10

ISBN 978-0-9745676-0-0

This book is dedicated to my dear family whose love and faith sustained me, and to all families touched by the Vietnam war, and by America's war against terrorism.

May it promote healing for all that has been lost, and appreciation for all that has been gained.

Foreword

The Vietnam war divided and compartmentalized society, often obscuring those elements of commonality by which we define ourselves as family, be it our immediate family, our national family, or our family of man. Although I dedicate this book lovingly to my immediate family, the writing has caused me to see beyond my narrow definition of family to include those with whom I served, those for whom I served, and even those I served against.

The perspective of nearly two decades has expanded my appreciation for the human side of the story: the personal lives and experiences of captives and captors alike, and the lives of the people with whom they are connected. These are the stories I have told in this book. In this more personal context, perspective and resolution come easier. It also sharpens our sense of urgency to learn and do better in the future.

Contents

1

I Surrender

Suddenly what I thought could only happen to the other guy became my reality. No matter how confident we are, none of us is exempt from trauma, from loss, from our world changing instantly without provocation or warning. Even while we cling to the hope that life as we have known it will sustain us, we can begin to find a depth of ourselves we didn't know existed. Imperceptibly at first, the emptiness and panic begin to be soothed by the stranger within. That stranger is our closest friend.

"Hi-dee-ho and away we go! Speedboat rides from the end of the Santa Cruz pier. Thrills and chills! Go skimming across the surface of beautiful Monterey Bay. Hi-dee-ho and away. . . ."

The loudspeaker droned on from the end of the pier as it did every hour or so, the mechanical spiel hardly varying. It blended with the more distant din of the boardwalk: the calliope tones of the old carousel, the roar-scream-roar-scream rhythm of the Big Dipper, which itself sometimes drowned out the belly laughs of the teetering mechanical clown over the Fun House door. The August sun was hot and the air was warm with the smell of ocean and taffy and baby-oiled bodies languishing on the beach beyond. So familiar.

The scorching heat of the San Joaquin Valley and the demands of summer jobs were so distant, as the tiny tongues of water lapped gently around my face. We floated limply side by side just beyond the break of friendly summer waves. Our breathing had eased after we'd wrestled and rolled playfully beneath the water's sun-flecked surface. My eyes were closed; I just let the sound and taste and feel of it all sink in. I smiled contentedly as I thought of her there near me.

Suddenly, as if that thought had distracted her from her own contentment, she rolled toward me, and with a playful chirp thrust my face beneath the water. I twisted away from the pressure of her hand and exhaled hard through my nose. There beneath me in the crystalline water was her lithe body swimming strongly down and then away. She was a water creature, this sweetheart of mine, and the silvery bubbles streamed up and behind from her dark hair like tiny pearls that had just been born there.

I gulped air and dove. I kicked hard after her through the colder, bluer water. Ahead of me she merged with and parted from the shifting prisms of sunlight as if she and the sun and the sea were one, then separate, then one again. Suddenly, in one swift motion, she stopped and turned and challenged, suspended motionless for an instant in her element. A few shining pearls were still breaking free, and she was smiling as I collided with her middle, wrapped my arms around her waist and thighs, and rolled her backward. Then again, as we had done in countless rivers and lakes and salty summer bays, we tumbled and rolled together; wriggling free from one grip, parrying another, holding tightly to an ankle or arm for a moment, then thrusting away defensively. The shivery blue of the deeper water, the swirling bubbles and sparkling rays of light, the firmness of her twisting body—all a sensual kaleidoscope of color and touch as in our sham struggle we inched toward the water's surface and the breaths we knew we would soon need.

I burst through the surface before she did and held her tightly with my legs for an extra second or two. She went limp; a sympathy tactic. As I released the pressure, her retaliation was explosive. The water she slapped into my face stung my eyes. "Rat!" she yelped, and again she dove, the bare parts of her tanned body glistening from the sun. She had an armlock on my foot now and was kicking hard straight down, trying to pull me under. I doubled forward to pry my foot from her grasp. But my right arm wouldn't move. And then she was gone.

The water beneath me was still deep blue, with fragments of sunlight dancing aimlessly from above. But she was gone. The pressure on my foot continued, however . . . from the nylon shroud lines tangled around my boot. My boot . . . ? Shroud lines . . . ? They were stark in their whiteness as they trailed off into the deep where, I was now aware, the dim shape of my parachute drifted downward. The nylon tentacles and undulating skirts of the canopy reminded me of a monster jellyfish trying to envelop me. What fantasy! This whole thing is fantasy! Where is Bea? Where did she swim to?

I lifted my stinging face from the water. The surface was gentle, the sun still high, but the rest . . . The calmness around me was eerie. What the hell was going on here? I floated higher now and vertically, but the pull on my foot continued to threaten, even with the flotation gear that encircled my torso.

Again I doubled forward, face in the water. God, it stung like fire now. I strained toward the tangle around my foot. Still my right arm wouldn't move. No pain. It simply dangled limp, ignoring my command to help out my other hand in freeing my foot. What's going on? My arm's broken, my face stings. What happened? Where am I?

Concentrating very hard, I finally freed my foot from the sinking chute. Several shroud lines had drifted loosely around my other leg by now, but in the space of one more breath, I was able to extricate myself from the deadly weight that had done in many an exhausted Navy pilot after all else had gone well.

Slowly I realized I was floating in the water with my parachute. Had I ejected from my plane? I couldn't remember. It was all so fuzzy. Green, sloping hills met the water ahead of me and behind me at some distance. I seemed to be in a very calm bay. It was absolutely silent at first, but then I was aware of the low rumble of a jet aircraft rocketing across and away from me, somewhere far in the distance. High overhead a thin trail of white smoke curved from the direction of the hills and ended in a darker cloud, all drifting slowly, benignly, out to sea.

No speedboat rides! No Fun-House clown or summer smells! Bea! Where had she gone? A tepid little breeze ruffled the water around me. Still; quiet.

My mind felt numb. Then vague reminiscences of the Sunday comics passed through it: Dick Tracy or Lois Lane coming to after being knocked out by the bad guy. *What happened? Where am I?* My arm floated limply before me. My face and neck were stinging like mad. I squeezed my eyes shut, straining to remember. Here I was in the water, in my flight gear and helmet. That was *my* parachute drifting in the depths below me. The first few shards of recall stabbed painfully as I focused harder, desperately seeking comprehension of my plight. A reconnaissance mission planned and approved. It was coming back now. . . .

Bob and I had manned our aircraft for the last launch of the day. We had found our way across the flight deck of the USS *Kitty Hawk,* stepping around tie-down chains and ducking under wings, jibing lightly about how much the other would spend on shopping in Hong Kong. The *Hawk* would be heading that way immediately after our 1600 recovery. Soon that same flight deck had been engulfed in an awesome symphony of sound and motion: an attack carrier's launch and recovery cycle. The jet engines from four dozen fighter and attack planes—all closely bunched toward the stern—screamed discordantly, gulping in tons of humid air even in idle. The hot exhaust from their tail pipes shot out across the catwalks at deck's edge. Their collective force alone could have powered the leviathan runway through the water at several knots. My own J-79 engines had checked out fine, their eagerness reflected in the quivering gauges before me. Pretaxi check had been complete, wings "spread and lock" to go. Bob readied the navigation and reconnaissance systems in his own cockpit aft of mine. This, too, had all been so familiar: countless evolutions from the carrier decks in the Atlantic and Pacific, Caribbean and Mediterranean; the same choreography—yellow-shirted plane directors; green- and red-shirted maintenance and ordnance personnel; sophisticated warbirds, wings still folded vertically to conserve deck space, lumbering close aboard into position behind the sturdy jet-blast deflectors aft of each catapult, then straddling the steaming cats themselves.

Suddenly the goggled face of my plane captain had disappeared from the side of my cockpit and was replaced by that of my squadron mate, Lieutenant Bob Renner. I knew he had just landed two cycles ago and had been debriefing his film with the Air Intelligence guys from the attack squadrons. "Beef" (he was husky) put his face close to my left ear and shouted above the din, "Jerry, the A-6 guys need to do some target planning while we're in port. They need coverage of these areas just northwest of Vinh City." He had thrust a folded map in front of me, several areas squared off and bisected by a dog-leg flight line—all drawn hastily with a green marking pen. "Your flight is the last chance to get what they need. Can you do it?" My own mission was to get verticals and obliques of the seemingly indestructible Than Hoa Bridge, and more verticals of military and supply areas up the river to the west. Plenty of extra time and fuel.

Instinctively I flashed him a "thumbs-up." "No sweat, Beef. Tell 'em it's as good as got!" As I clipped the map beneath my own on the kneeboard strapped to my right thigh, I recalled—just for an instant—the map of that same area northwest of Vinh that I'd seen down in the briefing room. It was peppered with little red and white pins, red designating confirmed triple-A (antiaircraft artillery) sites, white the sites where they were only suspected. Okay, Coffee, I said to myself. Fly higher, faster, and "jink"—a lot. Make it hard for 'em to track you with their guns.

I had been looking forward to the flight in any case, but now, with this new challenge, my anticipation was heightened all the more. This would be only my second flight over North Vietnam. Having joined the squadron in early January, I had flown all of my previous missions over South Vietnam or Laos. President Johnson had extended the holiday cease-fire of late '65 through January as a gesture of goodwill to entice the North Vietnamese to the negotiating table, a recurring tactic that through the next several years would prove to be self-defeating. But on the first of February, there having been no conciliatory response from the Communists, we started hammering parts of the North again.

My missions over South Vietnam had been productive but uneventful. I had seen flak only twice but never felt threatened. At the prospect of actually meeting resistance on this mission, my adrenal glands were already pumping a little more than usual. I noted this while carefully taxiing the big sleek Vigilante onto the starboard bow catapult, making my last few checks, and saluting my readiness to the animated Catapult Officer on the deck below me. I thrilled again at the near instantaneous surge and sharp kick of the cat shot propelling my thirty tons of warplane to 170 miles per hour in less than three seconds. It was never "routine."

"We're on our way, Robert," I had said to Bob rather rhetorically. I eased the nose up into a gradually climbing turn as the early afternoon sun slowly swept its patchwork of shadow and light from one side of the cockpit to the other.

"Roger, Boss! Take up heading three five zero. Our rendezvous with Lion Eleven is at three four zero degrees, twenty miles, angels eighteen."

God, it was a sparkler of a day. The deep shining blue of the Tonkin Gulf seemed to intensify the more ethereal blue of the Southeast Asian sky. At the western horizon, where the blues would otherwise have met, ran the variegated green and brown ribbon of the North Vietnam coast. With the exception of a few low puffy clouds far to the north near China, the sky was absolutely clear. It stretched on forever. Had the earth been flat, I mused, I could have seen beyond that seemingly benign coastline to Laos, Thailand, Burma, India, perhaps across the Middle Eastern countries to the Red Sea and the eastern Mediterranean, where I had flown three or four years before on similar crystalline days and conjectured on my ability to see the Tonkin Gulf to the east . . . if the earth were flat.

I had established a left-turn, three-mile orbit at our rendezvous point. Scanning back over my shoulder toward the ship, I picked up our escort plane visually. The F-4 Phantom jet had been launched just after us and was now climbing toward the rendezvous point. All reconnaissance planes were escorted by an armed fighter in case it should be attacked from the air. (It was also operationally prudent to fly over enemy territory in flights of two or more so that one pilot could account for the fate of the other should trouble arise.)

Since the Phantom's wings were level, I knew the pilot was still heading for the prearranged electronic point in the sky.

"Lion Eleven, Green River Two. We're at your ten o'clock, slightly higher."

"Roger, Greenie Two . . . I've got you."

The instant the pilot of Lion Eleven made visual contact, he altered his course to turn inside my turn but adjusting his angle of bank to just a little less than my own standard thirty degrees of bank for rendezvous. This would make his turn radius slightly greater than mine, causing him to move closer and closer to me on the inside of the circle while adjusting his throttle in tiny increments to match his own airspeed to mine.

"Okay, Bob, he's as good as aboard. Let's check in on Strike Freq."

"Rog!"

The VHF radio clicked through several bands of static, a fraction of another airborne conversation, and then stabilized on the check-in report of a flight of A-6 Intruders from the *Hawk*'s all-weather attack squadron. When they were finished, Bob checked us in.

"Master Strike, this is Green River Two with escort at rendezvous. Over!"

"Roger, Green River Two. Contact! You're cleared on course. Strangle!"

"Roger. Out!"

I noted on my instrument panel the termination of the tiny blinking red light denoting the pulse of our IFF (Identification Friend or Foe) radar beacon as Bob "strangled our parrot," a code phrase for securing the beacon. No use giving the Vietnamese search radar monitors a bigger and more defined blip on their scopes than necessary.

By now Lion Eleven had slid smoothly out of his own radius of turn, hesitated briefly just off my port wing, and crossed under to my starboard side. There he took up a comfortable cruise position on the outside of the turn and slightly aft.

As my compass pointer swung to a heading of two nine zero degrees,

I eased my wings level. Lion Eleven matched me. Ahead, the tranquil coast stretched out on either side. At the Than Hoa River delta, the overall S-curve of the entire Vietnam coast ran close to true north and south. There, just a small course correction to my left and now at a slant range of about twenty-five miles lay our first reconnaissance target. I repositioned the folded map on my kneeboard to put west at the top, matching the scheme of the world ahead of me.

I noted the flight line drawn on the other map clipped below this one. There had been no time to brief my escort pilot on the additional requirement. Mission security and radio discipline precluded informing him now. I knew he would wonder what the hell was going on when I deviated from our prebriefed flight plan, but he'd stick with me. That was his mission. I'd explain later over a cup of coffee in the Ready Room. Hell, I had thought magnanimously, I'll buy him a drink at the Peninsula's bar our first afternoon in Hong Kong.

The mission went like clockwork. Since there had been hardly any cloud cover over the lower half of North Vietnam, I had bracketed the husky steel and concrete bridge the way I had taught so many others as a recce training instructor in Florida. The actual targets for the attack boys had been less distinct, but I had flown the line and was sure of the coverage from my panoramic horizon-to-horizon camera. Although I had seen no flak, I had jinked frequently during the entire time I was over land, changing directions slightly with high G-turns often enough to keep any gunners from tracking me. Then, heading back toward the coast, my F-4 Phantom fighter escort spewing black smoke as he tried to catch up, I felt it. WHUMP! Hit!

It happened so fast—no flak or tracers, no warning! After the hit somewhere back in the aft part of the plane, I had felt a light vibration followed by the illumination of my master warning light. Uh-oh! Red hydraulic #1 light ON. Red hydraulic #2 light ON. Red hydraulic utility light ON. I pushed the throttles forward now to afterburner to get maximum speed toward the relative safety of the Gulf. Thu-thump. The burners lit off and, with a light fuel load remaining, the effect of their thrust was multiplied, pushing me back against the contour of my ejection seat as the Vigilante shot forward and slightly upward.

"Hit! I think we just took a hit!" I knew damn well we'd taken a hit, but years of being Top Gun-cool had tempered the alarm in my voice. Bob had heard my radio transmission and would be giving me a heading back toward the ship. The vibration had become heavier and the control stick sluggish. Still accelerating, the plane suddenly rolled to the left.

Control stick stiff—no effect. Jammed right rudder pedal. Left roll stopped but then immediate right roll. Left rudder—no effect.

Instinctively I reached for the yellow T-handle protruding from the side panel of the console near my right knee. I yanked it out sharply and felt the clunk of the two-in-one emergency generator and hydraulic pump extending into the wind stream from the starboard side of the fuselage. The wind-driven turbine pump should have regained the hydraulic pressure to my essential flight controls. Still no effect. Whatever had hit us must have severed both flight-control hydraulic lines, spilling all the precious fluid. Even with the emergency pump extended, with no fluid, there was no pressure. Still rolling, I tried to muscle the control stick into effectiveness.

Nothing! No control! Sky—land—sky—land—ocean. The nose had dropped now and we had picked up more speed. "Mayday! Mayday! Mayday!" Rolling rapidly! Speed 680! Red lights flashing! No more sky ahead, only the shimmering blue gulf spinning in front like a propeller. Christ! "Eject, Bob! Eject! Eject! Eject!"

I noticed that the water all around me was green now, bright chartreuse green. My dye-marker had come loose from its pocket on my torso harness. That should certainly make my position more visible from the air? The air! I scanned the ocean horizon to my right and there, as if materialized by my thought of rescue from the air, was an old UF Albatross sea-rescue plane. He was heading north just a couple of miles out to sea. Hey, fella, I know you must be looking for me! Here I am! Here I am!

Instinctively, I pulled my day/night signal flare from its pocket. The ring on the "day" end of the flare had to be snapped down hard over the edge of the tubular flare itself. This would break the seal so the ring could be pulled smartly away, igniting the flare and causing thick, bright orange smoke to billow forth. It could be seen for miles. The lumbering Albatross, my rescuer, droned on.

I struggled with the ring on the flare. I couldn't hold onto the flare and also snap the ring down with only one hand. My right arm and hand just refused to participate. The seaplane continued northward, expanding the distance between us. Frantically, I tried to smack the ring of the flare against the hard surface of my helmet but just couldn't get the right angle. "Turn around!" I shouted. "Over here!" He was barely a speck above the horizon now. With a final desperate bash against my helmet, the flare flipped from my hand, plopped into the water, and sank.

The loss of the flare caught me off guard. I had ignited flares a dozen times in training exercises, and once for real after ejecting from a crippled jet on a training mission over southern Georgia. Yet, throw in one variable—my disabled arm—and it was a whole new ballgame. Fixing upon the spot in the sky where the Albatross had disappeared, I suppressed my rising panic. I inventoried my remaining options, touching the pocket of my torso harness where each flare was stowed. I had my signal mirror and my spring-activated pencil flare gun, either of which could be operated with one hand the instant I caught sight of the next rescue craft. Somehow, even in this confused state of mind, I immediately realized that just because my primary and most natural course of action had been thwarted, I had resisted the paralysis of anger or shock and moved on to other possibilities. This was a principle inculcated by training and one that would serve me well in the immediate future.

The eerie stillness of both water and air enhanced the dreamlike aspects of my predicament. Indeed, as if echoing back out of some sheet-soaking nightmare came my urgent call—ordering yet also imploring: "Eject, Bob! Eject! Eject!"

Had he made it out of our doomed Vigilante too? Had the interconnect system between my ejection seat and his worked? I visualized the initiation of my own ejection activating the process of each little cartridge firing properly in series sending hot gases through the winding, bending lines to ignite the next cartridge, and the next. One caused the entire seat to pre-position for ejection, another activated the complex arm and leg restraining system, another activated a larger charge that blew the heavy cockpit canopy open and away, and finally the cartridge that activated the biggy—the seat rocket itself—propelling seat and parachute and Bob up and out of the plane, all a split-second before the same ingenious sequence had propelled my own seat out. A similar pyromechanical system would then deploy the drogue chute, braking seat and man to a speed allowing safe opening of the main chute without shredding, then a charge to instantly inflate the rubber bladders in the seat back, thereby popping the airman out and away from the seat to avoid entanglement between seat and chute. Finally, a barometrically activated cartridge deploying the main chute drogue and then the main itself.

All of this I reviewed in a few seconds almost as a backdrop for my immediate concern: Where was Bob?

SPWAT-TING! Something smacked the water a few yards away. SPLOCK! Off to the seaward. SPLAT! SPLAT! ZINNNG! The rippled surface exploded in two tall geysers ahead of me, and zinging sounds trailed off to my right. Instinctively, I twisted myself to the left, toward the shore. The puffs of blue-gray smoke hovered in the still air above the approaching boat. Now more flashes and smoke off to the right: another boat. THWACK! THWAP! THWAP! The spray flew around me. TZNNNG! TZINNNG! More flashes from the left: still another boat. Bullets whined above my head and fell into the water all around me, some skipping off the surface and going farther out to sea. Four boats were coming toward me, all very low in the water, each with a crowd of semiuniformed gunners. My instant picture was of rag-tag khaki and greenish clothing, some steel helmets, some pith helmets with cam-ouflage material; they were probably mostly militia.

The muzzles of their rifles and automatic weapons were ablaze and the smoke was incredibly thick. The air and water around me erupted with the deadly barrage so I could hardly tell the difference between the two. I couldn't believe that I, too, wasn't already riddled with bullets. I could feel their impact in the water, vibrating through my body. I had a sudden image of my own red blood swirling together with the bright green of the dye around me in wavy, concentric patterns.

In another agonizing instant, the reality of my situation crystallized: This wasn't a fuzzy dream. My aircraft had been hit. I had ejected but I was still alive, miraculously alive. Yet, how could I be? My plane had been plummeting into the Tonkin Gulf at just less than the speed of sound. Although more than eight years of military flying had prepared me to face a myriad of "what ifs" such as actually ejecting from a tumbling aircraft, my post-ejection actions must have been as much intuitive as trained.

Finally, I caught a glimpse of Bob floating low in the water between me and the boats. He was surprisingly close by, only a hundred yards or so away. He seemed to be inflating his tiny rubber raft as plumes of white water bracketed his position as well. Even if he had been conscious the whole time, he appeared to be too far away to have assisted me.

Yes, it had to have been almost instinctive: Somehow I had removed my oxygen mask and thereby hadn't suffocated. I had released the clips on my parachute harness, thereby—except for the entangled shroud lines that had almost done me in—allowing it to sink harmlessly away. And I had pulled the toggles on the CO_2 cartridges that had inflated my flotation gear. All the training and practice had left indelible patterns in my subconscious, and had assured my survival—even while uncon-scious and incapacitated. The survival instinct!

Now, could I evade? Could I keep from being captured? Could I resist? It was clear that to resist would be crazy. Obviously I couldn't outswim the boats even though they appeared to be no more than crude dug-outs, powered by single oarsmen sculling astern. With my arm apparently broken, weighted by the survival gear in the pockets of my torso harness and cutaway G-suit, and with the bulky flotation gear up under my arms, I could barely thrash away from them.

I was strangely oblivious to the threat of being torn to shreds by the continuing hail of lead. Just the thought of resisting drew my hands to the .38 pistol holstered firmly to the left breast of my harness. Grandpa had carried it for years as a deputy sheriff and had solemnly presented it to me before I left. "I've never once had to use this, son [he was very proud of that], and I hope and pray you won't have to either." He and I had been especially close when I was just little.

Every summer he'd put me to work with his migrant work crew in the peach orchards of the San Joaquin Valley. Sometimes I rode with him on his "ditch tender" rounds, scheduling irrigation water for the neighboring farmers. He'd talk politics with his cronies at each stop, and usually end up with "I tell ya the gov'ment's goin' to hell in a handbasket and we're gonna rue the day! You and I might not live to see it, but I feel sorry for this little kid here" as he poked the chewed-up end of his cigar in my direction. Is this what you had in mind, Grandpa? As if preprogrammed but still with a pang of regret, I slipped the steel-blue weapon from its leather holster and released it into the water. Better the deep than them, Grandpa. I watched it swirl down and down; it seemed to take forever. I still had that final image in my fuzzy consciousness as I realized the shooting had stopped.

The enveloping sound of the shooting had been replaced by the cacophony of words and shrieks in a language I realized I'd never heard before but might soon come to know well.

Regaining consciousness to find myself injured, confused, and so totally out of my element had been bad enough. But now, confronted by this hostile flotilla of natives, I felt like I'd been transported into some sinister world from which I might never return. Had I been able to think clearly, I would undoubtedly have felt the first pangs of fear, maybe even terror.

I was startled to realize how quickly they had drawn so near; they were only a few yards away now. Still they shouted excitedly, either to one another or at me; I couldn't tell which, and it would have mattered little even if I could. I just stared back into a couple of dozen pairs of eyes, all glaring widely above the muzzles of their rifles and machine guns.

For the first time now, I confronted my enemy face to face, an enemy that until now had been an abstract collage of Viet Cong, headlines of war, the Ho Chi Minh Trail, green jungle tops, road junctions on maps, and toy sampans on counterpane mirrors below. Now he had come alive and was real. These were men and boys of flesh and blood making hostile animal noises and gestures at me.

I felt more confused than ever. War was supposed to be clean—mechanical and technical, soldier versus soldier, rocket against tank, missile against plane, all crisp and decisive. Instead, I felt like some helpless cornered prey about to be pounced upon by a pack of savage animals as soon as they had sniffed out my fear.

Suddenly they were as hushed as the air itself as they contemplated *their* enemy. Had I until now been as abstract to them as they had been to me?

In how many movies, books, and dramas had I seen this first-time confrontation between foes, one with the drop on the other? How many times had I seen the intensity of their calculation: To kill or to spare? Revenge or forgiveness? Cruel bravado or compassion? What were the factors in their process now? The expression on my face? The emotion in my eyes? Would civility overcome the darkest animal instincts in us all, the hatred that I could see clearly in their eyes? But it was not hatred alone. Their eyes also reflected the same excited curiosity, and even some of the fear that I knew must be clearly evident in my own. Would I look into those eyes and kill if I had the upper hand? Could I?

In that instant of transfixion, we seemed to distill—they and I—all the centuries of human conflict of which we were now a part.

In a flash the deadly muzzle of an AK-47 automatic rifle erupted in blue flame and the water exploded in my face. This time the impact through my body was heavy and breathtaking. I was sure I had been shot. Two more shots in rapid succession. I felt the stunning CRACK! on my helmet as my head was knocked backward and a huge piercing strobe light seemed to bleach my brain. The image of the swirling blood and dye flashed hot across my mind. There she was again swimming down through the water, down and away, eluding the crimson and green swirls, down, down into the deeper blue—lending her own flowing grace to the thinning specks of sunlight and the spiral of silvery bubbles from her hair. The tiny silvery bubbles spiraling up around me were all that remained. Oh, God, Baby, I'm so sorry! I'm so sorry!

When I opened my eyes my left arm was extended out of the water and over my head. "Don't shoot! I surrender!"

2

The Enemy's Other Face

The absolute tests are those we face alone, without the support of others who believe as we do. There the beliefs we hold most dear are challenged—some to be strengthened, some to be tempered, others to be abandoned—but all to be examined. From deep within we claim the values that we know to be our own. Those are the ones by which we are willing to live or die.

My eyes opened and I was wide awake. I sensed my surroundings more than I could see them—dark, dingy, and unfamiliar—so I closed my eyes and thought for the next five minutes or so. The sounds and smells were familiar, from many, many years past; they were almost comforting. How many hours had I played and daydreamed in the hayloft of our old barn on the ranch, sharing the lives of my barnyard friends? Never before had that era of my life seemed so distant as now.

The scent of the fresh straw on which I was lying was very strong. I could hear more straw being sorted softly and munched by a nearby animal: a cow, my nose told me. I could feel a light chill in the musty air—unmistakably early morning. I heard two low voices nearby; one was that of my guard of the previous day, the other of a stranger. They were discussing who knows what. Their conversation was interrupted occasionally by the guttural bubbling of the water pipe they shared. The sweet, exotic smell of the opium mingled with the barnyard smells around me. The strange pipe sound seemed almost an extension of the conversation itself. I had decided by now that when spoken without anger, the Vietnamese language had a kind of careless, bubbly rhythm—like coffee perking. Coffee perking! God, would I love to have a cup of hot coffee!

Again my eyes opened. This time as I blinked, the dried sweat at the corners of my eyes cracked loose and began to sting again, like the day before when it was fresh.

I was aware of the roof now, close above me; the low side of what appeared to be a fairly large lean-to structure, maybe a stable. It was loosely thatched, and many of the sisal ties that held the dark, moldy straw to the crooked stick frame had rotted loose, dangling down in clumps and strands like grimy little stalactites. The thick bamboo uprights of the shed were polished to a dark patina from the rubbing of the tethered animals around me. Sure enough, a light brown cow—bony but content—was cudding away just a few feet from me, her breath making little steam puffs from black nostrils. I hadn't thought the air to be that cold, even though I had awakened covered only by the combat fatigues I'd been shot down in and was curled into a fetal S to ward off the chill.

A water buffalo stood near the cow in resigned stillness as three or four reddish chickens clucked and scratched aimlessly about its feet. A couple of scrawny milk goats tethered near the broad, open entrance seemed to complete my morning menagerie. As I lay there, quietly taking it all in, I was struck by the strange, dreamlike quality of the scene, the universal simplicity and serenity of the animals, the low bubbling of the opium pipe nearby, the unique mixture of smells, and finally, the incongruity of my own presence within it all, plucked suddenly from my familiar, professional environment and plopped down here in the middle of Southeast Asia among people we've been bombing and strafing. I've been captured by them. I am a Prisoner of War. I moved my head slowly from side to side, incredulous at my plight. God, I thought, I guess it doesn't always happen to the other guy. I think I'm going to need you a lot, Lord. Please stay with me.

I started to raise myself up on one elbow and tried, without much success, to repress the exclamation of pain. The water buffalo swung his stately head in my direction for a cursory check before raising its nostrils to test the dampness in the awakening air. My entire body seemed to beg: Don't move me again, please! My right arm and shoulder ached more than the rest. I couldn't remember ever feeling so sore and stiff in my life. How long had I not moved? Every joint in my body seemed to be fused in place to hold me mercifully still, as if in a body cast. Not surprising, I thought, since every limb and muscle had been wrenched—some past their limit—in that tumbling, plummeting ejection. Not to mention the subsequent pummeling at the hands of those first villagers as I had run their impromptu gauntlet up from the beach to the toolshed that had been my first "cell."

How long had it been now? Three days? Four? I wasn't at all sure. I wasn't even sure how long I had just slept. I seemed to recall arriving here at my stable the previous evening, but it could have been the one before that. The effect of having taken such a blow and being unconscious for a time was taking a long time to wear off.

My neck and both forearms were blistered crimson, and I imagined my face looked the same. I wondered, could I have been burned by the pyrotechnic charges in the ejection system? We had never been briefed on that as a hazard. Or had the plane exploded at the moment of ejection? So much for wishing I had delayed the ejection just long enough to get out over the Gulf, closer to our rescue forces.

Gradually, I groaned my way up to one elbow and then to a tenuous sitting position, leaning stiffly against the plaited bamboo that formed the back boundary of my little straw burrow. My grunts and expletives distracted the cow and the goats from their chewing. They stared curiously at their strange stable mate.

The morning-twilight space between the top of the rickety mat walls and the scalloped eaves above revealed the pinkish silhouettes of thatched ridges and gables of other huts. As we had approached the hamlet in the dusk of the previous evening (or whatever evening it had been), the variegated clumps of huts and trees and foliage had appeared as a homey little island in a serene pond of gray-green paddies—all crisscrossed by a network of levees like the one on which we had wended our way. Once inside the village, however, it had become a warren of twisting footpaths, prickly hedges, smelly little ditches, vegetable patches, and a maze of plaited walls and fences—all partly obscured by dense clumps of bamboo and shrubbery. In the fading light it had all looked so peaceful, yet quietly ominous. The air was pervaded by the salty, pungent odor of *nuoc-mam,* the fermenting sauce stored in crocks in every house and used in varying degrees to spice up food. I would come to know it as possibly the most memorable sensory characteristic of Southeast Asia, a lifelong reminder of my experience there. After the survival gear on my torso harness and in the pockets of my G-suit, my boots had been the next thing taken from me. As we had continued on through the hamlet, the duck and chicken droppings that squished between my bare toes were all that connected the scene to reality.

The straw beneath me was matted now into the shape of my sleeping form. It was surprisingly well defined, I thought; my sleep should have been fitful. My mind certainly had been alternatively embracing the hope of a terrible nightmare, and then trying to reject the all-too-evident reality. By now, the chronology of my final flight from the *Kitty Hawk* was clear: The struggle to control my disabled plane, the high speed, topsy-turvy ejection, the mad confusion of my capture, the unwitting strafing attack by our own A-1 Skyraiders as we scurried back to the shore as fast as the scrawny oarsman could propel us. And finally, the nagging uncertainty of Bob's fate.

We hadn't been together all that long. He had recently completed the transition syllabus in the training squadron where I had been an instructor for three years. I had taught him and others—pilots and bombardier-navigators—to know and operate the aircraft systems, and the flight tactics of the aerial reconnaissance mission. As I had rotated back to sea duty, I was pleased we had been paired up as a crew. Bob was good, and our Trans-Pac flight of a Vigilante from central Florida to Japan and finally aboard the *Kitty Hawk* confirmed his skills. Our three-day layover in Atsugi, Japan—*hotsi* baths and massages, and liberty time with our new squadron mates—had drawn us closer. His young wife, Pat, a schoolteacher, and Bea were probably in touch right now, sharing the uncertainty of their husbands' fates, and supporting one another as much as possible.

How many times had I relived it these past few days, that brief glimpse of Bob, alive in the water and closer than I to the shoreline and the approaching boats? Obviously he, too, had cheated the odds for surviving an ejection so far outside the accepted speed and stability parameters of the system. But had he survived the hairtrigger contempt of our captors? The straffing attack? Had his life been spared as miraculously as mine from the deadly swarms of 20mm slugs rained down upon us by the planes of our RESCAP (Rescue Air Patrol)? God, he was my responsibility! Have I gotten him killed? What could I have done differently? What emergency procedure or flight tactic might have saved us? God, please let Bob be alive. Please be with him, wherever he is.

I sat there in the half-light of the awakening stable, mentally wringing my hands and gnashing my teeth imagining all the things I might have done differently to avoid my present predicament and the apparent loss of my friend. The possibilities were endless.

Had I continued to harbor this line of thought, I would have become a member of a deadly club; a few POWs I would come to know who assumed personal blame for the loss of one or more crewmen in their aircraft. And with the self-blame would come a consuming guilt. In the coming years, I would find enough more immediate reasons for guilt without laying this on myself as well.

Somehow I realized, even at this very early stage, that what had happened was well within the range of risk we had all embraced. I was certain that had our positions been reversed, with Bob in command of the aircraft and responsible for our fate, he too would have accepted the addition to our mission with a positive nod and a thumbs-up just as I had. I struggled to the conclusion that if I was to maintain faith in myself to survive this ordeal—the ramifications of which I could not yet begin to fathom—I must learn to keep events in perspective and to keep the past behind me.

The crispness of the morning air around my upright body seemed to sharpen my recollections, subordinating for the moment at least my awareness of the painful stiffness of my calcified body.

Now, I couldn't seem to erase the scene from my mind. Our guys had been relentless in their attack, hoping, I'm sure, to keep the boats from reaching us farther out in the Gulf, where the wreckage probably had been and where they thought we would be as well.

I had pulled myself up along the shallow gunwale of the boat watching the A-1 Sky Raider aircraft roll in pass after pass, their bullets raining down. White plumes of water walked their way across our bow and then close aboard the stern. My captors never flinched, and returned the fire with their own weapons. The acrid smell of cordite stung my nostrils.

I couldn't imagine how the boat I was in made it safely to shore. The instant the bow had touched the sandy beach, we jumped into the shallow surf and ran toward the safety of the berm on the far side of the beach. The next strafing attack caught us halfway. With my bright yellow flotation gear left in the boat, there was nothing to differentiate me from the enemy. I scrambled like hell just as they did.

As others were frantically half dragging, half pushing me across the beach between wooden fishing boats and fan-shaped nets spread to dry, two or three went down around us. The mere sound of steel impacting flesh and bone seemed to slam their suddenly lifeless bodies to the sand.

I tried to coordinate my steps with the two who were jerking and pulling me across the soft sand. I would gladly have run like hell, but they wouldn't allow it. They were out of sync with each other, too, so we stumbled and scrambled toward the far side of the beach. God, it took forever. As the geysers of sand erupted around me, I instinctively tightened my sphincter as if to suck myself in and disappear. At least the tensing seemed to make me feel like a smaller target. Small comfort! Cradling my injured right arm tightly to my body, I had flung myself behind the levee, rolling as I hit the soft earth.

With my brain still numb from the concussion, I was in a strictly reactive mode. I seemed to be on the outside of all this—a detached observer—no pain, no fear, no other emotion, just a body trying instinctively to survive.

Just before they pushed my face down into the mud, I followed the terrified, over-the-shoulder glances of the last stragglers across the beach. There, boring down straight toward us, was the head-on view of an A-4 Skyhawk—the smallest and deadliest light-attack aircraft in the *Kitty Hawk*'s air group. In the space of a second I half-saw, half-imagined the face of my shipmate up there. Had we passed each other in the passageway that morning? Had he sat across the white-linened table in the wardroom last night? Right then in my mind's eye I saw his right eye quadrisected perfectly by the glowing crosshairs of a gunsight between us. I took into the mud with me the rapidly enlarging image of the warbird, wing roots engulfed by blue flame and smoke from his cannons. With my eyes closed, the sudden, rending scream of the 2.75 rockets was unexpected and even more terrifying—like the violent ripping of a sheet but magnified a million times. The rippling explosions were immediate. Four times in quick succession my body convulsed upward with the earth around me, my face making a new print in the mud each time I crashed down. The rain of sand kicked up by the 20mm slugs was replaced by heavy dirt clods and bits of wood and smoldering net. A rusted oarlock still threaded through a jagged piece of wooden gunwale plopped down on its edge a few inches from my face.

I remained still for a long time with heaving lungs and pounding heart, my body unwilling to release its straining clutch on the ground. The Vietnamese on either side of me were in no hurry to let go either, and I was aware of the commonality of our instinctive response to the prospect of instant, violent death.

Long after the last decibel of jet engine had faded into the distant sky, the Vietnamese who seemed to have assumed my charge eased off on the pressure of his rifle, which had pinned my neck and shoulders to the ground. Tentatively, I raised my head and looked down the levee to my left. We seemed like turtles, heads poking from shells, testing the air for more danger. The beach was strewn with the smoldering splinters of several boats and debris of fishing paraphernalia. It was scarred by deep craters, the damp sand yielding to the rapid seepage from the sea. But I was conscious mostly of several bodies that seemed to jump out at me in vivid color from this otherwise black-and-white war movie I was observing.

Strange, I had thought, here I am thirty-two years old and, not counting funerals, these are the first dead people I have ever seen. One was rocking gently in the shallow waves, while others were partly obscured by sand and wreckage. I still seemed to be detached, and they registered to me only as other people, people like me whose blood made the sand red and sticky.

With much shouting and jabbering, and with no one in particular in charge, they led me roughly along the edge of the beach toward the little fishing village and up what appeared to be its central lane. Others were running, wide-eyed, past us toward the water to aid their wounded and gather the dead. The villagers were hostile and excited. Spontaneously they formed a corridor lining the little dirt path up from the beach, clubbing me with whatever was handy: shovel and hoe handles, bamboo shoulder poles and a few rifle butts. As I stumbled and winced along through their gauntlet, each seemed to take his cue from the earlier one in line so that any natural restraint or compassion was overcome by the mob's momentum. Some threatened—or perhaps only feigned— fatal blows with pitchforks and scythes, but were restrained, sometimes at the last instant, by a uniformed cadre who emerged from somewhere to take charge. He walked ahead of me, half sideways and half backward, always watching for such threats from the people, even while inciting them with some sort of singsong chant. Although I only blinked and stared back dumbly, I was aware of the emotional extremes reflected in their faces and voices—men and women, children, even grubby little toddlers riding the hips of their mothers or older sisters. There was curiosity, uncertainty, fear, pity; but mostly there was hatred in them. Aside from those casualties on the beach, how many more of their fathers and brothers were drifting lifelessly out in their placid little bay where the fight for my capture had taken its toll? Which others of their sons and uncles would gradually be rolled and nudged up from the depths and carried up finally onto the beach by three or four successive waves, just like the ones they had played in as children? I was lucky these villagers were having at me right then, before the frenzy of their victory celebration gave way to the full realization of its cost.

Somewhere in the middle of the village, we turned off the lane and walked through a courtyard to the back of someone's house. There was a small shed, rows of green vegetables on two sides, and the fence and shack of an adjoining yard on the other. In the shed were various gardening and farming tools hanging on the walls and stacked in corners. A rack of sun-dried fish hung overhead, and the little hut smelled of fish and manure. The cadre motioned for me to sit on a pile of burlap sacks, and while one of the young militiamen took off my boots, he demanded my dog tags and my wallet, which held only my military ID card, my Geneva Convention card, and about ten dollars. This was my "combat wallet," the cards to identify me as an American Fighting Man—a combatant as opposed to a spy—in case of capture, and the money to buy a meal or a couple of beers should I have to divert from landing aboard the aircraft carrier to some military airfield in South Vietnam. My "blood chits"—which consisted of a written explanation in several Southeast Asian languages and dialects of who I was and the reward to be expected if turned over to friendly forces (a silk American flag, and several taels of gold for immediate incentive)—had been stripped from me in the boat. Fat chance of being turned over to friendlies by these hornets, I thought.

The loss of my dog tags and ID cards had been devastating to my morale. It would take a long time to realize that it had been only the first small step in the incremental peeling away of my identity, an identity built up over a lifetime but condensed on my dog tags to name, rank, serial number, date of birth, blood type, and religion.

The confiscation of my boots—probably in part to discourage me from escaping—increased my vulnerability, further compounding the sense of helplessness caused by my injuries. Under the crude scrutiny of the villagers, who took turns crowding up to the half-open door of the shack, I had never felt more naked and vulnerable.

Indeed, by then my brain was beginning to recover sufficiently from its trauma to comprehend more fully the real danger I faced. I was now beginning to feel considerable attachment to the situation; this was no dream or war movie. I was beginning to understand that all of this was *real.*

As darkness fell and the crowds became sparse, I was jolted from my simple prayers for strength and courage by the flat, metallic, nerve-rattling sound of a gong close by. Someone was beating on a piece of metal—like a triangle dinner bell, but with more "clank" than "ding"— each blow widely spaced at first, but then with gradually increasing frequency to an intense crescendo finished off by one final, distinct beat. I heard other gongs from distant villages, each with its distinct tone, but all signaling, in this case, the end of the formal work day and calling the people in from the fields and paddies. There was an alien savageness about it. Suddenly, it seemed the plug had been pulled on my remaining reservoir of confidence and I felt very, very far from home.

After talking with a villager who seemed to convey official instructions, the cadre ordered one guard to tie a rope around my neck and the other to blindfold me. He used a piece of rag found on the dirt floor of the shed and permeated with the same offensive smell.

We headed off, the cadre, two guards and myself, out of the village and inland, I guessed. The going was slow the first mile or so. Unable to see my way, I slipped down the sides of the muddy paths every few minutes, only to be yanked up each time by the coarse rope around my neck. It was cutting and chafing my already stinging face. Holding onto my injured arm with the good one made it even more difficult to keep my balance and, when I fell, to hurriedly wallow back up onto the path to ease the bite of the leash. Finally, the cadre became impatient with the slowness of our progress along the narrow levee and ordered the stinking rag across my eyes to be removed.

We traveled easier then, guided along by the beams of two flashlights and pale moonlight diffused by a layer of thin clouds. We still stopped frequently for the three of them to confer about our route. One time during a stop, we were approached by a young man who seemed to know our mission. He had come from the direction of a village just ahead on our pathway. It was marked by a cluster of dim oil lamps and the frenzied sounds of some kind of rally. There was chanting and cheering punctuated by a gong. The conversation had been in whispers and had obviously been about me. One of the guards turned to me and, with a smile that matched the menacing sound of the gong, pointed to the village then to me, making a slashing motion across his throat. "They want to kill you," I translated his accompanying words intuitively and marveled at how rapidly we pick up sign language, especially on issues of life and death.

The cadre took the messenger seriously. We reversed course and circumnavigated the village, always talking in whispers and sometimes crouching low along hedgerows to remain undetected. The sounds of the frenzied villagers ebbed and flowed as we crept along and I was relieved as the din faded behind us. At least the concern for my immediate survival was reassuring. They were taking seriously their apparent order to deliver me someplace safely.

Later, after moving along for some time at a steady pace, we encountered two old women shuffling along in the opposite direction. They both carried shoulder poles (I would later know them as *chogi* sticks) balanced at each end by shallow woven baskets, their obviously heavy contents obscured by cloth tucked in around the edges. The first woman also carried a small kerosene lamp with a wide conical top so its tiny flame could not be seen from the air. As they approached, the lamp swung quaintly to and fro with the rhythm of her bouncing load, like a scene described in a child's storybook. The path was wide enough for us to pass one another, but our lead man with the flashlight seemed to recognize the old lamp swinger. We all stopped as they talked softly but excitedly. They were exchanging news from the opposite ends of our path, his version animated by airplanes and shooting gestures. Several times the two women glanced guardedly toward me. The leader shined the light directly into my face and they moved closer cautiously for a better look at the "black-hearted American air pirate," as I was to be called frequently in the future.

In the reflected light, I saw their faces and was astonished at how much they looked exactly as they were "supposed to"—right off the page of some *National Geographic* of my youth, all delicate wrinkles and indented mouths where teeth should have been. In the shadows of their woven conical hats, little threads and tufts of gray hair—more silver in the soft light—poked from beneath the black scarves tied beneath their chins. Their little black eyes sparkled in the light, belying the tiredness of the sagging skin around them. They held no youthful fervor and certainly no hatred. One of them asked a question of the guard holding the rope to my neck, then clucked her disapproval of his answer.

Her face revealed the genuine concern and compassion of the grandmother she surely was. The gentleness of her touch as she reached up to test the tightness of the rope around my neck transcended the political and ideological conflicts that had led us both to this unlikely nocturnal encounter. She bubbled a few words to her companion, who immediately withdrew a banged-up thermos bottle from a shoulder bag. As the other woman poured hot tea, she stooped slightly, looked into my eyes questioningly, her hand held out straight, palm down, and level with her knees. She then stair-stepped it up, pausing briefly at three higher levels. She finished with her finger pointing at me and curiosity in her face. My mind searched for her meaning for only a second. Of course! Did I have children? I smiled wanly and held up three fingers, then four. No, three! How could I explain to her that my wife was pregnant with our fourth child? As she acknowledged my perplexity, I reemphasized three, then traced a bulging tummy with my good hand. Her eyes widened and the little wrinkles on her forehead furrowed even more deeply, as she shook her head slowly in comprehension.

She shared a few words with the other woman, but without breaking the link from her eyes to mine. Her expression was a mixture of compassion and wonderment. Again she clucked her puzzlement and wagged her diminutive head. I could imagine her thinking, "Why would a young American flyer come so far away from home when he should be back there with his wife and babies?"

The taste of the hot, bitter tea lingered on my tongue as my guards and I hurried on. Even the second cupful the crone offered hadn't quenched my thirst, a thirst I hadn't been aware of until it had been teased alive by the first swallow of the tea. I must have sweat much more than I had realized during the afternoon and evening.

With the blindfold removed, I was able to move along fairly well, head down, eyes fastened to the bobbing white light preceding us along the path. The night was otherwise very dark now, the previously misty-thin clouds having thickened to block out the moonlight. There seemed to be no light or activity ahead that might define our destination.

The Vietnamese were speaking sparingly now as we continued on rather mechanically. My thoughts wandered back to the old women and their kindness. Where had they been going on such a dark night? Probably returning to their own shabby homes after visiting their children or grandchildren. I would have many future occasions to recall them fondly, as well as my own naive assumption about their activities as the "party line" would be espoused repetitively on the VOV, the Voice of Vietnam radio:

> "In accordance with the enlightened policy of the Democratic Republic of Vietnam toward the equality of women in the revolutionary society, women are allowed to work equally, side by side with men. In the rural areas, older women, pregnant women, and women who are menstruating are allowed to work in dry paddies closer to home."

"Make watah! Make watah!" One of my guards from the previous evening, the one I heard chatting and smoking a while ago, stood in the doorway pointing to his crotch. I had so intensely projected myself back into the events of the past few days that I had not even been aware of his appearance. His half-question half-command brought me back in-

stantly to the reality of my humble accommodations. "Make watah!"
he repeated. I guess he's asking if I need to take a leak, I told myself.
I don't really, but I'd better take advantage of the opportunity. As it
turned out, he had anticipated the morning gong, for as I struggled to
my feet in the straw, the flat brassy clang of a tire iron on the 100mm
shell casing hanging from a limb in the adjoining courtyard assaulted
my ears, adding to the anguish of my effort. As the inhabitants of the
hamlet, My Xa, fell to their morning ritual, I pissed in the *binjo* ditch
sewer across the path from the doorway. My urine was deep amber in
color, and I realized this was the first time I had relieved myself since
my capture. I must have been really dehydrated.

To say the rest of the day passed uneventfully would have been true
in the normal sense, but for me, as I became gradually immersed in this
strange society, everything was an event. The soup and rice I was given
in the morning and early evening—my first food in North Vietnam—
were a major event. The soup had been made of coarse, bitter greens,
but was thick with pork and well seasoned. The rice was sticky. Both
had been served piping hot and I had found myself ravenous, but didn't
know it until the food was available.

I had "made water" a couple more times and learned that these two
words accompanied by crotch pointing made it clear that I had to take
a leak. And as I thought about the phrase "taking a leak," I realized,
with minor amusement, that it would probably be thought more strange
by a Vietnamese than "making water" seemed to me.

Various groups and individuals looked in on me through the day as
word apparently got around. To these simple people, I was obviously
quite an oddity, a subject of curiosity in any case, and a rare flesh-and-
blood sample of the Enemy. One group had been all children, I guessed
from the local school. I was the subject of their current events field trip.
Their young teacher had been as wide-eyed as her pupils when they all
squatted down a few feet from me as the cadre who brought me there
related—with considerable animation and detail—the odious crimes I
had supposedly committed upon their country. This was to be my first
experience of the incredible hold the Communists have on their people
when they control every input from birth on. Children were taught daily
that my government and country were the reasons for their need for
total sacrifice and deprivation in the defense of their homeland and for
the unending harshness of their existence. They needed a scapegoat to
explain away what, I would soon see at first hand, was actually the

inefficiency, unresponsiveness, and total failure of their state-controlled agricultural and industrial programs.

Just after the clanging of the gong that ended the nap period after lunch—around 2 P.M.—the cadre apeared in the entry with a very old man. The two of them talked with a great deal of intensity, pointing in my direction frequently. Finally the cadre left and the old fellow shuffled toward me and hunkered down a few feet in front of me. But for a lifetime in that flat-footed, knee-rending posture, eating, gossiping, gambling, and observing, there was no way that septuagenarian body could have swung down so easily into such a squat, at least not from my western perspective, which glorified chairs, benches, and stools. There weren't a lot of those to be seen around here.

Squatting there with his clear but somewhat watery eyes, he seemed to contemplate me and the reasons for my presence there. Finally, after several minutes—so many, in fact, that I was just beginning to ignore his stare—he blurted out suddenly, "Why you come Vietnam?" There was true inquiry in his voice and just a hint of hostility. "Why you come Vietnam?" I was startled both by his question and his English. "Why you come Vietnam?" His tone and expression indicated he was genuinely perplexed at why I'd come to Vietnam and also that he honestly wanted to know. I stared back at him, my mind grappling with the question.

Wary at first that this could be some very clever attempt to interrogate me, to trick me into saying more than my name, rank, serial number, and date of birth, as required by the American Fighting Man's Code of Conduct, I decided finally that there was no guile in the old man's questions. Why indeed had I come to Vietnam?

My mind raced back several months to the home squadron's weekly intelligence briefings. The Intelligence officer had intoned matter-of-factly:

"During the Japanese occupation of Indochina during much of World War II, the French presence had dwindled to a minimum. Their preoccupation with the European front had effectively left a colonial vacuum in Southeast Asia, which the Japanese had gladly filled for as long as they could. During the war, the Vietnamese patriot, Ho Chi Minh, organized the resistance against the Japanese. During his leadership of the resistance to the Japanese, Ho and his followers built up a strong and very nationalistic guerrilla movement. They were called Viet Minh (Vietnamese Communists) because of Ho's political background and ideology. Nevertheless, there had been many instances of cooperation against the Japanese between the Viet Minh and Allied forces, especially in the safekeeping and return of downed U.S. flyers in Indochina.

"After the war, the French were eager to reestablish their colonial presence. Ho Chi Minh—through unofficial channels, since his was not a recognized government—requested the support of Western nations in unilaterally establishing an independent Vietnam, Cambodia, and Laos. The U.S., however, mostly because we perceived Ho was at least as much a Communist as a Nationalist, and because of our knowledge of the brutal Communist regime in Russia after Stalin, chose to support our longtime ally, France, instead. During the early postwar years, the French, with our blessing and military aid, reoccupied Vietnam. And the bloody, protracted French Indo-Chinese War between the French Colonial Army, Legionnaires, and locally conscripted Vietnamese, and the Viet Minh Guerrilla forces began!"

It occurred to me that the old man squatting in front of me had lived a part of it all. He had probably lived that entire briefing I was now replaying in my mind. Where had he learned his English? From some American pilot whose plane had been damaged raiding Japanese forces in southern China, but who had been able to limp to a safe area where indigenous friendlies could help? Had he, an indigenous friendly twenty years before, rescued, aided, and ultimately helped repatriate an American airman like me? Was he, too, reflecting on this peculiar irony of history?

"After the French defeat, an international conference was called in Geneva to help decide the future of Vietnam. Because most of the French forces, infrastructure, and sentiment were centered in Saigon, in the South, and the majority of the Viet Minh forces and support were in the North, centered around Hanoi, the country was divided in two at the 17th parallel as an interim measure. The space immediately on either side of this line was declared a Demilitarized Zone (DMZ), a buffer to facilitate the disengagement of the two opposing forces. In 1956, there was to be a free national election to decide the fate of the entire country.

The situation polarized rapidly. However, with eleven million people in the North ruled with an iron hand from Ho Chi Minh's Hanoi, and only nine million in the South, ruled temporarily and barely by an aging mandarin, Bao Dai, who had been favored by the French, one could see the obvious outcome of any election.

The election was not held. The government in South Vietnam stonewalled the whole process, refusing under the existing circumstances to discuss arrangements for the elections or any aspects of reunification. Finally, the entire plan broke down and the international commission established to facilitate and monitor the reunification process disintegrated. The people of South Vietnam, through a series of governments succeeding one another due to abdication, coups, and classic Oriental intrigue, began building—albeit inefficiently—a free and independent nation. They had been blessed by the cream of Vietnam's agricultural land, natural resources, and beneficent climate. On the other hand, the weather in the North was more harsh, the land more stingy, and subsistence more difficult. These factors alone throughout history had kept the people of the North and South separate and sometimes openly hostile. The North Vietnamese, under the leadership of Ho's Viet Minh military council, stepped up the guerrilla infiltration and subversion of the South until finally the war between the North and the South was on."

The old man had smoked his third cigarette down to a tiny stub that he could barely pinch, then tucked it between the dirt floor and the sole of his rubber sandal to crush it. He lit another, and again I declined his offer, shaking my head and uttering the Vietnamese thank-you I'd picked up. *"Cam Ud!"* He shifted his weight—I thought in preparation to leave—but he just repositioned his butt on the inside of his ankles and closer to the floor.

"The fighting between North and South escalated over the years. Although in the early sixties President Kennedy never envisioned the use of regular U.S. combat forces in Vietnam, he pledged generous technical and material support to the South Vietnamese in their struggle to remain free of Communist tyranny. He also founded the Special Forces—Green Berets—and from their ranks sent advisors to South Vietnam. They were designated in noncombat roles, training the South Vietnamese army units, villagers, and even the mountain people in couterinsurgency warfare. Given the context of the time, the earlier anti-Communist warning of John Foster Dulles seemed well founded. Stalin's brutality had been well documented, and Khrushchev's nasty threat—"We will bury you!"—was becoming more than just rhetoric. The earlier Communist blockade of West Berlin, the defeat of the French by the Vietnamese, Castro's consolidation of his Marxist government in Cuba, followed by the Soviet's brazen introduction of missiles there—all combined to reinforce the need to make a strong stand against further Communist expansion. Besides, Kennedy realized that the Communists' typical strategy of consolidation in one country and infiltration and support of antigovernment guerrillas in neighboring countries made the domino theory worth heeding.

Gradually our advisors began taking casualties and we were slowly drawn in deeper, with greater commitments. After Kennedy's assassination in late '63, President Johnson held sacred his predecessor's pledge to the people of

South Vietnam. Johnson didn't want to box the North Vietnamese into a corner
with no option but to fight, so he escalated the bombing very slowly and offered
to negotiate at the same time."

With the thought of escalated bombing, my mind drifted to reports I
had heard of the first to be shot down in the bombing, Lieutenant JG
Everett Alvarez. I had seen newspaper articles about his shootdown
and capture. The columns had usually been accompanied by the soulful,
gaunt-faced picture of him as a prisoner. His loss in August '64 had
been big news, and the North Vietnamese had milked it for all the
propaganda the Western media would provide.

Bea and I had been on leave from Florida visiting my parents in
central California when we saw the news. I had been reading the Sunday
paper in bed and sipping my morning coffee. Alvarez's picture was in
the world section, and there was some statement from his wife about a
controversial letter she had received from him. Bea was brushing her
hair in the bathroom a few feet away.

"Honey, if I go to Vietnam and get shot down and become a POW,
when I write to you I'll put little dots under certain letters so they spell
out my secret message to you."

Bea said something like, "That's nice, dear. Do you want biscuits or
scones for breakfast?"

Hell, what am I saying, I thought at the time. She's right. Vietnam
will be history by the time I ever get back on sea duty.

The old man continued his intense scrutiny of me. For the first time I
noticed his scraggly beard, a few dozen wavy white threads hanging
down from his chin and from the outer edges of his upper lip, just like
the beard I had seen on Ho Chi Minh in news magazines. He would be
one of Ho's contemporaries. Maybe he had even worked with him
personally. . . . He obviously enjoyed some status, or the cadre
wouldn't have left him alone with me.

"Why you come Vietnam?"

He had apparently noticed that I was back in the present with him.

I knew why I had "come Vietnam," but how could I tell him? Even
if his English hadn't been limited, I felt helpless to explain. He no doubt
had his own historical version of the Intel briefing I had just reviewed
in my mind. I wanted desperately to explain to him that I and my
countrymen were involved in the affairs of his country for a good and

worthy purpose. How could I explain we had been asked to come by Vietnamese who didn't want to live under a repressive and tyrannical Communist regime? How could I tell him I believed they had the right to determine their own destiny, independent of their neighbors in the North? With his historical perspective, he probably would have fathomed my reasons far better than most of the younger generation of his country who had learned a distorted view of that same history.

I stared back at him dumbly, matching his gaze blink for blink. I felt the frustration of trying to help someone and having the effort go awry to make the situation worse somehow; of having my good intentions misperceived, and yet being unable to explain. Finally, the old man shrugged his thin shoulders and shook his head sadly as he added his final cigarette butt to the five already scattered near his right sandal. I heard his knees creak as he hoisted himself upright, then he turned and walked out into the ebbing twilight. I shook my own head sadly as I watched him become one of the shadows.

Later that evening, I was visited by a man and woman. They hesitated in the doorway and surveyed my situation, the woman speaking softly. By now the lengthening shadows had blended into darkness, and I could barely distinguish their forms in the opening of my shelter. Soon the man disappeared in the direction from which they had appeared. His companion stood quietly and waited. When the man returned he had a small oil lamp, the flame hardly bigger than that of a birthday cake candle. They approached together and squatted down very close to me. Only then could I see that they were a boy and a girl, probably in their late teens. The girl appeared to be the elder and was truly beautiful. They exchanged a few words in Vietnamese before the boy set the lamp on a cross-piece of the rickety little fence that separated my stall from the next one. Then he looked at me thoughtfully. After a moment, he spoke: "Her brother and her mother are killed by U.S. napalm. She hate you very much." The young interpreter shaped his words carefully, his boyish face overacting the emotions he felt appropriate for the statement. It was clear that he had practiced this opener. "She herself call Lan," he said more casually. "Lan . . . nurse! Different village. It call self Son My." His inverted sentence structure belied the French background of his English teacher.

The two of them sat low and side by side, their eyes slightly above the level of my own. The boy, like the old man, squatted squarely on flat feet; the girl knelt symmetrically on her knees, her hands pressed palms down against her thighs. But for the simplicity of her clothing, she exuded the elegant grace of a Tonkinese courtesan.

Lan! Even in the dim light I could see that her face was almost a perfect heart shape, with a delicate chin and cheeks curving gracefully up and around to the top of her forehead and the distinct widow's peak. Her jet-black hair was pulled to the back of her head in a bun, but the wisps that escaped here and there arched down over her delicate ears and forehead, adding to the weariness in her young face. A thin gold chain around her neck hinted at the femininity otherwise obscured by the coarse gray cotton blouse that buttoned down the front and was gathered into the small waistband of her classic black pajama pants. A webbed military belt cinched her waist even more trimly.

"She hate you very much! Nevertheless, her heart is in the right place." My eyes flicked to the boy's expectant face, then back to Lan's eyes. His well-rehearsed speech couldn't have seemed more incongruous.

Lan returned my stare with her enormous dark eyes, more round than almond-shaped. It's likely there had been a Frenchman in her ancestry, I thought. From the depths of her eyes I could sense her confusion; some hatred, yes, but more than that, searching and curiosity. She uttered a quick phrase to her interpreter without breaking our eye contact. "You must remove shirt," he said. While I did so—very painfully and laboriously working the sleeve down and off my swollen arm—she began methodically removing the small first-aid kit attached to her belt. I was struck by its resemblance to the play-nurse kit that my daughter Kimmie had received for Christmas less than two months ago. And Lan herself—dark hair and eyes and diminutive frame—caused me to recall for a trembling instant the bright effervescence of my little first grader now so far away in space and context. Lan's touch upon my arms and face belied whatever hatred she might have harbored. Her gentleness seemed to be the most natural part of her, both as Lan the nurse and Lan the girl.

From her touches and terse commentary I deduced my situation before it was interpreted to me—mostly by signs and motions—by the boy. My right forearm was broken; my right elbow was badly dislocated, probably shattered as well. There was a gash there—now crusted over— that had probably been caused by striking some part of my jettisoning canopy or ejection seat. My entire arm and shoulder were swollen to twice their normal size and were completely immobile, just as if in a cast. Lan applied Mercurochrome to the numerous cuts on my face and gently spread some kind of ointment on the burns there and on my neck and arms. As she finished knotting the gauze-strip sling around my neck and arm, she sat back in her best courtesan pose. She shook her head slowly from side to side, her huge eyes fixed upon mine, and then, like the old Viet Minh soldier who had visited me earlier, shrugged her tiny shoulders in helpless commentary. "Lan say you must wait more for doctors. You hurt very bad but you OK. She say you have very good fortune."

"Why does she say that?" She turned toward him to catch the gist of my question. "Because the brave army men of Tan Loc show they courageous. They shoot down your American piratical airplane on the spot." The airplane motions with his hands ended in a squirming tangle of fingers and flip-flopping palms. "It blow up over the water. Everybody think you must be killed, but I don't think so." He smiled as if happy for me.

"But there were two of us. What about the other man who was in the airplane with me?" Lan knew my question by the anxiety in my voice and my two upraised fingers. "He is . . . I don't know. He is somewhere else, I think." I could see more sadness creep into Lan's eyes and for the first time I doubted that Bob was still alive.

In an instant Lan's eyes became shiny with moisture and she lowered her gaze. God, she is actually sad for us! She may actually hate me but it's clear she is sad, too, either for me or for Bob, or about the whole damned situation. I didn't know if she had even heard my *"Cam Ud!"* croaked in the darkness behind her.

I thought of Bob and prayed hard—but without much conviction—that he was also alive and being treated all right. I thought of the seeming miracle of my own survival through it all; how I had removed my oxygen mask, released my parachute harness, and then inflated my flotation gear—all with only one hand and while unconscious. That was the miracle, the miracle of the subconscious. If I had been able to recall and implement the survival procedures learned throughout the years, could I trust my subconscious to recall all the patterns and processes I had ever learned in my life? Did it necessarily require unique life-and-death circumstances to bring them to the surface?

At this moment I began to realize, though not yet fully, that I had within me all the knowledge and intuitive resources that I would ever need to survive. Right here I began to trust myself and my capabilities.

This was to be the intellectual foundation of keeping faith in myself; that along with my faith in God's help and comfort—the spiritual foundation—I would be able to survive the incredible challenges that were yet to come. It would take even more time to realize that just surviving would be the minimum and that I would ultimately go beyond survival.

But for now, in February of '66, the short-term perspective prevailed. Surely now with our Marines in South Vietnam, and the resumption of our air strikes in the North following the Christmas holidays and January bombing pause, this whole mess would be wrapped up soon; it would take only a few more months at most. A political settlement—if not an all-out military victory—was very likely. Uncle Sam will have me out of here by summer, I told myself. I can hack it till then and if Bob is alive I know he can, too.

I didn't realize I had just exercised a critical survival tool. I had defined the first of many six-month increments by which I would measure my time remaining. Not "one day at a time," but one half-year at a time. How could I know at that point that there would be fourteen such increments, that these were but the first few days of a seven-year journey? Thank God I couldn't.

3
Forgiving Oneself

The decisions we make out of loneliness and pain, uncertainty and fear can take us to the extremes of shame and pride. The turning point that changes adversity into opportunity, defeat into victory comes when we are willing to forgive ourselves. Too often our unreasonable expectations lead to self-judgment and guilt. Our best is the best we can do.

"If you do not cooperate, there no reason to keep you alive." The province administrator, as he had called himself, shrugged as he said it, then commenced lighting a cigarette very deliberately. The click of his small metal lighter that he snapped closed deftly with one hand punctuated the silence that followed his words.

He still exhaled smoke through his nostrils as he continued, "And if you are to die, maybe you have some last words you are pleased to tell this man of the cloth." He flicked his head toward the man seated at my right, the only one dressed significantly differently from the other four at the table. The table itself was rough-hewn wood and looked almost as though it had been built hurriedly for the occasion. It matched nicely the tree-pole rafters of the low ceiling and smooth dirt floor.

We seemed to be in some kind of anteroom of one of the more important cadres' houses. The host was seated at my interrogator's right, probably a low party official, perhaps the political cadre of this tiny hamlet. He and one of the other men slouched at the table were dressed similarly, in clean but drab and threadbare work clothes. The army uniform of the fifth member of the delegation was so faded it looked like a khaki work outfit; only the bright red insignia on the collar—a red felt square with two gold stars—distinguished him as military. The insignia was like a dab of bright crimson pigment on an otherwise dull canvas. It must have been pinned on for the occasion. My two guards stood at either side and slightly behind me, their arms crossed and feet planted firmly at shoulder width apart, like eunuchs guarding a harem. Their stern pose appeared to be well rehearsed.

The head man at the opposite end of the table continued to stare from beneath his bushy brows and pale forehead; a forehead still marked by the red indentation from the headband of his dirty gray pith helmet, which now hung askew on the back of his chair. He had the only chair. The rest of us sat on very crude benches like the ones pictured in my Boy Scout manual that you hew out of rough logs in the wilderness with knife and hatchet.

"Well?" he said with a sharper edge to his invitation, "this is your last chance." Again he nodded toward the "man of the cloth."

I looked at the man to my right and he looked at me. His gaze was almost passive, slightly expectant. The faded brown frock that buttoned high in a stiff collar flowed loosely everywhere else and was as clean and threadbare as the work clothes of his comrades. After the two buttons at his collar, none of the other buttons down the front matched. Like the others, he smoked almost constantly. His Truong Son cigarette package, his lighter, and cheap souvenir plastic rosary were on the table in front of him. He looked like he could be a priest. He was older (there were no young priests here), and his eyes held the classic tired compassion of a priest in a war-torn country.

In the predawn darkness, the guards had shaken me roughly from a stonelike sleep. One had pulled sharply at my swollen arm. As the pain shot through my upper right quarter, I had cried out and bolted upright, searching the darkness for the source of the cry. The guard jumped back, himself startled. The pain or the cry—I hadn't been sure which—had brought me instantly awake and alert. The guards had laughed at my bewilderment and seemed to be in a nasty mood, out of character really with their previous attitude of curiosity and businesslike indifference. They had tied my wrists behind me with the same strip of cloth that had been my blindfold earlier. That would have been hard enough on my injured arm, but the stiffness of sleep on straw caused me to contort down and to the right as I tried to minimize the pressure and the pain.

For the next fifteen minutes they had yanked and jerked me along the little mazes of the hamlet, pushing me one way, then another, spinning me sideways, twice into the smelly *binjo* ditch that seemed to carry urine and feces nowhere in particular. Each time I had tried to roll with the fall, but the prickly bushes scratched and punctured my feet and hands and face. God, just what I need! More open wounds to attract the millions of deadly bacteria among which I was groping to regain my footing.

Finally, as one edge of the gray sky was tinged by pink, I was jerked to an abrupt halt in front of an open doorway. One of the guards went in and announced our arrival in a respectful monotone, received his orders, stepped back outside, and snarled at me: "Go through."

In the relative darkness of the room I could distinguish the five men at the oblong table, one at the far end and two on either side of it. The near end of the table was open for me. A small kerosene lamp like the one that Lan had used sat in the middle of the table, barely revealing their faces, the papers spread before them, and the emptiness of the rest of the room.

"Sit down." A hand belonging to the toneless voice at the far end of the table gestured toward the spot in front of me. "I am the administrator of this province, and these are my . . . my . . ." He searched for the word. ". . . my council." His hand made a small circle indicating the others at the table. I was surprised that he spoke English.

"You are captured by the people of the Democratic Republic of Vietnam and have been caught redhanded. You are the blackest criminal. You have no rights, no rights for medicine, no rights for anything. You are at the complete mercy of my government and my people. We can kill you at any time and your fate will be unknown. We can keep you in prison for many, many years. When the war is over in my country, and the heroic Vietnamese people have defeated the U.S. imperialistic aggressors and their lackeys, maybe you can go home and maybe not. It is according for us." He drew deeply on his cigarette and paused for effect, then continued in a more conciliatory tone. "On the other hand, if you have correct attitude, if you surrender your will—You understand 'surrender your will'?" I nodded. "If you surrender your will, you will receive humane and lenient treatment. That is the policy of our people, even though they hate you very, very much." He leaned back in his chair and looked at the others, then back at me.

"Do you understand?" I nodded again. "Good." He glanced down at several papers spread on the table in front of him and shifted one to the top of all the others.

"What was the name of your aircraft ship?"

I was silent.

"What kind of airplane were you flying?" More silence.

He said something to the others rather matter-of-factly, then lit another cigarette. This time he glowered at me as he snapped the lighter shut. "You must know you must answer my questions! You must show good attitude because the fat is in the fire!" It was becoming apparent that those Vietnamese who spoke English relied heavily on idioms in order to sound competent. Some were effective and some not. It could even be comical. I remained silent and looked at him as benignly as possible. Surely, I thought, there's a good bet he already knows what kind of plane I was flying and from which ship.

My mind flashed to the image of the six-inch-high black letters on both sides of the fuselage of my aircraft back near the tail: "RA–5C" and, below it, "USS *Kitty Hawk.*" This was standard for each type of aircraft on each aircraft carrier. The image focused more specifically on the last preflight inspection of our plane. As I had checked the control surfaces on the port wing, Bob had run his hand across the words *Kitty Hawk* on the fuselage, checking the security of the port engine access hatches.

Ignoring his question, I said almost reflexively, "Where is my crewman? Where is the other man who was in my airplane?"

With some exasperation he again shuffled through the papers on the table, extracted a stiff plastic card, and flipped it toward me like a Las Vegas dealer. It was Bob's military ID card.

"He has been shot." The words themselves were like a shot and I felt them in my chest.

Then he picked up my own ID card, which was also among the papers. Holding its picture toward me, he said, "And I think you are the very, very lucky one."

He snapped his fingers and said something in Vietnamese. The man on my left plucked Bob's card from my hand and returned it to the head of the table. Still I pictured Bob's face on the card I had just held. I didn't believe what I had just been told. I couldn't believe it. Surely Bob was alive. Perhaps even in this village in a different hut somewhere. He had probably been shown my ID card and been told that I had been shot, too. I couldn't give up on him.

"Now then," the administrator sighed heavily, "what kind of airplane were you flying?"

I wasn't about to answer, even though they may well have recovered some of the wreckage from my plane by now and could simply read the type and carrier from the pieces of fuselage. In any case, the information would have been reported by now in our own news media:

"AP February 3, 1966. The U.S. Navy reported today that an aircraft operating from the carrier USS *Kitty Hawk* was shot down just off the coast of North Vietnam. The aircraft, an RA–5C Vigilante, was on a routine combat reconnaissance mission. A spokesman said that aircraft exploded before hitting the water and one parachute was sighted. The two crewmen are officially listed as missing. Their names have been withheld pending notification of next of kin."

Shit, nothing is secret in this war. Even the enemy can read a complete account of everything to fill in the blanks, or know when one of us is lying to them. If Bob or I had been able to get to shore without being seen and was trying to evade capture, all these guys had to do was read the *New York Times* in Hanoi to know what they might not otherwise have known: There had been two Americans in that plane and one was still loose. My predicament was only a small example of the difficulties this would cause us militarily. There were virtually no restrictions on our media, and the military released information on combat losses as freely as if they had been training incidents. Since our nation was not officially at war, there was nearly unrestricted freedom of information, a state of affairs with serious implications for me as a POW, one I would soon come to curse.

I decided a courteous response would serve me better than silence.

"Under the Geneva Conventions on the treatment of prisoners of war, I am required to tell you only my name, rank, serial number, and date of birth. I am Lieutenant Gerald Coffee, 625308, June 2, 1934."

"I know all that," he hissed, as the cadre on his right interpreted my response to the others. "You have no rights under the Geneva agreements. You are not a prisoner of war. You are a criminal and you must answer my questions!"

He jammed his cigarette into the tabletop with two quick thrusts and purposely threw the butt on the floor beside his chair. I returned his stare briefly, glanced at the others, shrugged, and then looked down at the hole in the knee of my fatigue trousers, which had torn during one of my earlier encounters with brambles. I was becoming more and more distracted by the pain in my arm, which was still tied behind me. Fortunately, the severe swelling had the effect of a cast so my elbow and forearm, the focus of my injury, could not bend much; but that increased the pressure on my shoulders, and even the contorted position I assumed on the stool couldn't alleviate much of the pain.

Again, he pressed me on my type of aircraft and the name of my carrier. Again, I stated only my name, rank, serial number, and date of birth.

"Obviously you are a diehard so we have no more purpose for you. You might as well tell your last words to the priest here who is with us."

The priest looked at me almost pleadingly. He said, *"C'est nécessaire que vous répondez, s'il vous plaît."*

"I have nothing more to say."

With that, my interrogator slammed his fist on the table, startling even his comrades. He said something sharply to the guards behind me, who immediately grabbed me by the shoulders. Pain shot through the upper right side of my body. They jerked me off of the stool, and because the ceiling was low, my head bounced off the nearest rafter. I hardly noticed because of the pain in my arm. But even that was minor compared to what was yet to come.

The guards held me upright, waiting for further orders from their senior. They didn't have long to wait. He rattled off several sentences in Vietnamese and pointed outside. They immediately turned me and pushed me back out through the door toward the small courtyard. It was full dawn now, and I could see more of the courtyard. There were fewer shadows. The dirt itself had been swept clean, much like the floor of the room where I had just been. The entire courtyard was shaded by one huge *hau* tree, and although the trunk wasn't very large, it formed a large canopy over the courtyard about the size of a large living room or den. The three sides not bounded by the hut in which I had just been questioned were delineated by shrubbery and bushes and several clumps of bamboo. The yard sloped off to one side and then down into a drainage ditch that seemed to wander off into the paddies beyond.

The guards pushed me more urgently toward the trunk of the tree. I could hear shouting behind me as those who had been in the room followed. As they untied my wrists they pushed my back against the tree, and then retied my arms around the trunk. It was too big for them to reach all the way around, and I felt wrenching pain in my arm as they pulled my wrists within six or eight inches behind the other side.

The young officer with the red insignia on his collar was looking around the far side of the house, shouting orders to somebody I couldn't yet see. Finally, as the guards finished tying my hands, I winced at the one final tug on the rope and bit down hard on my lip to keep from crying out. I tried to imagine what was going on inside my arm. If I had a simple fracture at the beginning, I would be lucky to keep it from becoming compound, and my elbow felt like there was nothing left that would resemble the normal joint.

My two guards stood off to the side, and there was a great deal of discussion among the others as they looked at me and then toward the corner of the hut where the young officer had been shouting his orders. Finally, they appeared: five soldiers, each carrying a rifle of some kind, each in some kind of a ragtag uniform. It seemed as if nobody in this country had a uniform that matched. Nevertheless, the reality of the threat that had been made inside the hut began to be more clear. A firing squad was forming in front of me.

The officer shouted his orders to the five soldiers, actually all young boys. This, too, had probably been rehearsed beforehand, but they sure weren't remembering their moves very well. They finally managed to shuffle into a straight line about twenty feet from me. God, they were so young! Just kids really. A couple wore really baggy pants; none of their shirts seemed to fit. Their weapons were of the Heinz-57 variety: a couple of old American-made World War II–style M-1 rifles, a couple of French rifles that were worse for wear, and another rifle whose origin I didn't recognize. About all they had in common were the pith helmets that each wore. A couple of those had camouflage bits of cloth on them, and the others were bare.

About the time the officer in charge decided that they were in a straight enough line, a couple of women emerged from around the same corner the soldiers had come from. They stopped abruptly with wide eyes, startled by what they saw. Obviously, they didn't have any idea what had been going on in the courtyard. My interrogator saw them and shouted something. They turned around and fled back out of sight.

I was distracted from the pain in my arm now as I looked in the faces of the young boys with the guns. I could see that some of them weren't sure about what they were supposed to do, and one youngster with an M-1 rifle almost as big as he was didn't seem to be any more certain about what was going to happen than I was. They all tried unsuccessfully to look tough and serious.

The interrogator walked up to me, looked in my eyes, turned, and motioned the priest over toward us. He repeated, "This is your last chance. If you have anything to say to this man of God, you had better say it now."

I looked at the priest and again at the five young gunmen. My mind flashed back to survival training school in Brunswick, Maine. I'd been there less than six months before. There was a section in the POW training that talked about instances like this, and I remembered the words of the instructor: "No matter what they say or how they threaten you, they probably won't kill you because you represent something of value to them."

God, I hoped he was right. They're only bluffing, I said to myself.

I glanced back over my shoulder at the field. There was an open rice paddy—no wall, no fence, nothing to stop bullets. And since there was nothing out there, I supposed they could go ahead and shoot without worrying about hitting anyone behind me.

Again, the words came ringing back: "No matter how they threaten you, they probably won't kill you."

I looked at the interrogator, shook my head, and said, "I have nothing to say." He nodded his head decisively, took three or four steps back, motioned the priest out of the way, and said something to the officer with the red tag on his collar. The officer positioned himself off to the side of the line of gunmen, snapped an order that seemed to rouse them out of their stiff positions of attention and into a wider stance, rifles positioned across their bodies, much as hunters walk through the woods, ready to bring their weapons up at any time. Then he barked out the next command very sharply, and although I couldn't understand what it was, there was no question in my mind it was the first word of those three infamous words: "Ready. Aim. Fire!" Those three words that we'd played around with as kids, had seen in movies, and heard on the radio. We've read those words in novels and we've thought about the things that go through people's minds when they're faced with those three words. It conjures up notions of last-minute rescues of our cowboy heroes who are saved by a lifelong friend at the very last moment . . . .

But I could see no way that the fatal process would be interrupted now for me.

As the officer barked that first command, the squad brought their rifles up to eye level, partly sighting down the barrels toward me. I noticed that the kid with the M-1 was so undersized he'd hardly been able to heft it up to eye level.

"AIM!" The officer's second command seemed to fill the courtyard. I glanced around me and took in the scene.

"Whatever they tell you, they probably won't kill you. You represent something of value to them."

They're bluffing. They've got to be bluffing.

Five deadly muzzles pointed toward me, not very steadily. But steady enough.

They've gotta be bluffing. But if they're not . . . what a shitty way to die . . . so far away from home. God, let them be bluffing!

My heart thumped loudly and my body tensed for either the impact of bullets or the draining relief of the bluff.

The third command—"FIRE!"—rang out but was engulfed by the fiery roar of the kid's M-1. I viewed the scene as if it were in slow motion. I saw the kid slammed backward by the recoil of his weapon. His pith helmet jerked down over his face as he struggled to regain his feet while reeling back. Out of the smoke and flame emerged the slug from the muzzle of his rifle. I could see it coming. It should have been spinning from the rifling in the barrel of the gun and coming at me near the speed of sound, but for some reason—even though it was heading right toward me—that was not my impression. In fact, I could see the bullet wobble as it came closer and closer. For a moment, I felt I could even jerk my head out of the way before it reached me.

Instead, I closed my eyes in helpless resignation. Suddenly, I seemed to know in my gut that only my impression was slow motion and that there was truly nothing I could do to keep from actually being killed.

WHACK! The slug slammed into the tree trunk next to my ear. The splinters and pulp from the impact stung my neck and cheek. I kept my eyes closed and my body tense waiting for the impact of the next slugs. Surely they couldn't *all* miss.

I waited. The roar from the gun gave way to a great deal of shouting and jabbering. Everybody in the courtyard seemed to be yelling, but the voice of the provincial administrator rose above the rest. I opened my eyes. Still tense and disbelieving, I saw them all converging on the kid with the M-1, shaking their fists and their fingers in his face.

Overwhelmingly relieved, I understood what had happened. Now I was aware of my body slumping heavily as all muscle tone seemed to disappear. Totally limp, incredulous, I realized that they had indeed been bluffing.

But there had been a glitch. The chambers of all the rifles were supposed to be empty but the kid didn't get the word or had been careless. The other soldiers were standing there with their rifles at their sides in disbelief. The shot had surprised everyone, especially them—and even more especially, I suppose, the kid who had fired it, now being shaken by the collar of his shirt by the officer.

The administrator was really pissed. He stood there with his arms waving, ranting and raving, the soldiers and the young officers recoiling from his voice as if from a hot blast of air. They gathered themselves up and hurried back around the corner of the hut, hardly in the semi-military way in which they had appeared.

The administrator stood with his hands on his hips watching them go and then turned and had a curt exchange with two of his councilmen. He turned on his heels and strode toward me, seething in anger and embarrassment.

"So you think we are through with you!" He barked an order to the guards, who came around behind the tree and untied my arms. The release of the pressure was almost as excruciating as its application. As the guards twisted me away from the trunk, I noticed the gaping wound in the trunk of the tree, white jagged splinters sticking out stiffly, the sap already oozing. It was easy to imagine what my face would have looked like had the kid not missed.

Now they shoved me back to the other side of the courtyard toward the drainage ditch. With his rifle butt between my shoulder blades, one of the guards forced me down to my knees and finally flat on my face in the dirt. They tied the rope around my upper arms very tightly until it cut off the circulation; then with his foot behind my neck, he cinched my upper arms behind me. The strain and pain on my shoulders and injured arm was unbelievable. I could feel the cartilage begin to pop in my clavicle and my sternum and in the joints in my shoulders. Then, dragging me by the rope and the scruff of my shirt, they pulled me up toward a tree that was growing on the slope of the drainage ditch, threw the remaining rope over a low limb, and hoisted me up taut against the trunk of the tree until the tips of my toes were all that touched the ground. One of the guards secured the rope around the trunk of the tree, leaving me there in a semi-hanging position, my toes barely able to absorb the weight of my body. The administrator, who had been watching all this with his arms folded in front of him, moved closer, his face in front of mine, and said, "We will see. We will see." Then he strode back into the hut.

Except for the two guards the courtyard was empty now. One of them checked the tightness of the knot around the tree trunk, said something to the other as they looked at me, made a joke, then they too left. I was alone with my pain.

Now I longed for the dull, gnawing ache that had been my constant companion the past few days. Compared to this, it would have been blessed relief. I couldn't comprehend how they could leave me like this. The worst pain I had ever known until now was the tearing of cartilage and the twisting of ligaments in my knee while playing football: I had crumpled to the ground instantly, clutching my knee tightly to my chest while almost blacking out. But the pain had dissipated rapidly and continuously from that first blinding, wrenching instant. Now there was the same sharp, hot wrenching pain but no dissipation. It was constant, and getting worse.

Driven by the raw need for relief, my mind raced and contrived ways to alleviate the pain. I tried maneuvering my arms behind me, raising them up to get some slack in the rope. It worked a little bit, but I could only stay that way for a few seconds because I was barely touching the ground with my toes. I tried working my feet back up against the base of the tree trunk itself, hoping there might be some roots growing from the trunk on which I could stand to elevate my body and take the weight off my arms. That proved to be futile as well.

I could no longer concentrate on an intellectual solution. There was increased pain in my arms from the lack of circulation. My left arm—the good arm—began to throb and hurt as much as my broken arm. The pain was coursing through my arms in waves now, crashing against my consciousness. The muscles in my thighs and calves began to burn as I strained to be on tiptoe. As long as I could keep pressure on my toes, the pressure on my arms was less intense. But I couldn't stay focused. As my mind became more and more enmeshed with my pain, I seemed to be less and less aware of the world around me. The pain was blanking out the courtyard, the tree with the bleeding bullet hole across the way, the softness of the morning air. From somewhere came the guttural sounds of a wounded animal, grunts and whines and sobs. It was me.

The pain was all-consuming. I lifted my head to the sky. "Oh, God!" I implored. I realized that by raising my head and taking the pressure off my shoulders it helped to alleviate the pain in my arm. I stood as straight as I could and held my head as high as possible. It was the only way I could tolerate it.

Finally, the two guards came back, apparently with new orders. I guessed I'd been there twenty or thirty minutes, I couldn't be sure. Apparently, the administrator was becoming impatient, so the guards began their fun and games.

The tree was on the slope of the drainage ditch, and the side of the trunk that I was tied to and standing on was the high side. The guards began pushing me around the back side of the trunk so my feet couldn't touch the ground. I cried out. I cursed and I yelled and I tried to kick at them. The administrator appeared in the doorway a few feet away with the filthy rag that had been my blindfold. He held it out to them and said something. One of them retrieved it and began stuffing it into my mouth as a gag. I tried to twist my head away, but the other one held me by the hair and the ears while his companion shoved the rag into my mouth. I'm sure he was afraid I would bite him, so as soon as he got it in part of the way, he poked the rest of it in with the barrel of his rifle. On the final thrust of the barrel, I heard a crack and felt the sharp stinging pain of half of one of my front teeth breaking off.

Again I tried to reach them with a roundhouse kick, but that only made the pressure on my arms all the worse. I was so furious and demoralized and I was hurting so badly. My shouts and cries were nothing more than growls and gurgles lost in the wad of cloth.

My tormentors just followed through on the momentum of my kicks now and had a pretty good rhythm going. Down and around the downhill side of the tree with no ground beneath me, roll around to the uphill side of the trunk, touch my toes briefly, then they'd push me with the rifle butt back down around the far side of the tree again, just like a tetherball in slow motion.

My thoughts were fragmented: pain . . . Code of Conduct . . . aircraft carrier . . . type of aircraft . . . pain . . . name, rank, serial number . . . Bob—dead or alive? . . . pain . . . and more pain.

Oh, God, please help me to do what I need to do here. Help me to be strong. Help me to get through this, Lord. Please!

How would they even know if I wanted to give up? They didn't even seem to care. They just kept playing with me, laughing, taunting. The bastards really seemed to be enjoying what they were doing. I was soaked with sweat. My shirt and trousers were sopping wet.

Below where the ropes were tied, my arms were on fire. My shoulders seemed to be coming apart, and time stood still. I was consumed by the pain, aware of nothing else. The faces of the guards, the leaves of the tree that made the canopy over the courtyard, the smoothly swept dirt, the huts of the village, the hamlets, the sweep of the rice paddies as I swung across the downhill arc of the tree—it all became just a swirling manifestation of my pain.

Suddenly during one of those straining moments with my toes stretched as far down as possible and my head lifted to the sky, I became aware of the blurry face of my inquisitor standing in front of me. He grabbed my hair and pulled my face down toward him. The sweat stung my eyes. As it splashed off, I noticed a couple of spots on the shoulder of his shirt. The pain was causing me to gray out, like when pulling too many Gs in an airplane and peripheral vision narrows to a small, constricting hole. All I could see was his flushed and contorted face framed by the gray fog of my pain.

Somehow I was able to grunt my desperation and readiness to him; or perhaps he read it in my eyes. He pressed his palm against my sweaty forehead and pushed my head back against the trunk of the tree. He picked gingerly at the rag that had been stuffed in my mouth, unraveled it, and dropped it at his feet.

The relief was instant. I hadn't even realized how suffocating the gag had been, and how much it was contributing to my desperation. Instantly the tip of my tongue found the spot where the rest of my tooth should have been, but I was gasping for air and the pain made my broken tooth insignificant.

"Well?" he said. His eyes narrowed. I was shaking my head "no" as I heard a reluctant, raspy voice whisper. "RA-5C. *Kitty Hawk.*" The voice was my own.

When the rope was untied from the trunk of the tree and I was able to stand on my feet again, the relief of solid ground was immediate. But as soon as the ropes were untied from my arms and my circulation resumed, the pain came back with a rush. In the future I would find that this was always the worst part: the end of the ropes instead of the ropes themselves. It was a devilish twist: the relief couldn't come without the rush of excruciating pain first.

I was hardly aware of being led back to the little stable in which I'd spent my previous nights. The guards led me gently, not binding my arms behind and not blindfolding me again. I marveled at how they could be turned on and off. I plopped down on my little pile of straw totally exhausted. It had to be near noon by now. The pain in my battered arm had tapered off but remained at a high-level ache. I was given some water and a bowl of soup and then left alone. I couldn't eat.

My conscience began to work on me now. I was ashamed for not having stuck to my name, rank, serial number, and date of birth. I always thought I would be able to. It was such innocuous information I'd given them, I rationalized. But still, they shouldn't have gotten it from me. Had I given in because I really didn't think it was important information or was I just weak? Surely by now they would know what type of aircraft I was flying, the aircraft carrier from which I had been flying. Surely they would know the information from our own news releases.

What if they had wanted something important? Could I have held out longer? Could I possibly have beaten them? How could I live with myself if I'd given them our attack altitudes, the frequency spectrum of my electronic countermeasures equipment? What if they would press me for a future target list? I had been briefed on our probable target priorities and seen them designated on the charts in the Operational Intelligence Centers.

Coffee, you weak sonovabitch, you've got to do better. God, please help me to do better next time. I shuddered at the thought of a next time. Could I put my shame and disappointment behind me, to be stronger? To hold out? Hell, there hadn't even been any beating. There had been no bamboo slivers beneath my fingernails. There had been no hot brands burning my flesh. It had been just a variation of being tied up. My shame seemed to grow with each thought.

Finally, at some point that day, Lieutenant Gerald Coffee, professional warrior—trained in survival . . . evasion . . . resistance . . . escape—let go of his preconceived ideas of victory and defeat. Without really understanding it, I reluctantly acknowledged the first crack in my physical and psychological ramparts. But in my confusion and shame, it hadn't even occurred to me that I had just been brutally tortured.

4

The "Fiery Forge"

The only real security we have is the certainty that we're equipped to handle whatever happens to us. Too often we try to build strength through position, possessions, family or friends, social and religious rituals—all the outer trappings by which we form our identities. Stripped of them all, we have to draw from what is left: our basic sense of identity as human beings. From there true security is born.

The next evening my guards and the officer who had presided at my bizarre firing squad led me back along the levee paths to Highway 1, the main north-south artery in North Vietnam. We had actually crossed it a few nights earlier, but it was so insignificant I never guessed it could be that snaking red line on the briefing maps on which we had expended so much energy and ordnance. A few months earlier, Air Force General Curtis LeMay had suggested we bomb the North Vietnamese back to the Stone Age. In a few months, I would be convinced that most North Vietnamese wouldn't have known the difference.

Electrification outside the cities and larger villages was still a long way off. I supposed this contributed to the simple pattern of the people's lives: early to bed and early to rise. Their existence was as visually drab as it was routine. Thus far I had seen no one, except some of the small children who had visited me, wearing bright colors. The dominant schemes were dark blue, black, and white and uniforms of khaki and olive drab. Indeed, were it not for the tranquil tropical-agrarian beauty of the countryside and the sloping verdure of the mountains to the west, I surmised their lives would have been unendurable.

With the exception of military people and goods, mechanized transport was almost nonexistent. I had seen all sorts of people stopping through the village, weaving under huge loads of straw, manure, rice seedlings, and pieces of equipment. Even most bicycles were reserved for official transport. Eventually I would read of and see depicted in propaganda films the stories of famous bicycle porters, renowned for the huge loads they could lash onto their bicycles and then push across high jungle passes to South Vietnam to supply their troops there. The overall simplicity and almost total lack of technological development of North Vietnamese society contributed to their seeming indestructibility.

Our trek from the village took about an hour. We rendezvoused with a jeeplike vehicle on Highway 1, where I was turned over to another officer, a guard, and a driver, all with uniforms more matching than anything I'd seen so far. After receiving some papers and a small package—probably containing my dog tags and wallet stuff—the young officer in charge ordered me into the back seat alongside the guard, cuffed my wrists together in my lap, and ordered the driver to head out into the night.

We traveled northward for several nights. Like most of the other travelers, we spent the better part of the daylight hours beneath heavy tree canopies or, when such natural cover was not available, beneath intricate networks of camouflage netting. Almost all vehicles were heavily camouflaged as well. Headlights were seldom used but when they were, they showed only through the bottom third of each lens. The rest was painted over.

Although we traveled each night from dark to daylight, we seemed to be in no hurry. We stopped frequently at small villages and hamlets so the people who might be up and about could be rounded up for the treat of seeing firsthand the "black-hearted American Air Pirate" from so far away.

In the early evenings before getting underway, impromptu rallies were staged by the local political cadres. The villagers, young and old, were encouraged to take out their anger and frustration (whether they had any or not, it seemed) upon me. Their frenzy—like that of my original captors—was played like an instrument by their cadre, who exhorted them through chants to a near-crazed pitch and modulated their intensity while he lectured them.

One time a husky young peasant who appeared to be retarded became more frenzied than the rest. With what seemed like the strength of three men, he wrenched my cradled arm away from my body and twisted it back and upward. I spun my torso around and up, trying to diminish the pressure. Too late! I heard and felt the crack in my forearm where what little mending of the bone fibers had begun was instantly undone. The strobelike pain was blinding as I crumpled to the ground, hugging my bent forearm tightly to my chest. I hardly noticed the sharp kicks to my torso and buttocks that followed.

Another night we stopped at an isolated dwelling between villages and just off the road. The driver and my guard seemed to be familiar with the teenage girl who came out to meet us. She offered directions to the officer who trudged ahead up the road leaving the four of us at the vehicle. After the usual flashlight in my face and the relating of the pitched battle for my capture, and the wide-eyed "oohs" and "aahs," there commenced among the three of them the universal ballet of the sexes—the one rehearsed infinitely through the ages. There was the young warrior's boasts of heroics and dragons slain, the girl's flashing smiles and coy glances, their teasing threats to throw her to me, her mock horror and pleading little dance. It could have been at the local drive-in, the gathering place of my youth, or at a squadron beach party where young sailors flexed and preened for the nearby girls who pretended not to see. To the three of them at the moment there was no war, no captive to be guarded.

Their mood was almost festive as they led me to the largest hut of the small complex. Inside were five or six people and a boy of five or so. They were seated or squatting around a low wooden table with several bowls of rice, fish, and sauce. Two of the typical small oil lamps imparted a warm familial air to the room. After a light exchange between the girl and the others—perhaps introductions—I was gestured to sit nearby and was given a cup of tea and a sort of packet of sticky rice surrounding a core of pork and fat, all bound tightly by strips of banana leaves. I guessed it was a field ration because of its compactness and density, and it looked like it would keep well. A year later I would learn that it was a *bahn-chung,* a traditional delicacy prepared for and eaten only during the annual Tet, the twelve-day New Year's celebration for which this family was so happily preparing.

Their focus on this celebration was all the more understandable when I realized that it represented the only yearly break in an otherwise terribly gray and stoic existence. Tet represented not only the "new beginnings" celebrated by Westerners on the calendar new year, but was also a special time of reunion and family togetherness. The *bahn-chung* was one of several Tet delicacies that could be provided only by months of sacrifice and scrimping. The rest of the year's diet consisted mainly of rice, greens, gourd-type vegetables, and limited fowl and pork—all kept on the hoof. Cows appeared to be sparse and most milk must have come from the goats I had seen. All drinking water had to be boiled and was as often as not consumed as tea.

After more tea, I was ushered to a smaller room where the flickering light barely revealed a carved wooden bed that framed a wicker mat stretched taut. Two wooden blocks for pillows denoted the head from the foot. I accepted the invitation to lie down, not realizing it would be the last even remotely real bed I would feel beneath me for years. The child was brought in by his mother, who laid him down beside me. Although I must have looked scary with my hair singed and my face blotched with Mercurochrome, he had shown no fear of me from the beginning. Even now, after some reassuring coos and whispers from his mother he seemed nonplussed about retiring next to this foreign "monster from the South China Sea." The guard sat on the floor in the doorway so he could continue to chat with the others and observe me as well. Before dozing off, I was struck by the contrast with our previous stops, with the beatings and the hatred generated by the cadres trained for that purpose. That all seemed like another world, compared to the simple warmth and comfort I felt from the presence of my tiny bedmate. I slept soundly for two or three hours.

Traveling on to the North each night, we encountered convoys of trucks almost constantly, long lines of heavily laden vehicles heading South to resupply the Viet Cong guerrilla fighters and what regular North Vietnamese troops were already there. The convoys had the right-of-way, so we would pull off to the side of the narrow track. There the guards would smoke or talk with the drivers of other northbound jeeps and trucks. I was usually kept out of sight but not necessarily covered up, so I could observe the activities and surroundings fairly easily. I was struck by the accuracy of our intelligence reports, which had indicated huge volumes of resupply traffic under the cover of darkness. Even when the highway was illuminated by parachute flares to catch a convoy by surprise, the preplanned pull-off and camouflaged parking areas were spaced so frequently that from an attack pilot's viewpoint, dozens of trucks could seemingly disappear in only a few minutes.

It didn't take long to realize that most of these safe havens—used during the daylight hours as well as during threat periods at night— were in and around rural villages, and the suburbs of Vinh City and Than Hoa. Civilians, under the direction of military logistic supervisors, were always available to refuel both vehicles and drivers. In fact, I was fed fairly well during this time, with my cook or food bearer always rewarded with a glimpse of me and a description of my capture.

Several times during daylight stops I saw the results of our previous raids on these parking areas once they became known or even suspect. The areas were littered with the torn and burned hulks of dozens of vehicles bulldozed, or more likely dragged, by peasant power into isolated piles to maintain parking space for the next convoy after the recamouflage job was completed. The collateral damage to the nearby houses and buildings was extensive. Churches and schoolyards weren't exempt as truck parks, and I saw several such complexes damaged heavily by bomb blasts.

Truck parks and supply storage areas would have been primary targets in any wartime situation, but especially here where the actual enemy, the combatant, was so elusive. During many of our stops I translated in my mind's eye the topography, foliage, and buildings around me into the aerial image they would have imprinted on the film of my airborne cameras. I had spent hours with our squadron Air Intel officer poring over transparent negatives stretched across a light box, taking turns with the stereometric eyepiece that provided the 3-D image from two nearly identical negatives taken a second or so apart. A concentration of triple-A sites in a given area was a pretty good clue of a lucrative target. My daily observations enroute were confirming that.

I would later see propaganda photographs of heavily damaged or destroyed churches and schools—as well as pathetic pictures of maimed or burned priests, nuns, and children—with commentaries to the effect that these had been the primary targets of the "cruel and barbaric" American pilots. Worse yet, after piles of truck debris and the guns had been removed from the area, such church and school ruins were prime display areas for antiwar protestors and "international investigators" as they eagerly devoured with their notebooks and cameras the "evidence" that confirmed their preconceived opinions. Indeed, without their antiwar/anti-U.S. disposition, they would not have been welcomed by the North Vietnamese Communist government in the first place.

A few nights before arriving at our destination we became part of a long waiting line for a river crossing. A quarter of a mile ahead the overcast sky reflected the various lights of what appeared to be some major construction site. I could hear the harmonious growl of several pieces of heavy equipment, and the shouts and directions of construction supervisors and traffic monitors were constant. As we inched closer the angular hulk of the Than Hoa Bridge emerged, the hodgepodge of construction lights and flickering blue of welders' arcs casting shifting shadows across its cantilever flanks. Dozens of people were clambering over it, repairing the damage from the latest raid. In the pulsating reflections from the heavy sky, the bridge appeared like a great iron Gulliver with Lilliputian workers scrambling all over it.

The Than Hoa Bridge was famous. I recognized it immediately from the aerial photos I had seen, especially the ones I had used in planning my last flight. We had bombed the bridge frequently, and actually hit it several times, but it wouldn't drop. It was like a tenacious bulldog straddling the deepest channel at the mouth of the Than Hoa River. It was heavily fortified with 37mm and 57mm triple-A guns, and by now we had lost at least two or three planes and crews trying to destroy it.

We inched onto the span accompanied by much shouting and directing, and no wonder: I realized that we were actually driving on the railroad bed, tires straddling the rails and bouncing from tie to tie. Trains and trucks took turns using the same patched-up roadbed. It just took a little extra scheduling effort to make it work. The repair effort was probably increased to a near frantic pace on a night like this, as an illuminated attack through such a thick, low overcast would be improbable. As the driver felt his way along the narrow planks and steel plates that spanned the spaces where the ties had been blown and burned away, I could see the slabs of steel hurriedly welded across torn and twisted beams to maintain the load capacity of the battered trusses. Just as a broken bone heals even stronger than before because of the calcium concentration in the healing process, the Than Hoa Bridge seemed to grow stronger with the incredible mass of its repair. It was a discouraging revelation as I contemplated how many more planes and aircrew might be lost before the beast would finally be brought down.

Although much of the trip these last several days had been fascinating, full of new and strange sights and experiences, much of the time had also dragged on slowly and painfully. My shoulder, arm, and hand were swollen to the point of immobility.

Sometimes I spent hours during the day in a camouflaged vehicle haven, hidden from the sight of villagers and other drivers. I spent the time observing the scene around me—usually through a loose flap of canvas that was supposed to keep me from seeing anything. Or I would just sit quietly under my cover, thinking painfully about Bea and the children and the ordeal I must surely be putting her through.

Although the experience of the firing squad had been traumatic at the time, it had somewhat reassured me for the long run. I did represent something of value to my captors, but even that was a dubious comfort. Would I at some point in the near future wish that the scruffy kid with the M-1 had been on target and spared me the ordeal I was about to face?

During the trek, I thought back frequently to my survival training, more specifically SERE training (Survival, Evasion, Resistance, and Escape). So far I had been able to survive, but evading capture had been impossible for me. By the time I had regained consciousness out there in the water, my captors were upon me. Resistance and escape were my immediate concern. If the tetherball routine back in My Xa was any indication of things to come, I would somehow have to do better. I would have to be stronger and smarter, or something. Hell, that was just an improvisational little routine back there. What could I expect in a formal POW camp, where if I did in fact represent something of value to them that something of value might be extracted from me? My anxiety about resistance grew as we rolled on closer to our destination.

Escape had been on my mind almost constantly. The Code of Conduct specified as well: "I will make every effort to escape and aid others to escape." It was axiomatic that the best escape opportunities presented themselves between capture and arrival at a formal prison compound. At every stop along the way, in hamlets, huts, truck parks, roadside stops to "make watah," I had surveyed the circumstances quickly and calculated my chances.

Before my capture, in the anxious fantasies of my stateroom solitude or in Ready Room bull sessions, escape was a foregone conclusion: The bastards won't hold *me,* man; I'll be outa there! However, all those preconceived scenarios had you at full strength. Just having no boots, being handcuffed and blindfolded, confused and scared, let alone being seriously injured as well, had a devastating effect and seemed to diminish the number of circumstances in which escape might be feasible. Nevertheless, I had surveyed each new situation or holding place with escape in mind.

One night the southbound convoys seemed to be endless, and the Scoutmaster (the name I had assigned to the officer in charge of my delivery because the guard and driver were more like Boy Scouts than soldiers) led me into a two-room hut in some hamlet just off the teeming road. As with all the huts before, the floor was dirt and the walls were of plaited bamboo. Several soldiers and drivers were in the first room squatting around an open brazier, eating rice and something else with long chopsticks, drinking beer in bottles with no labels, and passing around a bubble pipe. The mood was festive—it was still Tet season— and I was offered a beer. Scoutmaster, in a magnanimous gesture for the benefit of the others as well as for me, unlocked one cuff from my wrist, apparently so I could enjoy the beer more. It tasted like soapy piss (I surmised, having never tasted soapy piss!), but I was thirsty so I drank it anyway. Then he sat me down against the back wall of the second room, removed a cuff from my good arm, and reattached it carelessly or kindly—it didn't matter—around my right ankle. He then returned to the party in the other room. It was apparent that he could hardly wait to regale the group with the story of my shootdown and capture, the exaggeration of which had by now, I was sure, reached near-mythical proportions.

As my eyes accommodated to the dim light, I could see this room was littered with trash from all the transients—drivers and transport people—who came and went. The sweet smell from the bubble pipe mixed with the smell of feces and urine in the far corner. The opium and the beer would surely have their effect and it seemed the word was that the southbound traffic would have priority most of the night.

As the party became more raucous, I began to realize this might be my final chance to escape. The bottom of the plaited wall I was leaning against was about eight inches from the ground, and the dirt was fairly soft. With my free left hand I began scooping it away from directly under the wall. Several bottle caps lay within reach; using the sharp edge of one, I was able to nick a bamboo sliver from the butt of one of the diagonal cross-pieces of the plaited wall.

God, I was only seven or eight years old when I had listened religiously to my favorite afternoon radio serials: *Jack Armstrong, Captain Midnight, Tom Mix,* and *Terry and the Pirates.* It had been Terry held captive in some Oriental horror chamber who had ingeniously improvised a bamboo sliver to release himself from captivity and a fate worse than death at the bloody hands of the infamous Pirate Chieftain. Using the bottle cap I shaved the sliver thinner and smoother until it was about the size and thickness of a plastic collar stay. The cuffs were hardly precision equipment. It was easier than I had imagined to slip the thin, stiff sliver between the side housing and the ratchet of the cuff on my ankle. As I depressed the spring-loaded claw on the inside, the ratchet slipped out. Way to go, Terry! Glancing toward the opening to the outer room, I repositioned the cuff loosely around my ankle so it would appear as it had been.

The dirt was scooping away easily and I soon had a trough deep enough for me to be able to slide beneath the wall to the outside. I hadn't the slightest idea what was on the other side except that it was the side away from the highway, the east side, so I would want to go straight away from the hut toward the Gulf. The options were limited at best. To go north meant to parallel Highway 1 and go deeper into North Vietnam. To go south meant again to parallel the highway for at least fifty miles before reaching the DMZ; then I'd need to somehow cross the Ben Hai River. After that I would have Viet Cong and possibly North Vietnamese patrols to avoid before reaching our own forces. East was the only possibility.

I figured the Gulf couldn't be more than twenty miles away through mostly farmland and paddies like I'd traveled along that first night. My plan was simple if somewhat naive: I would anticipate the dawns and conceal myself through the day, sleeping as much as possible. I could eat bananas and greens and young rice shoots. Night after night I would travel until reaching the ocean, where I would steal a fishing boat and row or sail or drift out into the path of radar coverage of one of our destroyers or carriers operating in the Gulf. Rescue would be an overwhelmingly joyful occasion, and my shipmates would be incredulous that I had escaped from deep inside North Vietnam. The message traffic would go out, and Bea would be phoned immediately that I had escaped and was safely back aboard the *Kitty Hawk* and would soon be back home for recovery from my injuries. She would hug the kids and cry with relief, and all my buddies back in the home wing would raise a toast at the bar during happy hour and say "Coffee, that slippery sonovabitch, we knew if anybody could do it, he could!"

I contemplated that thought: Could anybody do it? I knew no one had so far, but a year and a half later, Air Force Major Bud Day would be shot down and captured just north of the DMZ. Almost immediately—with the crudest of methods—a Vietnamese medic had set his broken arm and applied a cast from shoulder to fingertips. Then, in spite of a badly wrenched knee and a torn-up face, he escaped from an underground bunker and headed south. For over a week he moved through a barren and devastated landscape of bomb craters and charred trees. He survived close encounters with Vietnamese patrols, and a near-fatal B-52 bombing attack that left him vomiting and bleeding from the ears. He barely appeased his hunger by swallowing raw frogs and a few berries. After nearly two weeks of evasion, he crossed the Ben Hai River into South Vietnam and worked his way within a mile of a U.S. fire base. He could see and hear the helicopters ferrying supplies in and out. Reluctant to approach in the fading light and be mistaken for the enemy, he holed up in the bush for one more night. As he emerged from his concealment the next morning for the final run, he was spotted by a couple of North Vietnamese soldiers, shot in the leg, and recaptured. With one leg shot through and the other swollen to huge proportions, body emaciated and dehydrated, the cast on his broken arm crumbling, he was taken back into North Vietnam to be incarcerated for many years. His heroic attempt had fallen short by less than a mile.

The smile on my face was hidden in the shadows as one of the Boy Scouts looked in on me. It had been about fifteen minutes since he'd checked. Satisfied that I was hunched over asleep, he returned to the group. That was it. I'd have fifteen minutes to split this roach coach and get farther away than they would imagine I could get after they discovered I was gone. I thought, This is it, man, go! I took a deep breath, removed the loose cuff from my ankle, and snapped it closed so it couldn't snag something, leaned back into the trench I'd scooped out, and wriggled my head and shoulders through. The lower part of my body followed easily.

It was pitch-dark. Had I mistakenly thought there was a moon? I arose and stepped away from the wall—and smacked right into another wall. Shit! The impact was so loud I was glad for the noise of the party inside. I looked left and saw moonlight on the ground a few feet away. I'd exited right into the wall of a closely adjoining building whose eaves had obscured the moon. I crabbed to my left toward the moonlight, turned east at the corner, and stopped dead. Damn! It looked like I was on the west side of the hamlet and was about to go right down Main Street. Again I heard laughter coming from the shed. I figured that since the lane ahead was deserted, maybe everyone else in the village was celebrating too. I could see just well enough to jog cautiously down the middle of the path; there were houses and sheds on either side and lamplight glowing from cracks and doorways. Miraculously, I encountered no one. Way to go, Babe! You're gonna be outa here!

As the buildings became more and more sparse, it got darker and darker. The moon had become mostly obscured by a passing cloud and I barely noticed when the lane became a narrow path on a dike separating two paddies. My experience thus far had taught me that most of the dikes were laid out on cardinal headings, and I was reasonably sure I was still heading east. I was spurred on by the prospect of a straight path all the way to the Tonkin Gulf. I quickened my pace, so much so that I almost made it through midair across the three-foot ditch connecting the adjoining paddies. I'd completely missed the plank that crossed it and found myself flailing forward through black space. I crashed into the opposite bank with an incredible racket. There were several five-gallon water cans stacked right where my head and shoulders landed. The rest of me went into the ditch. The tin cans scattered noisily along the path and into the water. The sound of my splash and the cans hitting against one another was exceeded only by my subsequent thrashing and cursing as I tried to scramble back up the muddy slope to the level path. Christ! I couldn't have made more noise if I'd been in a bowling alley. Somewhere nearby a dog started barking as if it already had me cornered. Others joined in immediately. Soon it sounded like there were a dozen dogs for every house I'd passed, all of them deciding to celebrate Tet at the same time.

Watch where you're going, you dumb shit! You've really got to make tracks now!

Had it not been for the distracting crash of the cans, the din of the dogs behind me, and the desperation of the situation, I would have hurt more from the fall. I'd wrenched my good shoulder, knocked the breath from myself, and cut my lip on the rusty edge of one of the cans. It occurred to me, as I stumbled on down the path, that they might have been used to carry human fertilizer, so commonly applied in this part of the world.

A sliver of moon appeared through the clouds, allowing me to see about four to five feet ahead. Damn! I'd have seen that ditch if there had been just this much light! The increased visibility ahead and the barking dogs behind caused me to lengthen my stride. Still my eyes were fastened to the path in front of me as I watched for another cross-connecting ditch or for rocks or holes that could turn an ankle. Only last summer I had shown my sons Steve and Dave the fun of running along the rocks of the breakwater at Daytona, stepping and jumping from rock to rock, hardly knowing which rock we'd use next till we were there and our momentum forced us to choose, reacting with a long leap or perhaps two or three little mincing steps sideways and forward because that was all we could do. It was a sweet memory, their little five-

and three-year-old legs carrying them along, and they loved it. And here I was now, ripping along, picking and choosing spontaneously, as if my life depended on it. And, indeed, it might.

I could still hear the dog chorus in the distance behind me when the first gong made the hair on my neck stand on end. It sounded more urgent and savage than any I'd heard before. It had to be about midnight, and there was no reason for a gong except for some emergency. My early departure from the party had surely been discovered now and they were sounding the alarm. God, I hope I've gotten far enough away! If only I hadn't fallen into that stupid ditch! Did the dogs alert them? Make time, Baby, make time!

Other gongs chimed in, their collective dissonance like a howling banshee gaining on my heels. I fought back panic, the urge to run blindly into the darkness, anywhere away from the clutching sound. I glanced up at the moon, still weak but there. I riveted my eyes to the path ahead again and quickened my pace even more. I was flat-out running now, but I could see where the next couple of strides would take me. The whipping sound of my wet pants legs sounded their own cadence. I was really moving out now, putting precious distance between me and the dogs and the gongs and the Boy Scouts. Again I smiled as my mind raced forward to the ship, the debriefing, the medical care, a new front tooth, embracing Bea and the kids. Damn! I might even make it home before Number Four is born. The path was moving swiftly behind me. "That slippery sonovabitch Coffee, I knew if any . . . !" THUNK! A white-hot sun flashed through my mind, the lingering image vibrating with less and less intensity. In the black void that remained, tiny red and green balls wandered aimlessly through intertwined orbits and I was among them. I was one of them, floating just as aimlessly, no pain, no focus, no sensation of connectedness to anything. It seemed to go on and on, maybe for hours. I was just enjoying the silent, weightless life of a little red or green ball. I couldn't tell—nor did I care—which color I was.

Gradually the darkness began to grow gray, the reds and greens began to pale. I was becoming aware of sound and the weight of the earth pressing against my back and the throbbing in my head. The sounds became sharper: a dog barking and snarling, several dogs. Shouts! Commands! Excitement! Confusion! The graying consciousness was jammed with the noise, the dogs, the Vietnamese, the gongs in the background. Someone or something was pulling me up by the collar. I opened my eyes, or at least one eye. My left eye was stuck closed under some liquid. I tried to blink it away, but it was warm and sticky. With one eye I recognized the Scoutmaster. He was screaming something in my face, his angry epithets louder and more intense than the rest of the voices. The movement of several flashlights and lanterns made the whole scene appear illuminated by the flames of a giant bonfire.

Holy shit! What happened? What hit me? I tried to wipe my sticky eye clear. The congealed blood told me I'd been unconscious for several minutes, maybe a half hour.

As I was jerked up to my feet my knees wobbled, and I tried to reconstruct my last few moments of consciousness. Things had been going so well, I was really moving out. . . .

As I stood upright among the cacophony of barking, snarling dogs and high-pitched gibbering of the guards, drivers, and peasants who had gone from party to posse, I became aware of the structure that spanned the levee path on which we were all clustered. It was a bamboo-frame structure, on either side of which a person would stand and pedal a sprocket that drove little buckets on a chain, dipping water from one side and spilling it into a little sluice that directed it to the other side. It was a pedal-driven irrigation pump. In the flickering light of the lanterns and flashlights I saw the angle-iron crosspiece bracing and connecting the two sides and crossing the path at about eye level. It seemed to pulse a bright red warning light in time with the throbbing in my head. It spanned the path high enough for the average Vietnamese to walk under easily, but not the average GI Joe. As I traced with my finger the stickly split above my brow, I realized the crosspiece had nailed me right between the eyes.

Although I was sure they hadn't figured out how I had released the cuff, I spent the rest of the trip cuffed to the vehicle or to one of the guards. Someday I would learn that compared to Bud Day's brave attempt, and a couple of other truly heroic attempts from the formal prison to which I was heading, my own puny attempt at escape had been almost laughable. However, as the futility of trying to escape gradually became more apparent, I would be less discouraged by the failure of my own effort.

Certainly it had been my duty to try to escape. Escape was the most basic and desirable form of resistance, and I would hold my head just a little higher for having tried to escape in spite of the overwhelming odds against success.

Not until the last night of our journey did I pick up the word "Hanoi" in any of the conversations within my escort unit or with others along the way. Without knowing my destination, I half expected at each stop to have arrived at the POW camp in which I was to be held. My concept of such a camp was based partly upon the Hollywood versions that I had seen in movies such as *Stalag 17, The Great Escape,* or the TV serial *Hogan's Heroes.* They were all open compounds with rows of barracks for communal living and all surrounded by tall barbed-wire fences with guard towers at each corner. Although I had, of course, realized the slapstick nature of *Hogan's Heroes,* the image of roly-poly guards on whom tricks were played, volleyball games, and mess-hall dining tended to soften my preconception of what I was about to experience.

Hold on, I kept telling myself. Soon you will arrive at the POW camp where all the others you've read and heard about are kept. You will be together with them and there will be medical care. There will be Red Cross representatives and packages. You will be able to write home and let Bea and the kids know you're OK. This latter point was becoming more and more of a concern as I replayed the mental picture of the base chaplain, the Wing Commander, and my wife's best friend—the traditional triumvirate—approaching our doorstep to break the news that I had been shot down and was missing in action.

My love and concern for my wife and her circumstances were overwhelming at times. I found I was more worried about her and her grief and uncertainty than I was about my own condition. Sometimes I felt a near-panic desire to somehow let her know I was alive and was going to be all right. But I kept reminding myself that I'd be able to take care of all that once I arrived at the POW camp.

My SERE training at Brunswick, Maine, the previous fall had done little to alter my barracks-and-barbed wire expectations. It was laughable enough that my survival and POW training for combat in Southeast Asia had taken place in southeast Maine (that just happened to be the location of the East Coast survival training center); at the time, the compound environment replicated there had been based on our POW experience in World War II and Korea and had little physical resemblance to what we would find in North Vietnam. Undoubtedly, the principles of resistance taught there and the application of the Code of Conduct were extremely helpful ("No matter what they say or how they threaten you . . ."), but any physical resemblance between the POW compound there and the reality of North Vietnam would be strictly coincidental.

As I heard the word "Hanoi" more and more, I visualized the map of North Vietnam back in the Intel briefing room aboard the *Kitty Hawk.*

Hanoi was marked by the circled star symbolic of a capital city; it was right in the middle of the wide part—the northern third—of the country. I also recalled, in the same context and with a twinge of irony, the large red circle forty miles in diameter drawn around Hanoi. It designated the "no-bomb" zone, the sanctuary imposed by U.S. politicians from which the North Vietnamese government and military ran the war in the South.

On the same map was marked a complex network of circles around dams, dikes, canals, and irrigation facilities. There were shaded areas designating the flood zones should those facilities be destroyed. I had been told by the Air Intel officers from the A–6 squadron that the plan had been devised as a means to destroy the North Vietnamese capability to feed themselves at home, not to mention the Viet Cong and North Vietnamese regulars in the South. I had made the connection myself earlier in the trip as I counted dozens of trucks each night laden with sacks of rice going south. The implementation of such a plan would surely have broken the North Vietnamese will to continue the war effort. They could have negotiated for emergency rice from their "socialist brothers" in China, upon whom they were so dependent for most war materials as well.

Anyway, the plan had been sent off to Washington with the blessing of every major command in the operational chain. Any day now approval would be forthcoming, we would finally hit them where it would really hurt and make a difference. All the more reason, I thought, to consider my plight as little more than a temporary glitch in my normal career pattern.

I smiled wryly—maybe even optimistically—as I felt beneath my blindfold, touched the scab on my forehead, and recalled the irrigation equipment I'd almost wiped out singlehandedly a few nights before.

The final night of travel was a bitch. We proceeded more steadily, with fewer stops than usual, perhaps to make a deadline for my delivery. The closer to Hanoi the less damage to the road and the less congestion, so the driver was able to open it up. At higher speeds every rut and pothole caused the springless beast we rode in to lurch and bounce along crazily. Earlier I had been able to ride with my left hand curled around the front edge of the metal seat between my legs, holding myself tightly to the seat, like a bullrider trying to keep his butt in constant contact with the bull. However, with my hand cuffed now to the metal frame of the canvas top, I was at the mercy of every buck and toss and spin. My ass and hips were bruised to the bone, and it felt like my insides

were as well. Those few last hours of hell-bent-for-Hanoi were tougher
on my arm than any of the previous ten or twelve days. My arm and
hand were swollen taut and had begun to turn ugly shades of red and
purple.

With all the jostling around, I was able at least to nudge my blindfold
higher up without the guard at my side noticing. As we approached the
shabby suburbs of Hanoi, the shanties and lean-tos were crowded closer
and closer together. The living conditions on the outskirts of the capital
were even more appalling than I'd seen in the countryside. Gradually
larger and more substantial buildings appeared. Stucco and brick replaced bamboo and tar paper. A pall of smoke from morning cooking
fires flattened out just above the lowest buildings. Finally the buildings
blended one with the other to form a street of storefronts. Most had
been quite ornate and looked almost regal as the first rays of dawn
behind us cast them in hues of pink and pale orange. As we went deeper
into the city, it became apparent that there had been a time when the
buildings and boulevards might have been elegant. The clearly European
architecture, now crumbling and peeling from the neglect of wartime
priorities, was inconsistent with the Oriental character of the scene, with
its predominance of bicycle and pedestrian traffic.

I supposed we had arrived during the morning rush hour, because the
traffic was thick even on the widest thoroughfares. There seemed to be
no organized flow of vehicles, bikes, ox carts, or people, so our driver
leaned on the horn and the Scoutmaster shouted officiously as if trying
to scare cows off the track of an oncoming locomotive.

The din of the traffic, the shouts of policemen and vendors, the smell
of exhaust and burnt rice, the sight of woven conical hats and families
hunkered over breakfast in their doorways for light—it was all so foreign. I was seeing and hearing and smelling so many new things that I
almost forgot about my actual circumstances as I tried to take it all in.
It filled my senses beyond assimilation. I got the impression that my
Boy Scout guards were probably country boys, since they seemed taken
by it all almost as much as I, so much so that none noticed the ineffectiveness of my blindfold.

Finally we turned off the main artery. The traffic was less confused
now because there were no street cars. The side street had large sycamore trees on either side, stark and winter-bare. To the right was a
large building of three or four stories. It took the entire space stretching
to the next cross street. It was ornate and regal in design, but it too was
shabby with decay and had the coldness of bureaucracy about it. Indeed,

the signs and placards on the door indicated it was the musty head-quarters of some governmental bureau or agency. (I learned later that it was the Ministry of Justice.)

Midway down the block, just about opposite the entrance of the stately old place on my right, we braked abruptly, turned left into a driveway indented in the sidewalk, and stopped before massive faded green iron doors set back into a wall.

As the driver leaned on the horn to arouse someone from within, I glanced quickly to the sides. Although it seemed to resist doing so, my mind instantly assimilated the fact that we had pulled up to the entrance of a huge fortresslike prison. Mottled gray walls that might once have been white but were now streaked dirty from above stretched away in both directions, ending at the cross streets at either end of the block. The corners there were dominated by squat guard towers that looked both into the prison and out to the streets below. They were topped by weather-dirty terracotta tiles, as were most of the heavy masonry build-ings I'd seen. I recalled the high guard towers at the corners of Steve McQueen's open-air POW compound in *The Great Escape* and thought: Something's not right here! Where are the barracks, the other prisoners?

The iron locking bar on the inside of the door banged and clanked as it was raised to the open position. Just as the steel doors swung open, I noticed a weathered bronze plaque bolted to the wall to the right of the gate; the words HOA LO were cast in relief. With considerable shouting and revving of the engine, we entered the hungry mouth and proceeded into the cobblestoned innards of one of the most infamous prisons of the colonial era. I would soon learn that *Hoa Lo* means "fiery forge." The building had been aptly named by the Vietnamese themselves while incarcerated there by the French, who had built the place over sixty years before. It was now North Vietnam's main penitentiary and housed the headquarters of the country's entire prison system. The stench was immediate and distinct, a cross between evaporating urine and burnt chestnuts.

We emerged from the tunnel into a rectangular courtyard surrounded by the three-story wings of the main administration building. Rows of windows denoted administrative, living, and training spaces. Several semiuniformed military guards and an officer met the vehicle. A couple of them were armed with Russian AK-47 rifles, and one had a small machine gun. Still no uniforms matched, neither shirt to trousers nor one to the other. I stepped down stiffly from the back seat; the guard with the machine gun barked a sharp rebuke and jerked my blindfold back down into place. The officer (of the same rank as my would-be executioner back in My Xa) led me by the arm toward a corner of the courtyard. Looking down along my nose, I noted that we passed through a corridor, across the corner of another open courtyard, and into a dimly lit passageway. The ominous implication of the darkness cut short my passing sense of consolation that at least I was still under military control. (I hadn't yet realized that everything in North Vietnam was essentially under military control.) Almost in one motion my blindfold was yanked off and I was shoved roughly past the open door and into an even darker cavity of a cell.

Grabbing my shoulder, the guard spun me so I faced the wall. Inches from my face and practically plastered to the wall was a piece of yellowed paper with several faded paragraphs headed CAMP REGULATIONS. The guard who had followed behind jabbed at the paper with his finger, shook his fist in my face, and said something that sounded like "Obey! Obey!" Then he stepped back and swung the heavy wooden-beamed door closed, letting it slam shut by its own weight. An iron bolt clanked in the lock outside. Over the next few hours the psychological assimilation of my plight would be the most depressing experience of my entire life.

The cell in which I found myself was about three feet wide and seven feet long. With my right shoulder against one side wall I could touch the other wall with my left hand. The length could be spanned with three shuffling steps. Along one wall was a discolored concrete slab jutting out about two feet, at thigh level—the width of my reclining body. That would obviously be my bed. At the foot of it were ankle stocks—dark, sweat-stained wood on the bottom, and a heavy, roughly forged manacle that clamped down over the top. It was locked in place by a flat iron bar that slipped over it and through a hasp. The bar was channeled through a slot in the wall next to the door, and could be slipped in and out of the hasp and locked from outside the cell.

The ceiling was very high, and near it in the back wall was a tiny window with a double row of iron bars. As I craned my neck upward, all I could see through it were the filthy shards of green and brown broken glass imbedded in the concrete on top of the sixteen-foot wall that apparently surrounded the prison. There were kinky strands of rusty barbed wire stretched over the glass, and judging from the ceramic insulators at least one strand was hot.

Almost invisible in the shadows of the corner was a battered bucket. The rim was serrated from rust, and I could see and smell from the contents left by a previous occupant that it was to accommodate all my toilet needs. A bloody gauze bandage floated on the top. Another lay crumpled on the rough cement floor partly under the slab. My hope spiked briefly. Had another wounded American been my predecessor here? Or could it have been a Vietnamese? Same color blood.

The walls of the cell were grimy and sweat-caked. Whitewash—heavy with lime—partially covered the peeling coats of plaster and paint, in some places as thick as cardboard. A few V words or names were etched here and there and a curious little patch of letters in the shape of a square had been hastily whitewashed over. A squiggly cross had been scratched deeply into the wall just above the far end of the slab.

That tiny dungeon just reeked of the human misery endured there before me. Decades of human misery. I could see and smell and hear it. I could taste it in the stale, damp air. It permeated the pores of my skin.

I stood there between the wall and the edge of the slab, having never moved since the door had slammed behind me. I looked up toward the window, straining to focus upon the sliver of morning-blue sky pinched between the bottom of the wide eaves of the roof and the top of the wall. A pitiful, almost primordial, sound—part wail, part prayer— erupted from deep within me as I called out to God to please be with me.

5
Passageways through Fear

Loneliness and despair lead the deadly retreat into withdrawal. Time must be taken in manageable chunks—an hour at a time, a day at a time—whatever we can handle without panic. Each step we take down the unknown passageway leads to a door waiting to be opened. Each new door we open moves us through another barrier of fear.

God, it was cold. I shivered as I wondered if I would receive clothes in Red Cross packages from home. With so little food I was more vulnerable in this morguelike temperature.

How can men stand it here? Where are the other men? Surely they couldn't be far away. How soon would I see them? I prayed. Nothing lofty: I prayed for something to eat. I prayed to be warm. I prayed to not be alone.

"You must carefully learn and obey the camp regulations. If not, you will be severely punished!"

All I could see through the rusty narrow bars of the little peephole in my plank door were the snarling chops of the speaker outside. His bony finger stabbed like a bayonet toward the piece of parchment papered on the wall near the door. Since being herded into the tiny cubicle that morning, I had been hugging myself against the meat-locker chill while awkwardly pacing in the narrow slot between the slab and the wall. So engrossed was I in my misery and self-pity, I hadn't even heard this guy slide open the little door.

After a few glowering seconds, he slammed it shut and thumped the door with his fist. I paused occasionally in my pacing to read—in no particular order—and ponder the camp regulations. I had no intention of taking them too seriously, but they did provide my first real insight as to what I might expect here.

For starters, calling this place a camp was the height of irony. It was my first clue that many things would be different from what I expected. Camp Commander, Camp Doctor, and Camp This and That would be constant reminders of the incongruity. Apparently, they had begun collecting American pilots in Hoa Lo without much of a plan or policy. They had held hundreds of French POWs in prison camps after Dien Bien Phu had fallen, so I supposed that they called any place with POWs a camp, be it a few acres bounded by a barbed-wire fence or a medieval fortress.

The thrust of the ten regulations was ominous:

> 1. All U.S. pilots shot down and captured over the Democratic Republic of Vietnam are black-hearted criminals caught red-handed on the spot. They must answer all questions by the Camp Authorities. All attempts to evade answering further questions will be considered hostility and a bad attitude by the criminal and will be severely punished.
> 2. The criminals must absolutely and seriously obey all orders and commands from the Vietnamese officers and guards in the camp.

One regulation required prisoners to greet all camp officers and guards politely by standing at attention and bowing. As much as anything, I would come to hate the bowing. "In our country it is simply a sign of respect," I would be told, but I never saw one Vietnamese bow to another. We ultimately figured it was simply their way of getting even. After decades of forced submission to the French, they now had the upper hand over white men and relished rubbing our noses in it, the bow being the symbol of our submission.

Maintaining silence was another regulation—no talking or tapping on walls. If there was need to contact an English-speaking officer, the criminals must say only "*Bao Cao*" ("I must speak to someone in charge"). He must not keep anything in his room other than what has been issued; must keep his belongings carefully and must keep the room neat and clean; must go to bed and arise in accordance with the gongs; if sick, must report this to the Camp Doctor. When allowed out of the room, each criminal must strictly follow the path indicated by the guard. "Any criminal so imbued to reveal the identity of other criminals who violate these regulations will be properly rewarded. On the other hand, if criminal doesn't reveal such violations he will be punished all the more severely. Any escape attempts will be seriously punished." Finally:

> 10. Any obstinacy or dark schemes to violate these regulations in any way or to get out of the detention camp without permission are seriously punishable. On the other hand, any criminal who strictly obeys the camp regulations and shows his true submission and repentance through concrete acts will be allowed to enjoy humane and lenient treatment.

"Concrete acts": I thought about what that might mean and the speculation was not pleasant.

It was clear that the camp regulations were designed specifically to make it impossible to obey my Code of Conduct. They were mutually exclusive.

The Code consisted of six articles that prescribed behavior for POWs, much like a checklist to be referred to in times of stress and adversity. Over the years as a military officer I had been trained in the Code of Conduct, including a review just the previous fall at survival school. Although I could not recall the articles verbatim, I knew the gist of each and had at least memorized significant phrases:

> Article I: I am an American Fighting Man. I guard my country and our way of life . . . prepared to give my life in their defense.
> Article II: I will never surrender of my own free will . . . never surrender my men while I still have means to resist.
> Article III: If captured I will resist . . . escape and aid others to escape . . . accept neither parole nor special favors from the enemy.
> Article IV: I will keep faith with my fellow prisoners . . . give no information or take action harmful to my comrades. If senior I must take command. If not . . . obey lawful orders of and back up my senior officer.
> Article V: When questioned, I am bound to give only my name, rank, serial number, and date of birth. I will evade answering all further questions to the utmost of my ability. [Painfully, I recalled my shameful breach.] I will make no statements disloyal to my country or its allies.
> Article VI: I will always remember that I am an American Fighting Man responsible for my actions and dedicated to the principles of freedom. I will keep faith in my God and in the United States of America.

I could pace no more. The soles of my feet were still too tender and my legs ached. I spent the rest of that first day in prison hunched on a frayed straw mat that did nothing to buffer the cold concrete slab from my sore ass. The colder black of night came early, almost enveloping the feeble little light bulb high overhead which would remain on day and night.

Finally I slept some, never for long, and frequently aware of the dark eyes surveilling me through the peephole. My dreams were as fragmented and tenuous as my sleep: There was Bob's face, then the mongoloid kid in the village who'd wrenched my arm, the M-1 slug wobbling interminably toward my face, and demons from the South China Sea. Many, many demons.

In spite of the harsh glow of the spotlight that was focused directly into my face, I could see "Rabbit" smiling cynically. His two front teeth were slightly oversized, so much so that I had begun thinking of him as the Rabbit from the beginning. On top of the fatigue and cold of last night, I found the interrogation especially intimidating.

"Well," he said, "you say you have a medical problem and I say you have a political problem. When you are ready to take care of your political problem, then we will talk about your medical problem."

His head bobbed up and down lightly as he savored the cleverness of his response to my concern for my arm. The swelling and ugly discoloration were rampant from fingertips to shoulder. The foot of his crossed leg beneath the table between us matched the bobbing rhythm of his head. The low wooden stool on which I was seated stiffly guaranteed for him a downward line of sight from his eyes to mine—supposedly a position of subordination and surrender for me.

Considering the previous two hours of this first interrogation, I wasn't surprised by Rabbit's conditions for medical treatment. His lecture had been nothing more than an expansion of the harangue delivered less adeptly by the provincial administrator down in My Xa almost two weeks earlier.

"I remind you again, you are not a Prisoner of War; you are a common criminal. When the war in the South has been won by the determined and courageous Vietnamese people, you may or may not go home. You will be tried for your criminal acts by our people's court. Maybe our beloved president, Ho Chi Minh, will grant you amnesty and maybe not. If you show good attitude and strictly obey the camp regulations, your treatment will be humane and lenient. It will be well for you. But if you show bad attitude, if you choose to be a diehard troublemaker, it will be more harsh for you. You will be punished severely. I think you must recognize your position here. You have no rank of your military. Your so-called Code of Conduct has no application here. You must surrender your will to me. It is the only way for you. Do you understand?"

Here in the medieval context of Hoa Lo and the intimidating interrogation room, I was intellectually unpersuaded by his logic—but my emotional defenses were far more vulnerable. The room was about twelve feet by sixteen feet with a floor of large dark brown tiles. The grouting between them was black with grime, especially near the edges of the room. The walls, from floor to ceiling, were completely studded with clumps of rough unpainted plaster bunched closely together. At first it appeared to be an anti-graffiti treatment. If there were other prisoners here, there would be no terse messages of comfort and encouragement scratched by one prisoner to the other. Then I realized it might be some kind of acoustical treatment, and indeed I would soon come to realize it was. In the next few years the walls of the "knobby room" would reverberate back at them the screams of dozens of American airmen tortured there. When I first saw the dark blood stains on the clumps that protruded the most, however, my mind blocked out the chilling implications.

Before the guard who had escorted me from my cell clicked off the crude switch by the door, its frayed wires coursing up the wall between the plaster mounds to the bare bulb hanging down from the ceiling, I had seen the stains as well as the huge leg irons and coil of rope on the floor in one corner. As I had responded to Rabbit's command to sit down, he had adjusted the spotlight on the table to its most intimidating glare.

"Do you understand?"

His irritation was less disguised now. I sat as tall and straight as I could, and said with respect: "But your country has signed the Geneva agreements on the treatment of Prisoners of War. As a very minimum, under the Geneva Convention, I rate medical care and decent treatment, no matter what my attitude."

Rabbit forced a condescending smile and reached for his cigarettes. "I think you do not understand your situation on purpose. You have much to learn. I must reiterate to you in the first place, you are not a Prisoner of War. Your country has not declared war on the Democratic Republic of Vietnam and the Democratic Republic of Vietnam has not declared war on the United States of America. There is no war!"

Rabbit was cool and confident—confident bordering on arrogant most of the time. He appeared to be in his late twenties or early thirties, and

I wondered how and where he had become so proficient in English.

"Secondly, like other civilized and peaceful countries, the Democratic Republic of Vietnam is of course a signer of the Geneva Convention. However, my government is wise to the ways of colonialism and imperialism, and added its own condition. What is the word . . . yes, a caveat: If my country is at war defending itself against imperialist aggression, it is not bound by the agreements. So, you see, even if someone had declared war, it is a filthy war of aggression by your country against mine. For you, the Geneva Convention is a filament of your imagination!"

If that isn't a neat bit of Communist logic, I thought. What country would ever acknowledge a formal state of war for itself without claiming the other side was the aggressor?

I said as much in my terse response, and the interrogation went downhill from there. The rest of Rabbit's harangue for the day was about "the heinous crimes of Johnson, Rusk, and McNamara and their running-dog lackies in South Vietnam." About "napalm and white phosphorus bombs on the churches, schools, and hospitals of the Democratic Republic of Vietnam." About "the suffering of the Vietnamese people and their deep hatred" for me. About "the just cause of the freedom-loving people of the Democratic Republic of Vietnam and their indomitable determination to defeat the U.S. aggressors, whether it takes five, ten, or twenty years."

These sessions went on for the first several days in Hoa Lo, two or three times a day; the demands being to simply acknowledge my "crimes" and to "surrender my will to the camp authorities." To surrender meant "to repent of my crimes through concrete acts," a good indicator that the education sessions could give way to the action sessions at any time.

Most of these sessions were just between Rabbit and me and always an armed guard who stood behind me. A few times Rabbit was accompanied by a more junior officer—I began mentally referring to him as Spot because of the dark birthmark on his right cheek.

Two of the sessions included an officer more senior than Rabbit. He wore no insignia (nor did Rabbit for that matter). Rabbit's deference was obvious, even though tempered by his pride in his command of English as he interpreted the other's advice and admonishments to me. They seemed to be evaluating my responses to their lectures, which were always "Yes, I understand, but, no, I don't agree." This would always piss Rabbit off, but even more so when the senior officer was present.

"If you understand, then you must agree!" He would extend his hands toward me, fingers spread wide in confirmation of the clarity of his argument. But still, they made no specific demands for "concrete acts."

During this time my physical circumstances were abysmal. My clothes were filthy and ragged. All the jerking around of the previous weeks had shredded my shirt and ripped off most of the buttons. With no boots, my socks—which I'd been able to salvage—were barely recognizable. The soles were gone. Only a few threads around my toes kept them spread over my feet; some protection, at least, as I shivered through the cold nights curled up tightly on my morguelike slab. The stench from my own urine and feces in the open bucket made every breath an ordeal. I couldn't even imagine how it might be in the heat of summer. But then, I consoled myself, I wouldn't even be here by summer.

Again, without realizing it, I was breaking down into a manageable measure whatever time I might yet have to endure here. It wasn't just optimism, it was an instinctive survival technique. One day at a time, one season at a time. Surely this would be over before I knew it.

My conditions and predicament were so foreign to me, so stifling, so overwhelming. I'd never been so hungry, so grimy, and in such pain. Jesus, don't they extend *any* respect? I'm Lieutenant Gerald Coffee, United States Navy. I fly the hottest jets in the world's finest Navy. I wear the Navy wings of gold . . . Suddenly I was quiet: The stripping away of my perceived identity had commenced.

The hunger was a totally new sensation and made the pangs of fraternity hazing and survival school in Maine seem like mere samplers. I was fed only twice a day, about midmorning and midafternoon. This seldom varied except for a couple of times when the afternoon feeding was omitted for no apparent reason. Each feeding—as opposed to a meal—consisted of a bowl of soup, made apparently of whatever was in season and for as long as it was in season. I came in during pumpkin season, which would last another month or so. The raw gourd would be chopped up and barely cooked. Later there would be turnip soup, kohlrabi soup, squash soup, and three kinds of "greens" soup: slimy greens, sewer greens, and sour greens. There was usually a side dish with a little of whatever the soup was made of, fried in pig fat. Sometimes there would be one or two pieces of fat and rind about the size of a quarter. It was a cause for celebration if there was a morsel of pig flesh still attached to the fat. Finally, there was a bowl of poor-quality rice, which I learned early on to swallow without chewing because of the gravel and grit that would crunch hard on the teeth.

It is axiomatic among military aviators that flying is hours and hours of boredom punctuated by moments of stark terror. I soon came to realize that prison life was to be much the same.

My regular jailor, whom I called Sarge because of his almost professional indifference and methodical style, would clank open the heavy bolt on my door around 6 A.M. each day. I soon learned to anticipate it because it would follow in order the early morning gongs and the morning "people's exercise" routine, broadcast throughout the prison on the loudspeaker system—"*mot-hai-ba-bon, mot-hai-ba-bon,*" (1-2-3-4, 1-2-3-4)—and punctuated between exercises by explanations of and exhortations to do the next exercise with more vigor. Then there would be the stomp-stomp-stomp of the guards and other army personnel as they jogged in unison through the moatlike alley between the formidable prison walls and the buildings themselves, also in cadence: "*mot-hai-ba-bon!*"

Sometimes I would hear the food being ladled into my dishes in the passageway: two chipped enameled bowls and an enameled dish. My enameled cup and aluminum spoon, the latter supposedly forged from the wreckage of a downed American plane, I kept in my cell. The sound of the soup slopping would always heighten my sympathy for Pavlov's dog, and would trigger new gastronomic fantasies each time: cold milk, brownies, ice cream, a crisp apple, pizza, fried chicken, and on and on and on. As often as not the food would be left to grow cold before Sarge got around to me.

As my sense of hearing—like all my senses—became more acute, I sometimes had to acknowledge the sound of rats foraging around and sampling my congealing food. A couple of times my food was served up and left on the slab inside my cell while I was out. Even the opening clank of the bolt upon my return didn't seem to faze the family of rats feasting on my rice. Only when I entered the cell and threatened them directly did they grudgingly slither off onto the floor and amble out the drain hole into the alley. "We kill the rats many, many times but they just come back. They are a fact of life here. You will get used to them!" I was told. But I didn't. It always taxed my self-discipline to put them out of my mind as I gulped down the rice and pumpkin water they left.

Twice each day I would set my little water pot—with lid and spout—outside my door to be filled. It was usually ladled out hot, fresh from boiling to sterilize it. With any luck Sarge would let me at it soon so I could gulp down a disproportionate measure of my ration just to savor the warmth sliding into me.

Every other day or so, no more often in spite of my urging, Sarge had me set my brimming-over bucket—or *bo* as he called it—outside in the dim passageway, where eventually it would be taken away and returned empty. I always imagined the worst: that the food and water person and the *bo* person were the same.

The buckets were dumped in a raised, enclosed latrine area off the small courtyard outside my cell block. I was sent there once by Rabbit and locked in for an hour or so to "consider my crimes." The toilets there were nothing but foul-smelling, funnel-shaped holes in raised cement platforms that were really holding tanks. Slightly raised foot-shaped pedestals on either side of the holes marked the appropriate stance for an accurate squat. The cockroaches that infested the place were exceeded in size only by the ever-present rats. The filth and grime and stench were so oppressive that my eyes watered as I breathed shallowly and as seldom as possible. When I began emptying my own *bo* there, I held my breath the whole time.

The sheets of toilet paper that were grudgingly provided one or two at a time were the texture of coarse paper towels. The Vietnamese never wanted the paper put in the *bo* or latrine hole after use. It was to be saved for burning later. I finally surmised that since the paper didn't disintegrate in the sewage that was drained off periodically and used for fertilizer, perhaps on the very vegetables and greens that were raised for our food, it would be unsavory to have clumps of toilet paper dotting the vegetable patch. I never did set mine aside nor, as I found later, did hardly any other American POWs. It was just too foreign and distasteful to save our used toilet paper like that.

I kept seeing heaps of filthy, fly-infested bandages and pieces of plaster cast in the latrine and in various corners of the small courtyard and passageway. Although they provided evidence of some terrible wounds and injuries, and likely suffering, in a way they were an encouraging sign. First, it was apparent that medical care of some sort was at least available. Secondly, it was another indicator that I wasn't alone. I suspected there were also Vietnamese prisoners in Hoa Lo, but my routine and the food I was being given seemed to be geared for other Americans as well. There was a measure of comfort in just suspecting their presence nearby. The very day I came to this conclusion it was confirmed by the clanking of leg irons and the pleading screams of another GI from somewhere in the direction of the knobby room. Where would this poor guy be dragged off to? Where was he being kept? And the others: Where were they? In what condition?

By now I realized the extent of my naiveté in expecting to be put into a prison compound with other Americans. During my reflections on the POW information I had received during the months prior to becoming one, I recalled the newspaper article about Lieutenant JG Everett Alvarez, the first pilot to be captured as a POW in North Vietnam. They had had a very sobering impact. He was a fellow Navy pilot, and a native Californian like me. As Bea and I discussed the incident, our hearts went out to him and his young, attractive wife of only a few months. This was as close, personally, as the war in Vietnam had come for me. But at that time I still had almost two more years on my shore duty rotation as a flight and reconnaissance instructor in the Vigilante. The loss of Alvarez's A-4 Skyhawk and his capture were just an aberration in a small-time, low-risk "police action over there in Vietnam." His release would be negotiated and our objectives achieved there long before it would be my turn for sea duty again.

Six months later Alvie was still there and Lieutenant Commander Bob Shumaker was shot down and captured. His F-8 Crusader jet had been hit while strafing on a flak suppression mission. He, too, had bailed out into the hands of the North Vietnamese who made maximum propaganda on his capture as well. This incident really caught my attention.

Bob and I had been squadron mates on the USS *Saratoga* five years before. We both flew Crusaders, the hottest jet in the Navy's inventory of hot jets. He flew the fighter version and I flew the reconnaissance version. Our recce detachment shared the same Ready Room with his squadron because of the commonality of aircraft.

With his aeronautical engineering degree from the Naval Academy, Shu was a highly competent pilot and professional officer. He was respected and well-liked by all who knew him, and we had become close on the Mediterranean cruise in winter of 1959–60. The Air Wing had deployed with two extra Crusaders, a fighter and a photo version, to pre-position at the NAS (Naval Air Station) in Rota, Spain. In case either of the two aircraft carriers in the Mediterranean seriously damaged or lost an F-8, a replacement would be on hand.

When the *Sara* drew within sight of Gibraltar and the coast of Spain,

Shu and I were launched in the extra birds—the first launch of the deployment. It was a clear, crisp morning with calm, sparkling seas, and I was excited about my first look at Europe.

Now as I sat on the cold slab in my tiny cell, I drew my knees up under my chin and tucked my legs in closely, drawing a little warmth from the reflection upon that beautiful morning.

We had been shot off in quick succession from the bow catapults and I joined up on his wing in close formation. A few miles ahead of the ship, he called Pri Fly (Primary Flight Control), the ship's "control tower," and requested a low pass, bow to stern. We were immediately cleared by the cheerful voice of the Air Boss: "Roger, Swordsman Zero Nine, you're cleared. No other traffic. Keep it above the flight deck."

Great! That meant we could take it down to eye level of the flight deck crew and onlookers lining the catwalks, many of whom were first-timers like me. They had emerged from their inner city of steel bulkheads and decks to watch the launch and breathe in the sunshine and fresh salty air of the new day.

I was totally focused upon Shu's aircraft as I positioned my own with cockpit a few feet from his starboard wing tip so that my line of sight was right up the leading edge of his wing. This was the proper position and distance for a crisp parade formation. Even so, I was aware of the *Sara* getting closer as we accelerated in a shallow dive. About a mile ahead of the ship, we hit five hundred knots and leveled off at seventy feet. In the moist ocean air, ghostlike vapor shock waves danced off the leading edges of our wings and tail surfaces. We were really cookin' as we swept close aboard the port side of the ship. Although we weren't supersonic, at five hundred knots our sound would follow us by a second or so. The bare whisper of our rapidly approaching planes would seem almost eerie. Suddenly the thunderous roar would match the visual impact, as Shu smoothly eased our noses up into a three-G arc toward the sky.

"Burner . . . now!"

Simultaneously we slammed our throttles outboard to the afterburner position, directing raw fuel into the hot exhaust sections of the J-57 engines. As if welded into one sleek swooping mass, the two Crusaders leaped upward, the variable nozzles of our tailpipes dilating to accommodate the awesome cones of orange-blue flame stabbing out in shimmering heat rings. The shock wave from the screaming planes would be felt in the guts of every sailor on the flight deck.

We climbed steeply from the white, foaming wake of the ship.

"Roll . . . now!"

Shu rolled left and I rolled right, the first quarter of roll for each providing the lateral separation for safety. We each held it for three complete rolls; and just as we had briefed before the flight, we joined back up at ten thousand feet and headed for the sunny coast of Spain. That night in Rota and nearby Juárez, Shu shared all his favorite liberty hangouts with me. He had been there the year before on his first cruise.

Now, although far removed from those happy circumstances, it was comforting just to think that Bob Shumaker might be somewhere nearby, perhaps even here in the same prison.

There were others: Max Lukenbach and Glenn Daigle, the crew that Bob Hanson and I had replaced in RVAH-13 (Heavy Recon/Attack Squadron 13) aboard the *Kitty Hawk*. They had been lost only three months before, in November. There had been no word on their fate. I had supervised and conducted their recce training back at NAS Sanford, in Florida, the home base for the six squadrons of our RVAH Wing. And where were they now? Dead? Still evading somewhere near the Laotian border? Captured? Suffering somewhere near me right now in a different dungeon?

I spent a lot of time in a fetal position those first few weeks—sitting up or lying on my side—hunched close against myself for warmth and support of my arm. The boredom was oppressive, especially in view of the active life and routine to which I was accustomed. Squadron life aboard an attack carrier left little time for boredom. To fly a two-hour mission (usually about five per week and sometimes two per day) required another three hours of preparation and debriefing. Collateral duties could take several hours each day. I had just assumed the duties of squadron Safety Officer, responsible for the standardization, training, and supervision of safe aircraft operating and maintenance procedures. It was a position of serious responsibility, carried out almost autonomously, and answerable only to the Commanding Officer.

Personal time aboard ship was scarce, especially on the line in the Tonkin Gulf. Eating, writing letters, bathing, and tending to laundry were tucked into the nooks and crannies of the day and night. Sleep varied with the day/night operating cycle of the Air Wing, but was always welcome when it could be had.

Here, thrust into a totally different environment—foreign and hostile—badly injured, vexed between boredom, uncertainty, hunger, and pain, I struggled to adjust.

Much of the time, guilt and shame were my cellmates. It was becoming more and more difficult to believe that Bob Hanson had survived, and this was a major source of sadness and guilt for me. I continued to replay those last few minutes of flight, reconsidering options and "what ifs." Each session would end with a prayer that, in spite of the lack of evidence, he was alive and well somewhere.

I felt I had let down my squadron mates for sure. They were reeling from the loss of two aircraft and crews in less than a month—the other pilot and BN (bombardier-navigator) and their plane had simply disappeared one night over North Vietnam; there was no word of their fate, nor would there ever be. Squadron morale had been shaken, but the last-minute change in my sea duty orders to RVAH-13 had been a small shot in the arm. I had had a hand in training each of them. I had a fine operational reputation and was respected and liked by them all. My new roommate had been a good friend from before, "Bones" Morgan, one of the most senior and capable BNs in the Navy. Bones (so named for his resemblance to Gandhi) and I had become good friends, and we had a great deal of respect for each other's professionalism. We had been members of a small, elite task force of Navy pilots and crewmen evaluating the Vigis in their production phase at the North American Aviation plant in Columbus, Ohio. We had provided operational testing of the recce systems and provided recommendations for the engineers there. A collateral benefit had been the development for the Navy of an advanced operational recon capability as well as a recon training syllabus several months earlier than would otherwise have been possible.

Many times in my cell I visualized Bones gathering up all my personal belongings in the stateroom and from my locker in the Ready Room. Bea would receive them packed with TLC.

I was terribly disappointed in myself. I had violated one of my own maxims, which they had all heard me emphasize during training: "Never fly a recce route you haven't preplanned and briefed thoroughly." It had sounded very professional back in the training environment and certainly was an ideal worth striving for. Under the pressure of operational priorities, however, and in my "can-do" eagerness to provide the last-chance photos required for the attack squadron's in-port planning, I had altered my original mission route, unplanned and unbriefed. In the depths of my remorse, it mattered little that the deviation had been little more than the pursuit of a target of opportunity, an unexpected chance to photograph—or to bomb and strafe in the case of an attack mission—a target that had not been foreseen during the planning stage of the mission. And targets of opportunity were always fair game.

A few years earlier while flying low-level recce missions over Cuba during the '62 missile crisis, I had deviated from one of my planned routes after catching a glimpse of a camouflaged vehicle park and storage area off to the side of my flight path. At the last second I had pulled my F-8 Crusader into a hard port turn, leveled the wings with cameras covering the suspect area, and then pulled into a hard turn back to the starboard, picking up my original track. Later, through Air Intel and photo interpretation, I would learn that beneath the camouflaged netting I had imaged, for the first time in Cuba, several Soviet "frog" mobile surface-to-surface missiles. This disclosure enabled the revamping of our major contingency amphibious assault plans and earned for me a personal letter of commendation from the Commandant of the Marine Corps. So the consequences of the bending of operational rules really depended upon the outcome. In the case of the flight over Cuba, I had gotten an "Atta boy!" But now, having been shot down while deviating from my initial flight track closer to Than Hoa, I would get an "Aw shit!"

Finally, and most of all, my concern for Bea and her personal anguish and uncertainty was overwhelming. With her at eight months pregnant, I feared the emotional blow of my shootdown and possible death would be especially severe. She had always been a strong, capable woman and a supportive Navy wife. Previous Navy deployments and separations had reinforced her independence, but this might be too much. I felt that I actually had the easier of the two roles. I knew I was alive and would soon be home, but she had to live with the possibility of the worst. Again and again I reconstructed the details of our ejection and capture, not only trying to assess Bob's chance of surviving but also to determine the likelihood of our chutes being spotted, or of our being seen alive in the water—anything that might give Bea more hope.

"Soon be home!" That's what I had told her when she dropped me off at the flight line the day after Christmas. It had all seemed so routine. The *Kitty Hawk* had been deployed three months already, and would return in another three or four—a piece of cake compared to our previous separations of six or seven months. The central Florida sun was warm for December, and Bea had worn a sleeveless blouse, shorts, and sandals. Even with bulging tummy, her tanned face and limbs revealed her excellent fitness from tennis and waterskiing. Our parting had been almost casual. But now, on the opposite side of the earth, I found her image poignant and vivid: Standing by the station wagon, she shaded her eyes with one hand and with the other waved lovingly as I taxied the Vigi from the chocks and swung its needle nose toward the duty runway for takeoff.

Dear God, please be with my sweetheart and give her strength. Help her to get through this ordeal. Help her to know that I'm alive and doing fine, and that I love her so much more than I've ever been able to tell her.

6
From "Why Me?" to "Show Me!"

When we cannot change a situation, resolution comes through the way we choose to handle it within ourselves. To let go is not to deny but to accept. Letting go moves us beyond the unproductive lament of "What if?" and "Why me, Lord?" to the constructive acceptance of "What is" and "Show me, Lord."

Sarge stared thoughtfully at my swollen hand as I made sawing motions across the ring on my sausage of a finger. No comprehension! Next I made cutting motions as if snipping away at the ring with tin snips or metal cutters. Still he didn't understand. I tugged at the ring, trying to remove it, and contorted my face as if in pain. Almost like a faithful dog, eager to comprehend his master's command, he looked from the ring to my face and again at the ring. Nothing. I repeated the tugging, snipping, sawing routine.

Suddenly the intensity of his concentration changed to the brilliance of comprehension. Gently he took my hand in his own and tested the tightness of the ring himself. Then he nodded and motioned for me to set my brimming bucket outside the cell, his original purpose for entering.

After the door slammed, the iron bolt clanked home, and the padlock snapped into place, I looked again at my swollen hand and pondered anew the dumb mistake of wearing the ring while flying in combat. To wear a ring—or any other jewelry, for that matter—in a tactical Navy aircraft was taboo. There were horror stories, real or fabricated by resourceful squadron safety officers, about pilots slipping off a wing or fuselage surface during preflight inspection or even while disembarking from the cockpit, only to have a ring or ID bracelet snag on some protuberance, stripping their flesh away before the fall could be arrested.

No one ever knew anyone to whom this had happened, but it made good fodder for safety lectures. Aboard ship I rationalized that it had just been too much trouble to remove my rings for each flight. Besides, I figured, since I always wore my flight gloves from the Ready Room to the plane and back, the snagging potential was minimal. I certainly hadn't foreseen the problem I faced now.

After the injury to my arm, it had begun to swell immediately. In all the confusion and distraction, it hadn't occurred to me until too late to remove the ring. I had been at Hoa Lo for nearly a month. Surely my arm would be tended to soon and the swelling would go down. Now, from shoulder to fingertips, my limb was nearly three times its normal size. The circulation in my finger was becoming a real problem.

Until now, with everything else that had been going on, my concern had been slight. Now I was beginning to wonder if I'd ever receive any medical treatment at all. My mind wandered ahead to the prospect of a long, slow healing process, bones fusing in place misaligned and fragmented as they were, and accommodating to a new life with a right-angle arm. Well, maybe Sarge could dig up a hacksaw someplace.

I worked the ring around my finger until the oval aquamarine stone was again on top. In heavy 14–karat relief it was encircled by the words "United States Naval Aviator." Navy wings were sculpted on both sides in the triangular spaces where the gold narrowed to embrace the girth of my finger. It was the classic academy-type ring, worn by thousands of ring knockers across America.

The thin beam of midmorning sunlight, my welcome companion for a few minutes each day, pierced the gloom of my cell, stamping its golden seal on the dark wooden lintel of my door. I moved my hand slightly to focus the beam on the ring. The stone ignited instantly with the brilliant blues, pinks, and lavenders of its soul. As I sat mesmerized, the dancing colors became the lights and ornaments of our last Christmas tree. Bea and I had sat together on the ribbon- and wrapping-littered floor on Christmas Eve. We sipped eggnog and listened to carols and savored the afterglow of happy, sleeping children. They had been exhausted by the excitement and delight created by their floppy-eared basset hound Christmas puppy, herself depleted and sleeping a few feet away.

Bea had totally surprised me with the ring, her Christmas gift to me. It was both beautiful and meaningful, and I had been truly pleased. She said she knew I would be pleased because I was such a "Red Hot" about flying jets and being a Navy pilot and "all that stuff." And she was right.

I inched my hand along in pace with the turning earth as the tiny shaft of light beamed from the fulcrum of the prison wall, levering its way downward. The flaming prism of the aquamarine drew me even further through the years. . . .

It was a more delicate aquamarine that I had sought out for her high school graduation gift. How fitting, I had thought, that the icy blue of her birthstone should so beautifully complement the smooth olive complexion of her Portuguese heritage, the sable brown of her eyes and of her dark curly hair. We had slipped away from the rhythm and glitter of her graduation ball at the country club and meandered our way through moonlit gardens to poolside. We perched at the base of the diving board and were barely aware of the distant music slipping smoothly from "Mona Lisa" to "Some Enchanted Evening." Indeed it was enchanted.

The silver moonlight glowed from her tawny shoulders as I eased the sparkling ring onto her finger. She was surprised, and as she turned her hand slowly to capture the moonlight separately on each facet, her own smile added to the soft radiance, and we kissed. "This isn't an engagement ring, Sweetheart, but the more we're together the more I think it should be."

It might as well have been an engagement ring, for it symbolized our love the next three years, mostly apart at separate universities, she at San Jose State and me at UCLA. We came together as frequently as possible during those years: summer weekend rendezvous at Tahoe, where she taught waterskiing or camp-counseled younger girls; or at Pebble Beach, where I taught swimming and life-guarded. In the winter, we shared long weekend fun and wonders at the ski resorts of the Sierra Nevada as we competed on the ski teams of our respective schools.

The natural beauty of our work and play environments had complemented our shared love of the outdoors, sports, and an active life. It seemed as if the pristine beauty of these places—surely some of the most magnificent natural settings in the country—had enhanced the beauty and naturalness of our love.

During the summer of '57 after my graduation we had taught swimming in Beverly Hills, played two-man volleyball on the beaches of Santa Monica, and skipped out early on most of the laid-back parties at the Sigma Nu House at UCLA. We rambled around in an old '49 Ford convertible we'd picked up for a couple of hundred dollars. It had to be parked on a hill facing downward most of the time, and the ignition key was a popsicle stick, but it was a hard car to steal and it seemed to suit our style.

The sanctuary of little old St. Joseph's Church in Capitola, near Santa Cruz, warmly embraced the tiny gathering of family and a few friends who witnessed our wedding. Bea's narrow silver wedding band held a single row of tiny diamonds. I had slipped it onto her finger, snug against the graduation aquamarine. She had never expressed a desire to replace it with a diamond. Two weeks later I was off to Pensacola, Florida, to earn my Navy Wings of Gold. . . .

Now the little doubloon of sunshine in my cell had about run its course. Like a microcosm of the day outside, it had dawned upon my door, then cast its warm yellow beam just below the peephole whose tin cover the guards would quietly slip open to catch me at the transgressions of my solitude. Finally, the little orb stopped about knee-level as the eclipse of overhanging roof pared it down to a tiny sliver of gold. Today I had followed it all the way with the ring, keeping it centered in the spotlight, its sparkling depth my window to a world that now seemed almost never to have been. I stared at the stone as the final spark of color sputtered and died.

Some "Red Hot" I am, I thought, as I mourned the passing of my daily ration of sunlight. I couldn't have felt more dejected, more alone. My arm hurt and my stomach growled. The air stank and I was cold. I seemed to have so little control over whatever might happen next. I missed Bea and I missed the kids. I missed hot coffee and sunshine and fresh air and warm water and flying and laughter and life. How could I have known that my Red Hot life before would, by contrast, make my present existence all the more grim and debilitating?

So mired was I in my own misery that Sarge was standing in the open doorway of the cell before I had even heard him. No keys, no turning or slamming of the bolt. He was just suddenly there.

"Bow! Bow!" he shouted.

I dipped my torso forward and back, then obeyed his frugal motion to retrieve my empto *bo*.

He fished around in his pocket rather absentmindedly and withdrew a sliver of soap. From my water jug I poured the remains of last evening's portion into my cupped hand. It was so swollen that I could barely make a hollow in my palm. The soapy lather immediately revealed a part of me I hadn't seen for almost five weeks now: clean skin. I thought I had been keeping my hands fairly clean with water alone, but the mucky grime that appeared with the first application of soap was appalling.

So engrossed was I in my newly clean, pink skin that I almost forgot about the original purpose of the soap. Sarge grunted and prodded the ring with his finger. It was no use; the soap didn't work.

He hesitated briefly, shook his finger at me dispassionately, and left. He was back in no time with renewed enthusiasm and a piece of cotton twine about two feet long. The bugger seemed to be really taking this seriously, although the string was a mystery to me.

Holding my hand to steady it, he began winding the string around my finger at the knuckle, about a half inch below the ring. He wrapped and rewrapped the first strand several times to hold the end secure and to get it as tight as possible. Then, very purposefully, he continued to wrap toward the ring, each round very snug against the previous one. What the hell was going on?

His acne-pocked face was intense as he worked. He pursed his lips in concentration as a few greasy strands of his straight black hair fell down to the wide bridge of his nose. So that was it! I guessed his intent as he secured the last few winds up to and slightly under the widest part of the ring. He had compressed my swollen finger below the ring and was going to pull the ring over the compressed flesh as he unwound the string back toward the knuckle. You clever little bastard, I thought. I also realized how pathetic the whole situation was. If they'd just set my damn arm, the swelling would go away.

Well, the string didn't work either—but it might have. I was impressed by Sarge's resourcefulness. I had already watched him repair a burned-out light bulb. He had stood near the top of the rickety bamboo ladder, slowly turning and tilting the bulb until the broken end of the tiny tungsten filament reengaged the stiff wire post from which it had detached. Upon contact, the circuit was reestablished and the filament glowed as before and stuck there so long as the current flowed, which was normally twenty-four hours a day.

He had done it all so matter-of-factly, not even looking back up at the glowing bulb as he hauled the ladder out. Hell, I thought from my American perspective, if it had been me I'd have beamed brighter than the bulb, so satisfied with the magic I'd performed. Repairing a burned-out light bulb would be like effecting a massive technological breakthrough.

Now Sarge gathered the soap and string, and with a grunt and a shrug in the general direction of my hand, he exited. I was left to contemplate the fate of my arm and hand. I figured it would eventually heal on its own. That's why it had protected itself with enormous swelling, immobilizing the broken ends and fragments so they could at least fuse in place. The prospect of spending the rest of my life with an L-shaped arm was depressing, but by now I felt pretty sure that if it were not made worse somehow, I wouldn't die from it.

But how could I really know? I reflected upon the civilian and military medical care I and my family and, for that matter, everyone I had ever known had received for various ailments and injuries. Would we die if broken bones were simply left unset? I was beginning to appreciate to new degrees how resilient and self-healing my body really was. But up until now in my life, there had never been any significant test to prove that. Enjoying such a high standard of living, how little I had appreciated how physically tough and durable we can be!

Within the next few months I would appreciate my physical capacities even more as the full impact of captivity, near starvation, and maltreatment would be manifested. Because of the quantum change in my diet, for example, my fingernails suddenly became less than half their previous thickness. I watched with curious resignation as the little moon-shaped ledge on each nail grew from beneath the quick and, over a period of several months, moved outward like a tiny receding glacier. My body had higher priorities for the little calcium I was receiving now.

I began to realize that if I were to survive over the long haul—no longer than five or six months at most—I would need to maintain a balance between the food that I received and a daily exercise routine. I began walking back and forth in my cell, three short steps in each direction with a cramped, sideways turn at each end. I calculated the number of laps that would equal a mile, and set a goal for myself of not less than three miles per day. Even though I had to keep my torso fairly immobile as I continued to hug my injured arm to my body, the pacing increased my circulation and warmed me against the early March chill. The pacing was also therapeutic because it gave me something to do.

How many times had I watched zoo animals—lions, tigers and other wild cats, bears, sometimes apes—pace restlessly back and forth on a well-worn path in their cages, the swing of their haunches, the dip of their head establishing an invariable rhythm between the barriers that defined their pitifully scant horizons. Now, as I swung and bobbed through my daily journey to nowhere, I realized that the common animal instincts, evolved through a thousand ages, were the mesmerizing drive behind our study of our animal brothers. I vowed never again to add to their indignity by standing there, gawking, as they expressed their deepest stirrings.

My daily routines included deep breathing exercises, running in place on top of my slab, and one-arm pushups—push-aways, really, as I leaned into the wall against one hand and pushed my weight away from it as many times as my strength would allow. Although I realized I was losing weight, I decided I had to maintain my muscle tone and strength to the highest degree possible.

More than ever before, I began to appreciate the stringent fitness requirements for Navy pilots. I had been in good physical shape when I was shot down, and the importance of maintaining that physical edge became self-evident. Keeping fit became every bit as much my duty and a source of personal pride in imprisonment as it had been before in freedom.

The morning after Sarge had tried his soap-and-string tricks on my finger, I was pacing off my first three miles of the day. It was even colder than the previous days and my breath lingered on the air in filmy clouds of steam. How long would it be until warmer weather? How long had it really been now since the third of February, when I was shot down? I had lost track of time during those first few days and could never seem to get back on track. If those little alphabet squares scratched into the wall were some kind of calendar, they weren't working for me. I could only guess that it was about the first or second week of March.

Just over the broken slivers of old beer and champagne bottles on top of the wall I could see a few fragile brown shoots from a limb of one of the sycamore trees outside the wall. They were bare and brittle-looking. Hell, when does spring come to this . . .

"Yankee Doodle went to town, a-riding on a pony . . ."

The soft, melodious whistle could have been coming from the silver flute of an angel just outside my window. I froze in my tracks and strained to hear more. Silence!

I climbed up onto the slab and stood on tiptoes to be closer to the window.

Again the whistle: "Yankee Doodle went to town, a-riding on a pony . . ."

It had to be an American! I stretched my entire body upward toward the opening.

"I hear you, Yankee Doodle! Who are you?"

Immediately a clear, calm voice responded.

"This is Colonel Robinson Risner. I am the senior officer here at Hoa Lo. Who are you?"

My heart leaped and my spine tingled. It might as well have been God speaking. I couldn't conceal the excitement in my voice.

"Hello, Colonel. I'm Navy Lieutenant Jerry Coffee. Are you alone? Where is everyone else?"

With more of an edge to his calmness he replied, "We'll get to that. Yes, I'm alone and have been the whole time. When were you shot down? Were you alone? Are you injured?"

I tried to mimic his calmness and match his volume. "I was shot down near Vinh City on three February, Sir, off the *Kitty Hawk*. I'm not sure about my crewman, Lieutenant JG Bob Hanson. We were strafed by our own planes after capture. My right arm is broken pretty badly and they haven't done anything for it. Have you heard anything of Hanson, Sir?"

"No, nothing. Usually they bring men in together if they are both alive. Listen, we can't talk like this for very long. We have no clearing here. If we should get cut off, remember to keep the faith, and obey the Code of Conduct.

"This section of the prison is called New Guy Village. Almost everyone is kept in these cells initially. I don't know why they've brought me back over here, but I probably won't be here for long. There's another section across the main courtyard called Heartbreak Hotel. You may go there next. You'll see why it's called Heartbreak.

"You will need to know our communication system. There's probably a little square scratched in your wall with twenty-five letters of the alph . . ."

The clang of the door bolt on the outer door to the passageway that serviced our cells was followed instantly by a couple of sharp thumps on the wall that must have come from Risner. In a split second I was back down to the floor and pacing again as innocent-looking as my pounding heart would allow.

Without counting, I must have paced another six miles throughout the day as I replayed Risner's every word.

"I am the senior officer . . ." That meant there are others here at Hoa Lo and they must be together for him to know he's the senior officer. "Usually they bring men in together . . ." The exhilaration of the experience of talking to Risner was tempered by the heavy realization now that since Bob hadn't accompanied me to Hanoi, it was all the more likely he hadn't survived.

And finally, he had said, "Obey the Code of Conduct." My heart sank even deeper as I thought about my earlier transgression of the Code. It didn't matter that after the name, rank, serial number, and date of birth part the Code said, "I will evade answering further questions to the utmost of my ability." Had I really reached the utmost of my ability?

That evening and from then on I studied the little alphabet square scratched on the wall and thought of Risner's reference to it. It made no sense to me—the letters of the alphabet arranged in a little five by five matrix. Besides, the letter K had been left out. What could it all possibly have to do with communicating?

The next morning, and the next, I stretched up as close to the window as possible, whistled "Yankee Doodle," and listened. Nothing.

Four days had passed since Sarge's attempt to remove the ring had failed, and three days since Risner's contact. The swelling in my arm had seemed to plateau, but the feeling from shoulder to fingers continued to vary between a distracting ache and periods of intense pain. The arm was hot and blotchy, an ugly sight to behold.

One night it seemed to be especially painful and, in spite of my newfound confidence in the strength of my natural constitution, it was still difficult to suppress the sometimes paniclike anxiety. I was trying to decide exactly how many days it had been since my ejection and my body had been whipsawed like a rag doll in the clutch of a playful bull terrier. Thirty days was the closest round figure I could come up with— or was it thirty-five now?

Clank!

My entire body lurched as the sound of the door bolt shattered my reverie. Damn! Will I ever get used to that sound?

Sarge stood in the darkness of the open doorway, the scant protrusions of his features washed yellow in the glow of my little light bulb. As I completed the dip of my shoulders in a bow, he motioned across one wrist with his other hand. That hand signal meant: "Put on your long-sleeve shirt and your long trousers. You're gonna leave your cell."

I dressed as quickly as I could with one hand, fastened the top button of my shirt (the only one remaining), and left my right arm out of the sleeve. It wouldn't fit. Sarge eyed me thoughtfully. He wasn't sure if he approved of my partially buttoned shirt—not because of his personal sensitivities, I was sure, although by this time I had decided they were all pretty modest, but because of the possibility of offending his superior to whom I was being taken.

He motioned me out ahead of him, through the passageway, and across the corner of the small courtyard with the fetid latrine on the far side. I was still barefoot, and already thick calluses were forming on the soles of my feet. Still I cringed at the thought of the trash and filth through which I waded and I envied Sarge for his crude rubber-tire sandals, the type worn by nearly every Vietnamese I had encountered thus far.

We stopped at the doorway of a brightly lit room just off the main courtyard in which I had disembarked a couple of weeks before. I had expected to face the spotlight of another routine history lesson, starting with the indomitable Vietnamese (really Tonkinese and maybe even Chinese before the history books were rewritten) Trung sisters who, in something B.C., with their loyal elephants, repelled the northern hordes, thereby establishing the precedent for the "fierce determination of the Vietnamese people." What I saw instead startled me. I'm sure my hesitation was apparent as I entered the room.

My initial impression was of white—a lot of white cloth over the table where there was usually blue cloth. Three people in white, standing behind the table in white smocks, with surgical hats and masks in place. Another figure in white stood at the left end of the table while Rabbit, in khaki, faced him from the right. Several more senior officers, probably general staff, stood against the wall behind Rabbit.

Shiny instruments and enamel trays like multifaceted mirrors reflected the light up into the darker corners of the room.

"Co," Rabbit said ceremoniously—it was my Vietnamese name, pronounced "Caw"—"Co, in accordance with the humane and lenient policy of my government and people, tonight my doctors will give you some medical treatment. Sit down with your wounded arm on the table."

I sat on the stool and grimaced as I lifted the mass of my shattered arm up onto the table. Well, I thought, I guess this is it. It all looks a little impromptu, but I finally get this arm taken care of, thank God!

The medic or doctor or whatever on the left unfolded a white sheet. Instead of putting it beneath my arm as I had expected, he fluffed one end to Rabbit at the opposite end of the table. They lowered the sheet over my head and shoulders, tucking it in beneath my right armpit so only the right forearm resting on the table was exposed.

Strange, I thought. As a practical matter I don't see why they need such a sterile environment just to set my arm. In any case, a sterile environment anywhere in Hoa Lo was as unlikely as a rose garden on the *Kitty Hawk*. Having never had a broken bone set nor been witness to the process, I really didn't know what to expect, but the setup I had walked into just didn't seem appropriate.

There was much jabbering and rattling of instruments as they seemed to argue about what the first step should be. Through the whiteness of my shroud I could barely discern the veiled movement before me. If this operation was to be anything like the minor work details I had witnessed in the countryside, there would be one worker and several supervisors, hands clasped behind backs, kibitzing freely about how it should or shouldn't be done.

Not until the first prick of the needle did the sickening realization hit me. With my left arm, I pulled the edge of the sheet away from my face to confront the huge chrome and glass syringe with needle inserted between the knuckles of my hand.

"What the hell are they doing?" I was looking at Rabbit, but noticed the uncertainty in the eyes of the "doctor" administering the injection. His eyes darted between the two of us, fixing upon Rabbit for an interpretation of my rhetorical question.

"My doctor know best! The ring is dangerous for you."

"Just tell them to set my arm. The swelling will go down and the ring will be no problem."

"No! My doctor know best for you! You must be respectful!"

Sarge reached from behind with both hands and yanked the sheet back down over my face, twisting the long folds behind me until the cloth was tight against my face and chest. The serum—Novocain, I supposed—burned beneath the skin of my hand as the injection was hurriedly completed.

In the half hour or so that followed, the sheet across my face became soaked. The medic sliced my ring finger longitudinally in three places below the ring along each side and on the palm side. Then they literally squeezed the swelling of lymph and blood from my finger like pus from a gigantic pimple, twisting my hand as if the Novocain had deadened my whole arm, which of course it hadn't. I rose from the stool several times, trying to neutralize the torque. In any case, the stuff wore off halfway through the suturing process. I had nothing to compare it with, but I am sure it had to be the dullest suturing needle in the realm. Stoicism comes hard in the course of such wasteful, meaningless pain. I was exhausted and ready to throw up when the last stitch was clipped and Sarge released the tension on the limp sheet that had been as much a straitjacket as a hood.

I would come to know the young medic as "Ben" (for Ben Casey, the popular TV surgeon of the time). I watched him bandage my hand with strips of cotton cloth, sopping wet from the alcohol they had been soaking in for sterilization.

Rabbit held up the bloody ring as if for all to see and proclaimed almost triumphantly, "You see, Co. The people of the Democratic Republic of Vietnam care about your health." With an ominous inflection, he added, "And I think you will show your appreciation in the future, the very near future."

Late the next night, I was taken blindfolded through the darkening streets of Hanoi to the Bac Mai military hospital. My broken arm was set after a fashion, a cast was applied, and the swelling went away.

7

A Letter Home

Where does one go to give up? If we knew, would our answer be there? I think not. The answer comes from moving forward, even through confusion and fear. To try to go back—even if it were possible—is certain defeat. To give up on something you believe in or desperately want guarantees you won't get it.

My General MacArthur medal was a red-and-white striped ribbon bar from which hung a circular gold-colored medallion with a bust of the General in relief. I wore it with exceptional pride just over the Wolf, Bear, and Lion insignia on the left breast of my Cub Scout uniform. Our entire den had won the distinctive medal for exceeding our quota in the collection of scrap newspapers, tin cans, old toothpaste tubes, and anything rubber. We were proud of our "war effort." Every kid on the block could sing every word of "Let's Remember Pearl Harbor" and "When the Yanks Raised the Stars & Stripes on Iwo Jima Isle." My first full-size bicycle was called a Victory bike because the handle grips and pedals were of wood instead of rubber, the tires were synthetic, and there was no aluminum or chrome. It contained no raw materials essential to the manufacture of weapons and other war materials. We tended Victory gardens and endured the rationing of gasoline, sugar, and meat. In school we bought and saved defense stamps to be collected and ultimately redeemed—like green stamps—for a war bond to finance the war effort.

All the movies during World War II painted our adversaries as the cruel and heartless aggressors, to be defeated and punished at all costs. In playing our war games as children, we would always fall to the ground and writhe in agonizing death when we were impersonating Hitler, Tojo, and Mussolini. To have been captured by such enemies was considered a terrible fate, beyond imagination. In that war the thought of torture at enemy hands embodied the worst combination of Oriental and medieval horrors, depending upon which major foe—Eastern or European—we were facing.

From my boyhood perspective, the concept of torture at the hands of the enemy was always physical in nature. The Chinese Communists introduced "brainwashing" in Korea, but that was separate from torture. In all of my military training, the "R" ("resistance") in "SERE" had focused upon resisting the surrender to physical pain. All classroom instruction and field exercise had been conducted upon that premise. None of it prepared me very well for the actual physical torture I had experienced or would yet experience. What I was just beginning to realize now, however, was how ill-prepared I was for the mental torture as well.

Isolation and degradation were the psychological cornerstones of my captors' program to "change my thinking." And, of course, the constant leverage of prospective torture was mind-harrowing. The stripping of my rights as a POW and the threats of imprisonment "long after the war in the South is finished" weighed heavily, even though I maintained faith in my country and government to not allow such a thing. But through all of this, at least I knew I was alive and doing okay, and that I would survive the ordeal. In a convoluted sort of rationalization I could even convince myself that now I was probably safer than if I were still facing the missiles and flak over North Vietnam and the pitching deck of the *Kitty Hawk* on black, stormy nights. Although I couldn't yet be sure, execution didn't seem to be a part of the official policy here, and I was gradually learning to fight in the catacomb combat of Hoa Lo, continuing to pursue my duty as best I could as an American Fighting Man. At least *I* knew I was okay and was reasonably certain that someday soon I would return home.

What I was least prepared for and what was more devastating than any of the rest of this was the mental torture—the guilt, anguish, and sense of responsibility for what I was putting my wife and family through.

It all seemed so unfair to Bea. My duty was difficult but clear-cut. But for her there would be so much uncertainty. Her life would suddenly be in a holding pattern, not even knowing for sure for what she was holding. My concern for her overwhelmed any concern I had for my own well-being. The pain of imagining her pain was greater than any associated with my hunger or cold or injuries. God, I was desperate in my desire to reach out to her, to comfort her, and to help her define her task as mine was so clearly defined. Even though my faith in her to carry on never wavered, my desire to somehow reach and reassure her became almost obsessive.

Rabbit was solicitous as he offered me a cigarette from the pack of Truong Sons he was smoking. As usual, I declined politely even though I had begun accepting cigarettes offered by Sarge three times a day; they were the first I had ever smoked in my life. I didn't even know how to inhale so I figured they couldn't hurt me too much. And they did provide some diversion to help pass the time. I was pleased as hell with my first smoke ring. I would later learn to accept the cigarettes in any case. As incongruous as they were in an atmosphere of torture and degradation, they constituted an amenity that could be withheld as an initial increment of punishment, thereby postponing by one level the withholding of more important "amenities" such as bathing, food, and water.

The staff officer sitting next to Rabbit was the most squared-away Vietnamese officer I had seen thus far. He had removed his rank insignia, but his age and bearing distinguished him as a man of considerable authority. Nevertheless, I decided to think of him as "Blank"—for his blank collar where his rank insignia should have been. I immediately picked up on Rabbit's seemingly genuine respect for him, no small thing considering his usual imperious manner. The Staff Officer spoke and Rabbit translated.

"How would you like to write a letter to your family?"

I was so surprised I almost blurted out how my heart was aching for Bea and her plight and of my need to reassure her in some way, and yes, yes, please, I would like very much to write a letter to my family.

"According to the Geneva Convention on POWs I am allowed to write to my family. I expect to write to my family. It is just a matter of time."

This, of course, elicited from Blank a rehash about the unjust war— I was not a POW, I was a common criminal, the Geneva Convention was irrelevant, I might or might not go home after the war—all of which Rabbit translated by heart, sometimes not even waiting for the clichés from their parrot source before he "translated" them.

The two of them continued in their earlier solicitous tone as if my comment had never been.

"As you know, the Lord Bertrand Russell—an eminent English . . . no, British philosopher—is a famous peace activist and a staunch ally of the Vietnamese people. He has written many articles and made many speeches about the U.S. war crimes in Vietnam."

Blank interrupted Rabbit with a question and nodded to me.

"Surely you have heard of the Lord Bertrand Russell!"

I had heard of him, but I really couldn't recall how or why, and certainly not in any antiwar context. When I left the States in December 1965 for my tour in Vietnam I hadn't even been aware of any true antiwar activities. I could recall some isolated TV shots of scraggly hippies in front of various buildings in Washington protesting the Vietnam war. They were always protesting something, especially anything military. I also recalled some statements by politicians around the country warning about the danger of an all-out conflict with China if we weren't careful. And there had been some general disenchantment with the musical-chairs government in South Vietnam and its inability to organize its own credible resistance to the VC, but as far as I had been concerned, that was mostly misunderstanding of the painful process by which most Third World countries make the transition to a more democratic process. The thought of a major antiwar movement was alien to me and seemed to be no more than wishful thinking by the Communists here.

"No, I've never heard of him," I said cautiously.

Rabbit sneered at my apparent ignorance as he translated my response. Blank needed no translation. "No matter," he said, and they continued. "The Lord Bertrand Russell"—he enjoyed saying "the Lord"—"has sent his personal ambassador to Vietnam to convey his best wishes to the Vietnamese people, and to document U.S. war crimes so all the world will know them. He will be talking with many of the Lord Bertrand Russell's colleagues in the United States when he leaves Vietnam. He has offered to deliver a letter to your family while he is there."

Again my throat tightened and my mind raced as I visualized Bea actually reading to the kids a letter from me, tears of relief and renewed hope glistening in her eyes. It was more difficult to disguise my emotion now. I also thought of the Code of Conduct: "I will accept neither parole nor special favors from the enemy."

"Are the other Americans allowed to write to their families as well?"

I recalled the grim mug shots of Alvarez, Shumaker, and Commander Jim Stockdale, who was the senior Navy POW, in the newspaper. I was pretty sure their families had received letters from them, but there had been speculation they had been tortured to get them to include propaganda in their letters.

"Yes, of course. All captured Americans are allowed to write home, even though we hate them very, very much." My initial excitement at his response was immediately stifled when he relayed this exchange to Blank, who chuckled an "If he believes that he'll believe anything" chuckle.

"If I am allowed to write to my family it can be mailed from the DRV like any other mail." Rabbit bristled at "DRV"—he always said "Democratic Republic of Vietnam." However, Blank was anxious for the translation and he let it go as they jabbered to one another.

"But with the war the mail is very undependable. Sometimes it may take months for a letter to get there. Sometimes they become lost. This way your letter could be mailed in your country and your family could get it very, very soon. And furthermore [Rabbit glanced sideways toward Blank], you can give your letter to the Lord Bertrand Russell's personal secretary yourself. He can tell your family that he has seen you and that you are receiving the humane and lenient treatment from the government of the Democratic Republic of Vietnam."

"I would see him myself?"

"Yes, yes! He would like to talk to a captured American pilot who has been in the United States just recently and who has seen the outrage of the American people against Johnson and his criminal war waged against the innocent people of Vietnam. And also you can tell him yourself where to deliver your letter to your family."

God, it seemed too good to be true, to actually get word to Bea and to send her my love. But I must be cautious. Rabbit and Blank seemed awfully anxious for this to happen, and I was rapidly learning that what was in their best interest wasn't in mine. Was I being set up for something? But the Geneva Convention prescribes that men be allowed to correspond regularly with their families. What difference does it make how a letter might be delivered? I knew I was rationalizing and picking my way through a minefield. Yet with Bea's peace of mind—and mine, perhaps more than I realized—on the far side, the risk might be worth it.

The interrogation stool was placed in my cell and my slab became my writing table. I drafted the letter several times, impatient with my tedious, left-handed scrawl as I printed reverse slant letters into the words and sentences of my heart reaching out.

*   *   *

When Rabbit read my final draft he made some derisive remark about how childish it looked.

"Is this the best you can do? You can't do better?"

"I have never written with my left hand before. It is the best I can do since my other arm and hand are healing so badly."

My right arm and hand were, of course, useless still, but even more so than necessary. Even though most of the swelling had gone down almost completely, the limb now rattled around loosely in an oversized cast. I had stuffed whatever paper and rags I had scrounged up into the space between my arm and the cast so the healing would be as rapid and true as possible. Of course, the slashes in my finger had become infected—just like the whole damn filthy prison was infected—and the flexor tendon was fusing tightly to the bone. I had reconciled myself to the probability that both arm and hand would be deformed forever.

Rabbit continued. "But you must say about your humane and lenient treatment!"

"When my wife reads this letter she will know that I am alive and have received humane and lenient treatment. As you see, I told her I have received medical care."

"No, you must write it. And you must also say about the fierce determination of the Vietnamese people to defeat the U.S. aggressors and their lackeys."

God, I thought. What bullshit. I should have known it wouldn't be that easy.

"No. I'm not going to say all that stuff. This is just a simple letter to my wife in accordance with the Geneva Convention. The fact that I'm alive and have received medical care will make all my family grateful to the people of the DRV."

"No, you must write as I say about the humane and lenient treatment you have received!"

Shit! I went ahead and wrote it. I'd really only been tortured once officially. I'd received medical care after a month or more, and my arm was mending after a fashion. I suppose, since I wasn't dead, one could call this treatment lenient and humane.

Rabbit left hurriedly with the letter and was back in twenty minutes. He had obviously consulted with Blank.

"I think"—as if it were his own idea—"I think you must still say about the fierce determination of the Vietnamese people to defeat the U.S. aggressors and their lackeys."

Again I pictured Bea, reading with relief the unexpected letter, the carefully chosen words of love and concern far outweighing the propaganda. I wrote the crap about the "fierce determination," parroting the blatant hyperbole I'd endured during Rabbit's lectures. Surely Bea would see through all this other stuff for what it was.

Rabbit read the new draft.

"Now you must tell your family to become activists and to join the struggle against this dirty war."

"No! This is all I'm gonna write."

"You must write as I say. You will meet our guest this night and give him the letter to deliver to your family."

"That's fine, but this is all I'm gonna write. If you don't want to send it, it's okay with me!"

I bit the lie into my lip as Rabbit stormed out.

"Wass!"

Sarge made a circular scrubbling motion against his chest and pointed to the water in the cement cistern. It reminded me of the old watering trough on Grandpa's ranch, a relic of earlier days when he and Dad had milked a small herd of dairy cows.

"Wass quigly!"

My first Vietnamese bath. With only one arm functioning, the process was slow and tedious . . . and cold. I stripped totally, dipped water from the mossy tank with a soup bowl and poured it over my head and body, bathed with the coarse soap, and rinsed one dip at a time, all the time keeping my casted arm elevated. Inevitably some water ran into it anyway because the space between my arm and the inside of the cast was now twice as big as it should have been.

After the initial shock, the water felt good; being clean felt good. But now, as Sarge returned, I was shivering so uncontrollably I couldn't even get my clothes back on. Sarge waited as I hobbled into my shredded skivvies, then motioned me to pick up my shirt and trousers, and led me back to the cell.

There on the middle of the concrete slab was my first prison issue. There were two sets of khakis (long-sleeved shirts and trousers), two sets of shorts (short-sleeved shirts and bright blue cotton shorts), a pair of rubber-tire sandals (the feet had been cut from a discarded tire, tread down, and the straps from an old inner tube). There was a brownish stickery cotton blanket, an olive drab mosquito net, and a small hand towel. Best of all, there was a blue turtlenecked sweatshirt that I promptly named Old Blue. We would become best friends.

Sarge had me throw the leathery remnants of my fatigues and my skivvies into a corner of the passageway, and there went my final material connection to my past life, another increment in the process of stripping away my identity—the total significance of which I was yet to understand.

The uncurtained windows of the shabby downtown "conference rooms" were crisscrossed with paper tape as if prepared for high winds or a hurricane—in this case, bomb concussions. The small low table in the center of the room held a tray of fruit: bananas, oranges, and tangerines. There was also a plate of plain cookies, a teapot and teacups, and an open pack of Truong Sons and some matches. There were straight-backed chairs on both sides of the little table. An old floor lamp stood to the side, the paint smudges on its shade casting weird shadows on the walls, which were painted a classic bureaucracy green. Little bits of trash—paper, filthy mop strings, dust—littered the shadowy corners of the room where the cleaning utensils failed to reach.

Roger Schwinman entered rather awkwardly from a side room as I sat down in one of the chairs. It was clear he had no more idea of what to expect than I did. Our greeting was stiff, more of an acknowledgment, really, and there was no handshake. Probably just as well, since both of my hands were already juicy from the orange I had commenced peeling immediately.

He introduced himself as Bertrand Russell's personal secretary. Schwinman was apparently an American; he had no accent of any kind. Rabbit, Blank, Sarge, and a few others—all in their best uniforms—stood just inside the room from which Schwinman had entered, and were all within earshot of everything that might be said. A Vietnamese photographer in civilian clothes flitted about obsequiously for the first few minutes.

Schwinman appeared to be in his early thirties, maybe a little younger than I. His hair was cropped closely and was especially dark in contrast to his pale complexion. He wasn't a person you'd notice in a crowd, and his clothes too were dark and nondescript.

I poured one of the small teacups full, drained it, and filled it again. Then I began peeling a banana. I knew Schwinman was watching me but I didn't look at him. Finally, he cleared his throat and asked rather tentatively how I was. That initiated a stiff exchange of "pleasantries." Between bites of banana and gulps of tea I answered his questions courteously but sparely; where I was from, where my family was, how my arm was healing, and so on.

I could almost feel my deprived stomach wrap itself around the orange and banana I had already devoured, and the hot tea was sweet and soothing. I peeled a tangerine and stuffed it into my mouth, four sections at a time. The bandage on my hand was soaked with citrus juice but I didn't mind. Schwinman waited until I'd swallowed the second half of the tangerine, then continued.

"My sponsor, the Lord Bertrand Russell, is convening an international tribunal to investigate the war crimes committed by the U.S. government here in Vietnam. How do you feel about these atrocities carried out by your government?"

"I am not aware of any war crimes committed by my government," I said, selecting several cookies and eating them in multiples of three.

"But surely you yourself have seen and heard of the suffering of the Vietnamese people perpetrated first by the French colonialists and now by American imperialists."

"Listen, I am very sorry about the suffering of the Vietnamese people. War is hell no matter how it is carried out. But my government doesn't commit war crimes." I poured myself more tea.

"But these people here tell me that you yourself were shot down carrying out such crimes. Your war planes have bombed schools and hospitals and churches. Thousands of innocent women and children have been killed by U.S. napalm and cluster bombs. Even an unborn baby has been killed in its mother's womb by a U.S. cluster bomb."

I thought back about the truck parks and depots I'd seen in and around villages off Highway 1. I'd seen a great deal of collateral damage around the debris of shattered trucks and road repair equipment, and fuel storage tanks north of Than Hoa.

"It is inevitable that civilian casualties occur in wartime and they are unfortunate. I truly feel sorry for the suffering of these people just as I feel sorry for the suffering of people in South Vietnam who have been terrorized by the VC."

Schwinman glanced at Rabbit and looked a little bewildered.

Peeling another banana, I continued. "I can tell you for a fact that my government targets only military targets and our pilots bomb them as accurately as possible."

I didn't know then that in the coming years I would be shown propaganda films extolling the combativeness of all the Vietnamese people.

Women would be manning antiaircraft guns and "children and old folks," all civilians, would be happily passing ammunition through the trenches in the heat of battle. "Every man, woman, and child is a combatant, fighting in defense of the motherland." But I would learn further that as soon as one of those combatant women, children, and old folks became a casualty they were suddenly "innocent civilians scurrying to take cover from the barbaric attack on their poor village."

Schwinman had been taking notes on my comments, as I continued devouring bananas and tangerines as fast as I could peel them and shove them in. I drained the last few drops from the teapot, removed the lid, and looked inside as if I couldn't believe it was all gone. The photographer came in with a full pot, poured a cup for Schwinman, and backed out again. I refilled my own cup. Schwinman went on for about twenty minutes or so, telling me about all he had seen; all the evidence of U.S. crimes against humanity. I was sure he had seen exactly what the North Vietnamese had wanted him to see and no more.

"My friends here tell me that you have acknowledged the humane treatment you have received at their hands."

"I told you at the outset that I finally received medical treatment." I paused slightly after the word "finally."

"And you have witnessed their determination to be victorious in this dirty war of aggression against their country?"

Dirty war of aggression? What the hell was this guy talking about? This was one of Rabbit's favorite clichés. He and the others hissed it out in nearly every other sentence. But this guy was an American. This is America fighting against Communism—where the hell has this guy been? He's talking about "his friends here" and the enemy being "victorious." I stopped peeling the last tangerine and shook my head.

"If there is aggression it is on the part of the Communists. They are the aggressors in South Vietnam."

He responded quickly. "No. The war in the south is a civil war among the Vietnamese themselves. The United States has no right to be here."

The "camp authorities" in the side room were listening intently. Although Rabbit was probably the only one who could understand everything, I was sure the others could easily detect the tension in the conversation. I knew I was at risk but I continued.

"We have been asked by the government of South Vietnam to help them defend themselves against Communism. President Johnson has offered to stop all bombing and withdraw all of our troops if the Communists cease their aggression. You know he extended the recent holiday cease-fire in the south and the bombing pause in the north as a sign of goodwill, to encourage negotiations. But the North Vietnamese just used that time to repair their transportation lines and resupply their troops. We don't want to be fighting in this country but we will help our friends in the south for as long as they ask us to."

Schwinman had been sipping tea that was poured for him. I could almost see his mind locking onto his own preconceived impressions of the war just as mine did when he was parroting the Communist slogans. Jesus, we could just as well be debating over a cup of espresso in some esoteric Soho coffee den. Could it have occurred to him that I was practically starved? Did he think I just had some strange obsession for fruit, cookies, and tea?

He returned the little cup to the table emphatically and leaned toward me.

"If Johnson is so interested in negotiations, why does he keep sending more troops to South Vietnam? To prop up an unpopular dictator, Nguyen Cao Ky, that's why. There are more than three hundred thousand troops in South Vietnam already. Many Americans see what is happening and are demanding an end to this folly. Young men are refusing to fight Johnson's criminal war. Many are burning their draft cards. In fact, one who has done so, a young man named David Mitchell, will be tried in court soon. His trial will be a cause célèbre for the antiwar movement in America. There is a ground swell of resistance in America. You are in the minority. You are foolish not to see the truth. The Lord Bertrand Russell's war crimes tribunal will make that truth more evident throughout the entire world."

He paused and glanced back at the shadowy group crowding the wide doorway to the other room.

"My hosts tell me that you have been taught the history of the Vietnamese people's struggle for freedom and independence; that you have spent many hours with them learning the truth of the situation."

I'd eliminated the third tangerine while he was speaking, and wiped the nectar from my chin with one of Old Blue's sleeves.

"Yes, I have spent many hours listening to their version of history and truth."

He leaned forward even more, almost to the center of the table.

"You see! You are in a unique position to bring enlightenment to the American people. You could contribute to the defense of David Mitchell. You could contribute to Bertrand Russell's tribunal. You have been an innocent victim of your government's propaganda machine, but now you know the truth. You have been in North Vietnam and have seen the suffering of the Vietnamese people. Your testimony would be invaluable."

I couldn't believe what I was hearing. Just because I hadn't actually spit in their eye all that time they had told this kook that I believed them; that I had seen the truth. That just because I had expressed gratitude for minimal medical care, I should be willing to join an antiwar movement.

Undeterred by my look of bewilderment, he continued with the same fervor.

"My hosts also tell me that you have witnessed firsthand the incredible determination of the Vietnamese people to defeat Johnson's aggression in support of his lackeys in the South."

I pondered the intensity in Schwinman's face. The pale skin around his mouth was drawn taut and his eyes shone brightly with conviction. I sensed my shoulders relax as I sighed my realization of the futility of this discussion. I finished off the orange I had been peeling, shoved the last two cookies into my mouth, and washed them down with the remaining tea. He was watching me, and I sensed for the first time that he may have considered my voracious appetite for what it really was. I said as calmly as I could, "Yes, I saw and experienced their determination out in the countryside near where my crewman and I were shot down . . . By the way, speaking of my crewman, do you know his fate? Have they told you what happened to him or where he is? His name is Hanson."

"No, they haven't mentioned him."

"Could you please ask? They may tell you the truth."

He looked away, and seemed uncomfortable with the subject.

"Perhaps."

He glanced back at Rabbit and the others, shifted gears, put on his first smile, and said as affably as possible, "Listen, I understand you've written a letter to your family. I'd be happy to take it back to the States with me and mail it from there."

"Yes, thank you. I have been allowed to write and I would really appreciate that."

The instant we started sounding like a couple of ordinary Americans talking in normal tones, Rabbit stepped forward and said to Schwinman, "I will deliver the letter to you before you depart Hanoi. I don't think Coffee is quite finished with it."

Schwinman was draining the last of his tea and didn't see Rabbit's menacing glance toward me. I didn't like the glance or the sound of that "not quite finished with it."

We said good-bye as perfunctorily as we had said hello. I was led out of the room and back to the vehicle, was blindfolded and returned to Hoa Lo.

En route I thought back to our conversation. I was puzzled and depressed. How could two men born about the same time in the same country develop in such totally different directions, form such opposing views and convictions? He was welcomed here as a friend, I was reviled as an enemy. Finally, my darker thoughts gave way to the realization that only in such a free and pluralistic society could we have traveled such diverse paths to intersect on the opposite side of the world in some squalid Southeast Asian capital and argue the merits of a war that in my own mind was so clear-cut, so inarguable.

As the ominous clanking of Hoa Lo's gates jerked me back to reality, the depression returned heavier than before. Shit, he still hadn't been given my letter. For the first time, I suspected that if I were lucky, there would be no letter. If I were unlucky . . .

For nearly two hours I stared at the tiny mesh squares in the top of my new mosquito net. Each hundred squares—ten by ten—was bordered by a slightly heavier weave, so the entire pattern was one of subtle checks about one inch square. In the future I would spend hours staring up through the porous membrane working out chess and checker tactics, math problems using the ones and tens as an abacus, constructing floor plans of dream houses using the combinations of squares to show room relationships in position and size.

The warmth from my body heat trapped within the net as well as from my new cotton blanket provided welcome relief from the shivering cold of previous nights. Still, my stomach churned with uneasy feelings of impending crisis. Finally, my eyes closed. Reality and dream began to intermingle, each maintaining fragments of integrity like oil and water.

Voices . . . keys . . . dream or reality? The voices were muffled, the jingling keys purposeful. Suddenly the bolt on the door slammed open sharply. Reality! And I realized I'd been expecting them.

Sarge glared at me as I fumbled beneath the folds of the net. I could see that with only one arm this simple routine will take some practice. My bow was stiff and the roving gun guard looking over Sarge's shoulder snarled derisively.

As I worked my new long-sleeved shirt on over my cast, I noted its cold clamminess from the earlier sweat. I sensed it might be nothing compared to what was about to come. With a sideward jerk of his head, Sarge commanded me to follow the guard into the darkness of the passageway.

Rabbit was furious, and I figured I was in deep *kim-chee*. He was pacing back and forth and practically frothing at the mouth.

"You said wrong! You always said wrong! But now you will write a proper letter to your family. My superiors have promised the Lord Bertrand Russell's representative that you will write a proper letter to your family."

"I have already written the letter. Why didn't you give it to him?" My heart was sinking, not only with the disappointment that my letter was still not on its way to Bea, but also because of the ominous implications of Rabbit's term—a "proper letter."

He sneered.

"Do you think I would give him that letter? It says nothing about your education to your crimes, or about your repentance. It is not a concrete act of repentance."

Still seething, he slammed his fist on the table, making the gooseneck spotlight lurch off the edge. He caught it awkwardly by the cord and fumbled as he put it back into place.

"You must say as I tell you! You must tell your family to tell their friends to write to Senator Fulbright and Senator McGovern and to your President Johnson to end this dirty war. You must tell them that you have learned the history of Vietnam and of this filthy"—he always pronounced it "feelthy"—"war, and that it is an unjust and criminal war."

"No. I have talked about my humane treatment and about the Vietnamese determination. If that isn't enough, forget about the letter." I tried to ignore the tightening in my throat as I blurted out those last few words.

Rabbit stood centered behind the table, hands sternly on hips, and glaring down at me sitting on the lowly stool.

"We will see!"

He snarled a command to Sarge, who was standing behind me in his usual unobtrusive style. Sarge summoned another guard from outside. Together they went to the far corner of the knobby walled room and dragged out a coil of rope, some handcuffs, and the long thirty-pound iron bar with its U irons to go around the ankles. The new man slammed the end of the bar he was holding to the floor. I shivered at the recollection of the same sound I had heard several times now, followed by the sound of men screaming.

Sarge, still as matter-of-fact as if simply opening my door for morning *bo* call, said "Co!" and pointed toward the floor. As I arose from the stool the other guard let me have it right between the shoulder blades, both hands clenched together in a common fist, like an iron maul. I dropped heavily to my knees, and as it was registering that I might have a crushed vertebra, he spun me around to a sitting position. He moved with a vengeance, this guy. Short, stocky, and strong, he had stripped down to an old-fashioned undershirt with thin shoulder straps. He had a face like a pig: I could see straight into his nostrils about six inches. One of his eyes was haywire. The upper lid didn't come down very far, so the entire iris was always visible. It made him look like a wild-eyed pig, but he operated more like a pissed-off Tasmanian devil. I would learn later that this little torture specialist was known appropriately as "Pig Eye." If any Vietnamese ever acted like I personally had bombed and strafed his village, killing his mother and sister, it was Pig Eye.

Before I knew it he had my ankles threaded into the heavy irons held by the bar and had cuffed my wrists behind my back. He had crunched the cuff into the plaster cast that encircled my right wrist, totally oblivious of the strain on my casted arm—or maybe acutely aware of it. Sarge held me firmly from behind with an arm lock around my neck while all this was going on.

Rabbit walked out of the room, not deigning to dignify this most undelicate process with his presence.

Pig Eye was sweating already and mumbling half to himself and half to Sarge as he uncoiled the rope with a practiced flick, dropped down behind me, and began tying the rope around my upper arms very tightly. He tied the right one a little higher than the left so he could get it on above my cast. Somehow he used slip knots on both arms so that he could cinch them down tighter and together simultaneously. I tried to tense my biceps and triceps against the constricting strands but he was patient, pulling every few seconds to catch my arm between flexes. When the ropes seemed to be touching the bone in my upper arms and the tingling had begun in the lower arms, he cinched them together so that my elbows were touching. He wrenched and jerked and yanked my arms closer and closer behind me. The stiffness of my right-angle cast caused my wrists to overshoot behind me and the cuffs bit into both wrists as well, even through the cast.

With his foot between my shoulder blades he began pulling with all his weight, cinching my shoulders closer and closer to one another. Each vicious yank on the rope gradually blended the pain from separate blinding flashes to a more constant burning sensation. It didn't take long before every joint in my upper body—especially my previously dislocated shoulder—began to cry out separately in pain and outrage. Tendons and cartilage in my chest, rib cage, elbows, shoulder blades were all straining, stretching. Below the ropes, my arms were tingling intensely. My entire upper body felt like it was going to crack open. The pain brought me back to My Xa, where I had been hung from the tree and had answered their stupid question about the names of my aircraft and my ship.

But Pig Eye had only begun. Like someone having an out-of-body experience, I watched almost disconnectedly as he brought the excess rope over my shoulders and down to my feet. The pain almost separated me from the actual process. He applied his specialty knots to my ankles then, and still with excess rope in hand, stepped back around behind me.

My arms and shoulders were on fire now, like my burning thigh muscles when I skied an entire hill without stopping, only multiplied many times.

Pig Eye slapped his sweaty bare foot up behind my neck and began cinching my head and upper body forward toward my feet, pulling in the slack in the rope between my shoulders and ankles. Sarge stood on the big iron bar to keep me from scooting across the room as Pig Eye cinched me down tighter and tighter, the air being forced out of my lungs with each constricting jerk. As my head got closer to my feet my knees were forced wider and wider. Now I could feel the rending of tendons and cartilage in my hip sockets and my lower back. My ankles wedged against the U irons at an ever-increasing angle. My knees were straining outward at an awkward angle. Still the little bastard pushed and cinched and cursed and sweat.

I could hardly breathe, so constricted were my lungs from being bent over into a tightening little ball. Between my grunts with each cinch on the ropes, I was panting like a bitch in labor. Tears and sweat pooled in the grouting between the terracotta tiles below my face.

Pig Eye began sort of jumping up onto the back of my shoulders and pulling the web of rope tighter each time my torso would bob a little closer to my feet.

"Co! Co! Co! Co!" He was yelling my name with each jump and cinch. "Co! Co! Co!"

The pain was all there was. The pain in every joint, bone, muscle in my body filled my entire consciousness. My body exploded with pain; the most intense was the burning in my arms from lack of circulation. God, I thought, I've got to get outside myself. I've got to detach someway. Detach! Detach! My thoughts broke free. Briefly, I was in a sunny sky at forty thousand feet. I was flying right down the middle of Florida, the Atlantic to my left and the Gulf on my right. Huge columns of roiling cumulus clouds formed rounded peaks and caverns around me, and the sky above me was blue forever. And I surveyed this from the cockpit of my sleek Crusader jet and thought, Sonovabitch, I can't believe I'm getting paid to do this! . . . paid to do this! . . . to do this!

Suddenly the pain slammed shut the window to my Florida sky. I felt the pressure increase on my arms and shoulders. I'm being pulled upwards by my arms, I thought. I remember the hook in the ceiling. I had never imagined what it was for.

More rope, threaded through the hook. The two of them begin hoisting me off the floor by my arms.

They bounce me up and down. I am pulled between the pressure of their yanking and the weight of the iron bar on my ankles. They never get the irons off the floor but most of me is in midair.

I gasp and cough and cry out. I watch the drops of sweat bouncing from the tip of my nose, making little dark spots on the tile. Would two drops ever land in the same place? Can I make 'em land in a pattern? Do I have any control? Over anything? I bounce. I hear as much as feel the snapping in my shoulders. "Co! Co! Co!" Again I cry out. I yell "Stop it! Oh, God, stop it! Please stop it!"

I am graying out again, just like back in that village hanging from the tree. My mouth is invaded—a piece of dirty rag wadded around a stick to shut me up. I had seen it tossed aside in a grimy corner and had wondered what it was. Sarge shoves it farther into my mouth. I gag and try to twist my head away. I cry and growl in pain and anger and frustration. I can't stand it anymore. Break out, Jerry, break out! Get outside of it! Break out! I muster all my concentration . . . the window opens.

Bea, sunshine, sandy beach. We're unclothed, embracing each other. The sand is warm and soft on our bodies. She feels luscious in my arms. Her face in the crook of my neck and shoulder, her tears moistening my skin. "Oh, Honey, I'm so glad you're home again. I didn't know if you were alive or dead." I didn't know if you were . . . I didn't know . . . I didn't know . . .

The pain sears the window shut like the burning film on a stuck projector. God, she doesn't know! She doesn't know! The pain is from the inside out now. Every cell of my body is straining to tear apart one from the other. Oh, God, stop it! Stop it! She doesn't know! She doesn't know! Hail Mary, full of grace, the Lord is with thee. Hail Mary . . . I'm tumbling through the blackness of pain. No control!

I feel my bladder let go, warm and wet, but it doesn't matter. The rag wad in my mouth seems to grow huge. I can breathe only through my nose now, and then barely. Jesus, Coffee, don't throw up! I envision my corpse lying stone cold on the terracotta tiles of the knobby walled room, drawn tightly into a rigor mortis clump, with cold, strangling vomit caked around my mouth and nose and on the floor around my face. Jesus, don't throw up or you'll die!

In a lucid moment I realize I am on a medieval rack: a simplified, compact, mobile version of the rack. I tumble end over end through the vermilion and black splotches of pain, my entire consciousness fills with a foreign, strangling voice screaming words I disclaim: "Stop it! Stop it! Please, stop it! I'll write it! I'll say it! I'll write . . . Please . . ."

March 15, 1966

My Dearest Family,

I pray to God this letter reaches you very soon. My desire to let you know that I am alive and well has been almost overwhelming, as I have wanted to spare you the grief of thinking the worst, and the worry of just not knowing. I understand I will be allowed to meet with an American visitor to North Vietnam who will carry this letter back to the States and then mail it from there. So, I am confident it should reach you before our baby is born.

I am in good basic health both physically and mentally and, Darling, I pray this finds you the same way. I do have a problem with my right arm and hand, however, hence the left-handed writing. My arm was broken but after arriving at my present location, I was taken to a hospital where my arm was set. It seems to be healing OK. You can see I am very grateful to the people and the doctors of the Democratic Republic of Vietnam for the medical care I am receiving. It is an indication of their humane and lenient treatment.

Since I have been here I have been taught some things about this war. The Vietnamese people are fighting a civil war. The North Vietnamese are not intervening in South Vietnam. They have a right to be there supporting their own countrymen. They are fighting for the reunification of their country. It is the national purpose of the people of North Vietnam. We don't belong here. We are here in violation of the Geneva Agreement on Vietnam and keeping the Vietnamese from realizing the fruits of their revolution. Further escalation will be catastrophic because the North Vietnamese are prepared and fiercely determined to fight forever. We are fighting an illegal, dishonorable, and unjust war here.

Our immediate future is truly in God's hand now, Darling. I pray to Him every day to watch over all of you and to take good care of you. Please give my love to all of our family and friends whom I know are taking good care of you and the children. Tell each of our precious children how very much their Daddy loves them and give them a kiss for me. You must know my thoughts of you sustain me from day to day. I'll be right there with you in April when that delivery time comes, so just think of me holding your hand. Also, Happy Birthday, Honey. You can be sure we'll make this one up. My love for you gives me the strength and courage I need each day, and I dearly hope it works the same way for you.

I love you
Jerry

8

Like Steel,
We Are Tempered by Extremes

Laughter sets the spirit free to move through even the most tragic circumstances. It helps us shake our heads clear, get our feet back under us and restore our sense of balance and purpose. Humor is integral to our peace of mind and ability to go beyond survival.

Two sleepless nights after my argument with Pig Eye about the letter, I was moved across the small courtyard and into the room by the cistern. I was still exhausted—my entire frame ached even worse than it had from our high-speed ejection a couple of months before. Pig Eye had dislocated my shoulder again and I had relocated it again. But now it popped and hurt with each movement, so I kept the entire arm hugged against my body. My hand was badly infected, and the stinking bandage was moist and sticky most of the time. No one seemed to care, not even Sarge.

At least this room had not been designed as a cell and was large and airy compared to the real one. I could pace several steps from wall to wall. The barred window was on the courtyard side of the wall. It was high but bigger. Each morning I would stand ceremoniously with my eyes closed and face fully toward the shaft of sunlight that beamed gloriously through for nearly two hours. When on my tiptoes near the opposite wall, I could just see the bough of a sycamore tree beyond the wall. Its longer twigs reached bravely toward me between strands of barbed wire. Fuzzy green buds were sprouting. The air was warming.

My bed was a wooden pallet on the floor. There was nothing to tie my mosquito net to, but the little demons were less intense here than they'd been over on the other side. Using the net for a pillow was luxurious.

For nearly two weeks—as best I could tell—I languished in "the courtyard cell" of New Guy Village. Although I could almost smell the water in the cistern just outside the door, I was not permitted to bathe. The food stayed the same—soup with crunchy sour greens, a small plate of the same greens fried in pig fat, and rice, twice a day. Still I was always hungry.

I was interrogated once. A Vietnamese Air Force officer—his rank patch was blue with one gold bar and three stars—and his own interpreter questioned me almost casually about the frequency spectrums of the Vigi's electronic intelligence recording systems. I had learned from the few times Rabbit had pressed me on military subjects that to feign ignorance or stupidity was usually effective.

"I have no idea of the frequency spectrum of that system. I am only a pilot. I follow the orders of the intelligence officer on the ship. I fly the flight path that he has drawn across my map. My crewman turns on the switch at certain points and turns it off at other points. When we return we simply tell them if and where we deviated from the flight path."

"And your cameras?"

"It's the same. I follow the line on my map, turn the switches on and off at the designated points and return to the ship. I am not allowed to know what my targets have been or to see any of the pictures my cameras have taken."

The Air Force officer—probably from Air Intelligence—had pondered my answers and apparently believed them, absurd as they were. In reality, I, like other American military airmen, took great professional pride in knowing all I could about every aspect, every system, every characteristic of the planes I flew, everything except perhaps the specialized technical details of maintenance and repair.

Once targets—recce or attack—had been determined by higher authority, we were in on every aspect of target ID and flight planning. We had considerable flexibility during the mission to change flight paths, sensors, and even targets (preapproved alternates) due to unexpected weather or operational considerations. Once a mission was complete, the aircrews participated in debriefings, again helping with target ID and location, assessing bomb damage and recommending tactics for subsequent strikes.

We were kept abreast of strategic objectives and alternatives, targeting philosophy, and most special plans such as the proposal I had seen on the *Kitty Hawk* to destroy hydraulic and irrigation facilities in North Vietnam.

Conversely, in most Communist military organizations—mostly due to the paranoid preoccupation with secrecy—expertise and information are quite compartmentalized. Generally, one is allowed to know only what one must know to do the job—a wooden peg binding the spoke to the hub, with no idea of the function of the hub, the spokes, or the rim, much less of the direction in which the wheel is going. With so little actual information on the big overall picture, the effect of the system's endemic propaganda on individuals—the lies and deceit—is magnified.

For this North Vietnamese Air Force officer, as with many of our interrogators through the years, my apparent ignorance was accepted. He could personally relate to it. He simply couldn't extort from me information he did not expect me to know.

In my new cell I began to immerse myself in routine. I began to realize that with structure, time passes faster. There was prayer and meditation. There was detailed introspection—the beginning of truly knowing and understanding myself. There was pacing and exercise and hygiene. There was entertainment—singing softly to myself every song I'd ever known, categorizing them, dwelling upon the memories specific to each. There was studying of the rats, the cockroaches, the ants, flies, and mosquitoes; watching and learning the habits of the little tropical lizards called geckos. When pacing I allowed my mind to idle in memory—of family, childhood, flying, achievements, disappointments—and already I had begun to think more deeply about my values and beliefs. This is not to say that the loneliness and boredom weren't nearly overwhelming sometimes, but I was gradually learning how to deal with them.

Underlying it all, however, was my chronic concern for Bea, my hope that somehow the letter that Schwinman was to deliver would reach her. There was also my guilt for having written it at all, for saying the things in it that Rabbit had dictated after the ropes had been loosened, but with Pig Eye standing over me at the ready.

Twice now I hadn't been strong enough. God, how do the others do it? Am I the only one who gives in? What will they think of me? What will Risner think of me? Christ, where are they?

There was another little alphabet square scratched into the bottom of my pallet, but I couldn't figure out what it had to do with reaching the others. It was maddening. The whole goddamn situation was maddening. I prayed. Please, God, let me have seen the worst of it. Let me get with the others soon, to be with them until we're released. Let it be downhill from here.

My hopes to that effect were dashed when a week or so later I was moved back into my original little dungeon where I'd spent my first six weeks at Hoa Lo. It was enormously depressing, a step backward for sure. And I didn't even know the boils were yet to come.

"You take care of your parachute and it'll take care of you, ya heah! You r'member that, boy. Take care of that chute, it'll take care a you! Ow! Ow! Oh, God!"

I opened my eyes, instantly wide awake. What the hell had I heard? An American voice?

"You take care a that parachute now, ya heah!" More groaning.

I bolted upright beneath my net, startling the rat near my feet. It sprang up and against the opposite wall, fell wriggling to the floor, and disappeared.

An American in the next cell . . . Southern accent . . . not Risner. I listened more intently.

"Don't evah f'get that, son. You take care a that parachute and it'll take care a you."

Who was he talking to? Himself: I'd been back in this cell for over a week now; no interrogations, hearing only Vietnamese. It was good to hear another American voice, but I was alarmed by its detachment from reality.

"Doncha evah f'get that, son, you take good care a that parachute. That's a cahdinal rule. You take . . . ahg . . . ahhh . . ."

God, he was delirious—in pain. He must have just been brought into Hanoi. Could have been his cell door slamming shut that had awakened me. He was moaning and bumping around over there now. These cells had so many hard surfaces . . . the ankle manacles had rough edges and jutted out . . . he must be bumping into all the hard edges. I heard a movement, a thump, and a cry in pain. More moaning.

"Take care a your para . . ."

His voice was weaker. I sprang from beneath my net and stood on my slab on tiptoes toward the window in the back wall, like the one in his back wall a couple of feet away. Even pulling myself up with one arm, I could barely see over the sill.

"Hey buddy! Can you hear me? I'm another American."

He was sobbing, making sounds like a wounded little animal. No reply.

"Hey! Can you hear me? Listen up! You'll be okay!"

"No! My parachute! Gotta take care a my parachute!"

He kept mumbling on, paying no attention to me. His accent was thick southern—Texas, maybe Louisiana.

Sometimes he thought he was a flight instructor talking to his students. Then he'd talk like the student. Still he seemed to be kind of thrashing around and moaning and yelping sharply as he bumped against things.

Suddenly he was quiet. I tried to reach him. No response at all. I jumped down and went to the peephole in my door.

"*Bao Cao! Bao Cao!*"

I hadn't yelled so loud since facing Pig Eye.

"*Bao Cao! Bao Cao! Bao Cao!*"

A guard came clanking through the entry door to the passageway.

"*Bao Cao* what! *Bao Cao* what!"

"Here! *Bao Cao*, here! Go get someone who speaks English!"

I thumped the inside of my door. He opened the peephole and glared at me.

"*Bao Cao!* Man sick! *Bac Si!* Doctor!"

I pointed my thumb toward the adjacent cell.

"*Bac Si! Bac Si!*"

"No talk! No talk!"

"*Bao Cao*, you little sonovabitch! You're supposed to get an officer! Get an English speaker!"

My outburst made him furious, and he shoved the unsheathed bayonet of his rifle at me through the peephole.

"Kip shilent! Kip shilent!"

"*Bao Cao! Bac Si!* Man over there needs doctor!"

Again I motioned with my thumb and my head.

"No! No! Kip shilent!"

He slammed the peephole shut and moved away.

I kicked the door. "*Bao Cao*, you little shit, *Bao Cao!*"

I peeked down through the crack at the bottom of the little peephole—saw his feet and then his legs move toward the next door, heard the peephole open, then heard it close softly. He ambled back past my door, through the outer door, and into the courtyard.

I went back to the windowsill and listened. I could barely hear the moans in rhythm with the man's shallow breathing.

"Hey, Jet Jockey, listen up! Can you hear me? I'm an American too. Answer me! Hold on, you can make it!"

Nothing, not even the moaning now.

I reared back my head toward the open window and yelled as loudly as I could: "*Bao Cao! Bao Cao!* A man here needs help! *Bao Cao!*"

My shouts echoed through the alleyway between the outer prison wall and the wall of the cell block, but were rapidly absorbed by their brick and plaster and the cobblestone pavement.

"*Bao Cao! Bao Cao!*"

Nothing. And from the next cell, nothing.

I paced for a while, praying for the guy and listening for some sound. The guard had returned and opened my peephole quietly. I looked up and saw him.

"*Bao Cao!* You bastards, you can't just let him die! *Bac Si, Bac Si!*"

Again he slammed shut the little door and sauntered out.

Periodically through the night, between prayers for him, I called to the injured man, tried to encourage him, but received only silence in return. I paced and prayed through dawn.

In the morning, a few minutes after the reveille gong, I heard voices outside in the passageway. The door bolt to the man's cell clunked open, there were a few seconds of silence, then urgent orders and shouting. Peeking down through my tiny crack I saw a stretcher arrive. Still more voices—inquiring, but in tones of resignation. A blanket covered all of the limp form on the stretcher as it was hefted back out past me.

For the next hour Vietnamese prisoners worked next door, sloshing the cell with water, scrubbing and sweeping it down. Then more water.

I was depressed and furious. The dirty fuckers just let him die of neglect. What could I have done? How could I have helped him? He must have been bleeding, but he could have been saved. The bastards let him bleed to death.

That morning, among my usual prayers were many for the GI next door who hadn't made it through the first night, and for his family somewhere in Dixie. And I pondered my own blessings of survival and hope. I thought about the huge difference that just a split second or a fraction of an inch somewhere along the way can make; the difference between life and death.

You've spared me thus far for some reason, God. There's got to be a purpose in all this. Please help me to see it, to learn from it, and to understand what it is you are preparing me for.

*   *   *

Several nights later Sarge came and gave me the "roll up" moving signal he'd taught me earlier, rotating one hand over the other like a paddle-wheel. I was to roll my belongings securely into my rice straw mat so the bundle could be carried under one arm.

Sarge had been averting his eyes from mine all week during our routine. I was sure he had been told I called for help the night the man had died. If I hadn't figured for myself that he had died, I would have guessed it from Sarge's behavior—almost embarrassment.

With the usual blindfold in place, I was taken out of New Guy Village, through the main courtyard with the rose bushes, and into a drive-through. Halfway through we entered a door to the right. I knew before the blindfold was removed that we were in another dungeonlike cell block; the smell of unbathed humans mingled with the odor of the *bos*—all confined to a minimum of space. The contrast with the fresh air I'd just packed into my lungs was incredible.

Yep, this must be Heartbreak Hotel that Risner had told me about. I began to see why he had said I'd know why it was called that when I got there.

There were four ominous-looking doors on each side of the stubby passageway. In the dim light I could barely see the dead end opposite the entry door. Immediately I wondered if other Americans were behind the doors. Sarge opened the third one on the left and motioned me in.

The cell was twice the size of the one I'd just left but there was a slab on each side, leaving a slot between them barely wide enough to walk in. The same medieval ankle stocks—operable from out in the passageway—were menacingly present.

I set my bundle on one of the slabs and turned to give my perfunctory bow, which Sarge accepted more readily than usual this particular day. But we weren't finished. He gave me the wash sign and motioned me back out into the passageway. He pulled open the door to the closest cell to the entry on the same side as mine, motioned to me and said "Whass!"

I stepped onto the wet, slimy floor. It was littered with rotting bandages and bits of garbage—mostly rice and greens. A huge black rat ambled out the drain hole at the base of the back wall.

"Whass!" He pointed to the rusty pipe running up the wall where one of the slab beds had been. It had a faucet at waist level but the pipe ran on up the wall about six feet high, where it was bent ninety degrees so the water could run on your head. A shower!

"Whass queegly!" And the door slammed behind me.

Okay, Sarge. I'll whass queegly. Who'd want to stay in this sump in the middle of the night for long anyway? As I undressed, the big rat kept poking his nose back in, impatient that I was still there.

The water was cold but the shower felt good. It was a real effort to keep my cast elevated out of the water until I realized I could rest it on top of the bend in the pipe, where it stayed dry. There was a sliver of soap on the algae-covered slab across from the shower. I lathered my body briskly. I realized it had been almost three months now since I had showered in that impeccable stainless steel officer's head on the 03 level of the *Kitty Hawk*. Little had I known that the hot steamy water that massaged my body that morning would be the last of its kind for a long, long time.

I shook my head at the thought of my life aboard ship, the camaraderie of my squadron mates—good friends, the fulfillment of a mission well flown and capped by a perfect "OK, 3 wire" or recovery, the fun of the evening Ready-Room movie when we weren't on the flight schedule, the midnight snacks always available in the wardroom, and reading letters from Bea and each of the kids on the aft catwalk out over the blue water of the Tonkin Gulf during stand down from flight quarters. And now here I was in this dismal, stinking hole, body broken, totally uncertain of my future, pressure to do this, do that, hostility for my daily fare. Men dying in adjacent cells, my crewman possibly dead. My family totally uncertain of my fate.

I thought back to the previous months and to what had transpired and realized I just hadn't been as tough as I thought I was. I hadn't done as well as I should. I was disappointed, devastated.

I rinsed the last of the soap from my body in awkward motions. The cold water had become even more tolerable now, and I let it run over my neck and shoulders as I held the pipe with both hands, head lowered in pensive dejection.

Finally I raised my head. And there at eye level on the wall in front of me, scratched indelibly by some other American who'd been there before me, were the words "Smile, you're on *Candid Camera!*"

Well, I couldn't not smile. Even with what had gone on in the past week, I smiled broadly. I laughed out loud, enjoying not only the pure humor and incongruity of the situation, but also appreciating the beautiful guy who had mustered the moxie to rise above his own dejection and frustration and pain and guilt to inscribe a line of encouragement to those who would come after him. He couldn't have known how many scared and broken GIs would pass through that miserable cubicle, see his impudent reminder that they weren't alone, and pull themselves together to face whatever life's candid camera might have in store. I would never know which of my fellow POWs had left that bizarre greeting, but, by God, he deserved a medal for it.

9

The "Commune" of Communicating

Few things are more basic to our survival than to communicate, if only with our God. To communicate without protection or pretense puts us on the most common ground with our fellow man. Nothing is more exhilarating or comforting than communication based wholly on truth. Once we understand this, our challenge is not tearing down the walls that stand in the way of authentic communication but not allowing them to be built in the first place.

"Man in cell number six with the broken arm, listen up! Can you hear me?"

Instantly I was up into a sitting position on my slab; my body tense, the hair on the back of my neck straight out. Risner! I was sure it was him.

After settling in the night before, I had prayed that there would be other Americans behind those foreboding doors out there. During the morning routine, I had heard some of those doors open and close but they could have been V prisoners like the ones I'd heard that morning in the huge open compound behind my cell. Even though my hope for contact today had become anticipation, I was still excited by hearing the voice, almost certainly Risner's.

"New man in cell number six, can you hear me? It's safe to talk. We have clearing."

I sprang up to the transom over my door, straddling the space between the slabs and balancing precariously with my good arm. I had already decided the small space beneath the wooden panel covering the barred transom would afford the best view of the dim passageway.

"I hear you, Colonel. I hear you. It's me, Lieutenant Jerry Coffee."

I was startled by the urgency in my own voice. And it was much louder than I had intended it to be.

"Hi, Jerry. Welcome to Heartbreak. Try not to talk so loud. The man in the cell closest to the door is Larry Spencer. He's clearing for us by watching for the guard's shadow as he approaches the entrance. If you hear a single cough or a thump on the wall, it means danger. Stop talking and get away from the door."

The tone of his whisper was dead serious but soft, and I could hear him clearly.

"Colonel, when we talked briefly over in New Guy Village over a month ago I asked if you'd heard anything about Lieutenant JG Bob Hanson, my crewman. Any word yet?"

"No. I've been out at the Zoo for a few weeks and no one out there had his name either. . . ."

"The Zoo?"

He chuckled softly. "That's an old French film studio out in the suburbs of Hanoi. They've made it into a POW camp. There are about forty men out there." Then his whisper went from thoughtful back to urgent.

"Listen, Jerry, you must learn to communicate through the walls. We could be cut off here any moment. You must learn to communicate by tapping on the walls; the system is called tap code. It's the only dependable method we have."

He said "we" and he had said "the man in the cell closest to the door." There are others. Thank God, now I'm with the others. Rabbit had implied there were others, and of course there were the pictures of Alvarez, Shumaker, Stockdale, and Risner I'd seen before. But I was beginning to wonder if I would ever really be in touch with another American.

"How many others are there?" I blurted, ignoring his remarks about tapping on the walls.

"Shhhh! Not so loud! If they catch us communicating like this they'll torture us again just to extract an apology for breaking the stupid prison regulations. Then it can go downhill from there."

"Okay, okay, sorry!" I whispered back, matching Risner's volume as precisely as I could, and truly sorry for having put us at risk. But my curiosity about others persisted.

"How many Americans are here in . . ."

Thump! Thump!

The "danger" thumps on the side wall reverberated like thunder and were unmistakable in their meaning. They had quickly followed Spencer's single phony cough down near the entrance. I practically catapulted off my tenuous perch, half because I had been startled by the thumps and half because of the adrenaline burst.

A guard entered the passageway and stalked from cell to cell, quietly sliding aside the flaps of rusty tin that covered the little peephole in each door. I was sure I must look guilty as hell sitting there on my slab, my heart pounding loudly. We waited ten minutes.

Finally, a double cough. "Jerry, listen up!" I was back up at the transom instantly.

"Jerry, the tap code is our only dependable link to one another. Somewhere on the walls of your cell you will probably find a little square matrix with twenty-five letters of the alphabet; five rows of five letters each, one row on top of the other. We leave out the letter K because we can use a C for the same sound most of the time."

My mind was scanning back across the letters on the walls of the cells I had been in. Those damn little alphabet things had driven me bonkers trying to figure them out. Now the mystery was about to be over.

The first five letters, A through E, comprised the top row. Then came F through J in the second row, and so on. The rows were numbered top to bottom and the columns were numbered left to right:

	1	2	3	4	5
1	A	B	C	D	E
2	F	G	H	I	J
3	L	M	N	O	P
4	Q	R	S	T	U
5	V	W	X	Y	Z

The faceless whisper from across the dim passageway continued. "If you want to communicate the letter A to the man on the other side of the wall, you tap once for the row and once for the column. So A is one and one. If you want a B, tap once for the row and twice for the column. B is one and two. For F, tap twice for the row and once for the column, so F is two and one. N is in the middle of the square, row three and column three, so N is three and three. Z is down in the last corner, row five and column five, so tap five and five. Call up the man next door by tapping shave and a haircut."

He demonstrated on his own door so I could hear it: Tap-tap-tap tap-tap.

"And he'll answer with two bits." Tap-tap.

"Then you go on with your message."

My mind strained to comprehend and retain all I had just heard. Risner continued: "When you are receiving a message, just as soon as you understand the word being transmitted, interrupt with a roger (tap-tap) and the man will go right on to the next word without finishing that one. We use lots of abbreviations for . . ."

Cough!

Thump! Thump! Thump!

The same guard reentered the cell block. He was suspicious. The afternoon sun was lower now and the entire cell block was in shadow. There would be no more talking today. It became apparent my first communication lesson was over, but I would soon realize that Risner had provided the single most important lesson of my POW life. I didn't know at that point, however, that he would soon provide even more— one of the most inspiring leadership examples as well.

As I sat in the yellow gloom of my tiny light bulb that night, I recalled what I had been able to piece together from memory about Risner since he had first contacted me. In the Korean conflict he had shot down eight North Korean MiGs, making him an ace—the ultimate operational achievement for any fighter pilot. More recently he had been the commander of an F-105 squadron—the hottest new fighter plane in the Air Force inventory—flying missions over Vietnam from Da Nang, the huge airbase in northern South Vietnam. Sometime not long before he had been shot down, *Time* magazine, in its effort to inform the American people about their fighting men in Vietnam, featured him on their cover, a "red hot" portrait of him wearing his flight helmet with the squadron insignia emblazoned on the front. The feature article described Risner accurately as one of America's most dedicated professional warriors.

As Robbie was to regret, the North Vietnamese had access to *Time* as well. Of course, they were especially interested in him. When Robbie was shot down and captured alive, you could imagine their gleeful re-action. Robbie later described Rabbit rubbing his hands together, and with that "last laugh" smirk on his face, saying, "Ah yes, Risner! We've been waiting for *you*."

Robbie would spend many agonizing hours in mental and physical torture, many years in solitary confinement, months in darkness, but they never broke his will. Robbie lost battles—as we all would—but he never lost the war. They ultimately forced him to write statements and say things he wouldn't have otherwise, but they never got him in their pocket, never forced him to surrender his will to theirs, to conform— without torture—to their program of extortion and exploitation. As for many of us, his deep spiritual convictions, as well as his patriotism and love of his family, helped him to hang on. Possibly more than that, however, it may have been his profound sense of duty to be an example to the rest of us and to lead us that kept him going.

Much later I would smile at the irony of one of Robbie's comments to me there in early '66: "We must do our very best during this short time. We will only be here a little while. This whole Vietnam issue will be decided by fall. Surely we can all hang on till then and return to our country and our families under circumstances that will make them proud of us."

Over the next few days we had sufficient clearing that Risner was able to talk to us briefly each day. There were only four of us in those seven cells of Heartbreak Hotel at the time. Navy Lieutenant JG Larry Spencer was down in cell number one. Larry was a Radar Intercept Officer (RIO)—the back-seater in the F-4 Phantom jet. He was doing all the clearing for us. The man to my right in number seven was Navy Lieutenant Commander Render Crayton.

Risner did most of the talking during those sessions. Spencer had to concentrate on clearing, and Crayton had already filled Risner in on news from home since Risner had been shot down the previous fall. Both Spencer and Crayton had been shot down within a week after I had, so we really had no news to exchange. Spencer's Phantom jet pilot had been killed, and Crayton had piloted an A-4 Skyhawk alone.

Risner would remind us: "Don't forget that Communists look upon propaganda as being every bit as important as combat readiness, intelligence, and logistics. They look upon us dispassionately as resources to be exploited for propaganda. They don't even seem much interested in the gold mine of military information they are sitting on here. Their preoccupation is to win us over to their way of thinking and use us as propaganda tools. Otherwise, frankly, I don't think they'd bother to keep us alive. Torture is becoming more and more common, some for military info, but, again, mostly for propaganda statements. It took them awhile to get their act together and decide what to do with us, but now it's pretty clear what they have in mind. They are launching into the exploitation game full steam."

When he told me this, I immediately began doubting myself and having second thoughts about my own actions. How severely had I been tortured compared to the others? Had I given in too easily to write that damned letter? Maybe I could have held out longer, averted the whole thing.

"How have men been doing? How do you resist the torture?"

He picked up the uncertainty, the edge of anxiety in my voice.

"Have they tortured you, Jerry?"

"Yes, but I don't know how bad it was compared to anyone else. I've felt terrible that they got anything out of me."

Risner came back quickly. "Listen, it's not how anyone else does, it's how you do. Once they've decided to break a man down they've done it. The key is how you come back. Jerry, the V have been brutal. They've broken some bones, dislocated shoulders, elbows, and knees, popped cartilage and broken teeth. But we're doing okay. They aren't very sophisticated and will believe almost anything. Don't give them anything for nothing. Make them force you every time, but you don't have to let them make you a cripple. Lie, deceive, act, equivocate, distract, and when you are absolutely forced to give something make it as useless as possible. Just follow the Code: resist to the utmost of your ability. If they break you, don't just stay broken. Catch your breath, lick your wounds, and bounce back at 'em again each time. That's the key. That's what we need to strive for. Try to never let yourself get down after a torture session. Just talk to someone if you can and you'll be reminded we've all been there. The other man will know exactly how you feel. We need to take care of each other like that."

Render Crayton ended that session on a lighter note when he broke in, "Jerry, as you now know, once you learn the ropes it's all downhill!" I could even hear Spencer chuckling down at the end of Heartbreak Hotel.

I thought about what Risner had said. Yes, we do need to take care of each other. When isolated we tend to magnify our own shortcomings, but when interacting with others we can more easily see that everyone is human, has weaknesses and regrets. I could see that being in touch with the others, communicating with one another, would be essential for us all to keep our own self-doubts and guilt in perspective.

Later on it would be apparent that when held within and not shared with others, guilt and shame would be some men's undoing. We would see them begin to withdraw, impervious to our efforts to keep them in the community. They would cut themselves off from what they needed most: a word of encouragement and understanding from a fellow POW. When the prison authorities recognized the symptoms of withdrawal, they would tend to isolate the man even further so that supposedly the rest of us wouldn't know they had driven one of our comrades over the edge. In the coming years I would hear of the officer who had been my jet engines instructor in preflight training in Pensacola, a most likeable fellow. He was shot down about a year after I was, tortured, isolated, and then the usual pattern followed—he'd refused to communicate, stopped eating, and disappeared. Several others dropped out of sight the same way. One man would be brought back to live with others; he would be fed and bathed forcibly and given as much TLC as possible. To no avail; he was taken away again, never to return. Another man, to minimize his vulnerability to exploitation, would feign derangement and amnesia for years until—we believe—he actually became what he had faked, as the V would finally trip him up and then in punishing him would beat him to that actual state.

In the coming years I would slog through my own valleys of depression and guilt, so ashamed of my weakness. But there would also be peaks of satisfaction and pride in the courage I had somehow summoned.

Risner said that New Guy Village, where he had contacted me briefly before, and Heartbreak Hotel—the cells we were in then—comprised the main areas for American POWs. There were a few makeshift cells off the main courtyard, one of which had contained Alvarez during much of the year and a half he had been the only POW. The rest of Hoa Lo, especially the huge compound behind my cell, held Vietnamese prisoners.

Indeed, I was fascinated by the daily routine in the big prison yard behind my cell. Balancing shakily on top of my *bo* on top of my slab, I watched over the sill of my high window as local men and women were interrogated at open-air desks. I spied on their twice-daily feeding process: Collapsible tables of planks on sawhorses were used for serving tables, set up and put away each time. I had studied a group of fourteen or fifteen young boys brought in wide-eyed with curiosity or fear, who squatted down in a cluster to face a scathing harangue by a husky prison official with a croplike whip in one hand smacking it into the palm of the other. They disappeared into one of the cell blocks that surrounded the courtyard.

Our little contingent in Heartbreak could talk no more than a half hour or so each siesta time, but, sure enough, we could tap softly on the wall much of the rest of the time.

When there was enough light, Render and I could clear for ourselves by watching for the guard's shadow through the space under the door.

We also learned to pour a little water there to increase the reflectivity—like a mirror. When retrieving our food we would spill just a little rice near the cell door to attract the rats. They'd then squeal as they scurried off when a guard entered the cell block, a primitive but fairly effective alarm system.

I spent hours on the wall with Render Crayton in the adjoining cell. He had been shot down four days after I had, but had made contact with Risner and the others early on. He told me that the report of my shootdown had reached his ship. He recalled reading that our escort had reported seeing my Vigi rolling and tumbling out of control and that it had exploded before hitting the water. Only one parachute had been seen, but no survivors had been determined. Bob and I were listed as missing in action.

Render taught me to use abbreviations for our most commonly used words. We used "T" for "the," "F" for "of," "N" for "and" and "in," and "TD," "TN," "TM," "YD," for "today," "tonight," "tomorrow," "yesterday," and so on. I would come to think and speak of the Vietnamese only as the "V." Almost all commonly used words were abbreviated. The classic was the frequently used word "interrogation," which was reduced to "quiz" and further reduced to "Q." A typical message might be: "This morning I was interrogated by Bug Eye. It was mostly political indoctrination, but he also claimed many American pilots were shot down yesterday." That would be tapped as "TS AM I Q W BUG SOS [same old shit] BT [but] HE SA MANY JOCKS [pilots; jet jockeys] DN YD."

Even at this early stage I was beginning to decipher far more than letters and words from my unseen comrade. From subtle variations in his tapping I could feel urgency, longing, sadness, excitement, and humor. I could tell if he liked my joke, or if it had bombed depending on his extemporaneous scratching, drumming with the fingernails, brushing, or light thumping. What was he doing, laughing or groaning? I was really beginning to know.

We talked about many things those few days of my apprenticeship: our families, our Navy careers, other POWs we knew, how we killed time in prison. Eventually my problem would be not how to kill time, but how to accomplish within each day everything I would set out for myself to do.

Tap code had never been taught formally in any of our military survival schools. Most of that training had evolved from the Korean experience, and solitary confinement had not been used as extensively by the North

Koreans and Red Chinese as it was being used with us here in the prisons of North Vietnam. As it turned out, it is a code as old as prisoners themselves, sometimes even called the "prisoners' code." Fortunately, Air Force Captain Smitty Harris, the sixth American to become a POW here, had recalled it from his stint at the Air Force survival school. It had been mentioned by an instructor almost as an afterthought. When it became apparent that solitary might become the norm, but before the V had actually established it formally, he taught it to the other five men, who all agreed to pass it on to every new POW.

Ideally it would be passed on verbally, as Risner had passed it to me. The next most efficient way was by note, whereby you would draw out the matrix on a piece of paper, writing it with a burnt match stick, a piece of red brick, or (best) with a piece of pencil lead extracted from a pencil left carelessly available in the drawer of an interrogation table. The lead, along with assorted wire, string, nails, and bamboo cuff picks, could be easily concealed in the hem of a shirt or trousers, and thereby usually survive the frequent cell and body inspections.

The code was incredibly versatile, another reason for using it over Morse Code. Messages could be transmitted by sweeping, chopping, and raking, using the strokes in lieu of the taps. Almost anything that made sound could be used: squishing clothes as you wash them, even as a guard was watching, or flapping clothes before hanging them to dry, or pounding on the bottom of your *bo* when you emptied it.

The most sophisticated variation we called "vocal tap." The normal everyday sounds we make as people were isolated to mean a certain number of taps, one through five. A single cough equalled one tap, two sniffs two taps, a throat cleared three, a hack—as before spitting—four, and a sneeze five. I would have many occasions to communicate my initials, J. C.: "sniff, sniff—sneeze, cough—throat cleared." This was significant, because if I should just disappear from the prison system— and several men would—someone would know when and where I was last accounted for. The roving guards and jailers were always hacking and spitting anyway. They had no idea we were communicating.

When standing in a courtyard waiting to be interrogated, or later in an exercise yard, I would always know I was being watched by another GI through some tiny crack or peephole in his door or boarded-up window. With my hand nonchalantly at my side I would communicate with him with subtle finger combinations, one through five. This was often the only link between cell blocks and would keep all apprised of what was going on throughout the prison. When the man watching me understood my message he would cough or sniff twice. If he didn't understand or got lost translating, he'd cough or sniff once. Generally two of anything meant yes, go ahead, clear, I understand. One would mean danger, I don't understand, or repeat.

Sometimes a situation would preclude aural or visual use of the code so a note drop would be established. Notes could be written with the usual materials, but if more security was necessary, tiny knots could be tied into a piece of thread drawn from clothing. The knots would be along the thread in number combinations one through five and could be read visually or by feel like Braille; it was especially helpful for men isolated in dark cells, as Risner would be. A piece of wire was sharpened by scraping it on the coarse iron surface of the ankle manacles and then used like a needle to prick tiny holes in a piece of paper in number combinations. The paper could be wadded up and tossed into a corner and if inspected by a suspicious V would appear to be blank. But the GI who knew better would hold it up to the sky or light so the holes would be revealed and easily read: "FNG N DI SA UCLA BT OSU N RB SH." Translation: "A new guy in the Desert Inn says UCLA beat Ohio State in the Rose Bowl. Shit hot!" (FNG—Fucking New Guy— is the derisive term referring to a new man in a military unit or squadron; part of his "initiation.")

Actually, the most common form of generic communication I had already learned before my session with Risner. Nearly every man would ultimately develop his own unique signature sneeze. A normal sneeze would be turned to an expletive such as "Bullshit!", "Horse shit!", "Rat shit!" (my favorite), or "Fuck Ho!" meaning, of course, Ho Chi Minh. A man could gin up a good healthy sneeze and practically shout out his pent-up anger, contempt, and frustration. The guards never seemed to regard this practice for what it really was—insults really—and it would afford us some small pleasure in putting something over on them on a continuing basis. Strangely enough, it would become comforting to hear these expletives throughout the day and night; sort of a humorous little reminder that the family was all there, and things were normal; dismal as ever, but normal.

As military men accustomed to expressing our professionalism through leadership, problem-solving, bombing on target, in-flight refueling at night, and getting back aboard the carrier on the first pass, we found communicating the new challenge. I would come to measure my professionalism not just by resistance posture, outsmarting the interrogators, and sticking to the Code of Conduct, but also by how fast I could send and receive tap code, or by the creativity I could muster up to reach a FNG, or maintain the chain of command, or reach a comrade who was hurting and desperate for contact and comfort.

Cumulatively over the next several years I would spend hundreds of hours on the wall. For the most part, we seemed driven to communicate. I would realize more than ever that the human species is gregarious, dependent upon relationships and human interaction. As military aviators, the camaraderie and interdependence of squadron life had deepened our needs for togetherness all the more. And we understood that from that togetherness derived not just comfort, but strength as well.

In case it may appear that it was always a piece of cake to bring a new man into the tap code system, Render told me about his first attempt to teach a new man how to use it.

"He was a young Air Force navigator named Mark Mason—add him to your list—and he was in the same cell you're in. They moved him out a couple of nights ago, probably to the Zoo. Anyway, RR [Risner] wasn't across the hall then but LS was down in number one to clear and we had been whispering. I finally got this FNG to come up, tell me his name and to listen. The poor guy was really hyper. I explained tap code, the matrix and some examples—you know, A is one and one, N is three and three and so on. I asked him if he understood and he whispered back very positively, Yeah, yeah, I got it! I can do it! I said, Okay then, Mark, this afternoon during siesta—you'll see it's just like Mexico here; everyone naps from noon till two—you call me up with a shave and a haircut, I'll answer with two bits, then you start sending me a message with tap code. Got it? The guy's real eager. Yeah, yeah, okay, I'll call you during siesta. So the siesta gong goes and things quiet down, and I'm waiting for his call-up. Finally he calls me on the wall, tap-tap-tap tap-tap. I answered and put my ear on the wall so I can still watch for shadows. I'm waiting patiently for him to start tapping his message on the wall when I suddenly realize I can hear him whispering out in the hall: . . . two—three, two—four. Five—two, one—one, four . . .

"Jesus! I jumped to the door and said, 'No, no, dummy, on the wall, tap on the wall! That's why it's called tap code!' We were lucky there was no guard around. We both had a good laugh—his was a little sheepish—and he came along fine on the wall after that."

And now I found myself laughing at Render's story and I realized it was my first laugh in tap code. I scratched and squiggled and brushed my fingernails on the wall erratically so Render would know I was having not just a good laugh, but a very important one.

All that I learned about tap code those few days would become the heart of an incredibly effective system facilitating our mutual support and survival, to help each of us return with honor. By applying our communication system persistently and creatively, we would breach barriers of brick and concrete and vast spaces in between. We would console, encourage, sympathize with and even entertain one another. We would form close friendships through the walls of Hanoi's jails. I would come to know and love other men as my brothers, sharing feelings for families, hometowns, and hopes for our future, and still not even know what the other men looked like. We would not have the chance to meet, shake hands or, more likely, hug one another for years.

Many times in the next several years I would be down and hurting, being punished with my ankles in the stocks on my slab and with wrists cuffed tightly behind me and my buddy in the next cell would be up on the wall with a "GB!" "God bless!" But I knew it also meant, "Hang tough, Babe. I love you and I'm praying for you." And I knew he really was, and it helped so much. Then when he was being punished I'd be up on the wall for him as well: "GB!"

Each night before Render and I would go to sleep we would softly exchange on the wall. "GN," "good night," and "GBA," "God bless America." I never knew if we started that or not, but it became the custom—no, a ritual—for every man every single night throughout the entire system for as long as we would be there.

10
The Hanoi March

When times are good and life goes well independence comes easily. But we are all vulnerable to the sudden impact of the most bizarre curves life can throw at us. Especially in such times are we interdependent. Reaching down to help, and then up to be helped, we pull each other through the pummeling and the pain. And perhaps not until it is over do we truly realize the extent of our need for one another.

The Zoo was as Risner had described it: rustic, but a hell of a lot better than Hoa Lo. Based upon the time enroute from Hoa Lo, the number of right turns and left turns, the sounds of the city then suburb traffic, I estimated the place to be approximately three miles southeast of downtown. It consisted of about ten acres, several buildings laid out around a large courtyard—an acre square—containing a cement swimming pool full of stagnant water and extensive landscaping now gone to seed.

The buildings were almost Mediterranean with stucco walls, tile roofs and covered porches across the fronts. Some had terrazzo floors with inlaid designs.

Risner had told me that an interrogator had told one of the POWs that the place had been a French film studio, and indeed some who had been assigned to earlier clean-up details had thrown away hundreds of cannisters of old film, some into the swimming pool as well.

The pool now was little more than a mossy sump where the guards dumped leftover food to feed the fish—*frey* they called them—they were cultivating. Still, we would sometimes hear them plunging in, splashing and yelling and laughing like the teenagers they were. Even the guards and jailers, who appeared to be in their early twenties, were so naive and unworldly they seemed more like younger kids when at play.

Upon arrival I was isolated in the end cell of the building in the southeast corner of the prison. The first morning I had worn my knuckles nearly raw tapping shave and a haircut to the next cell but I finally decided it was empty. But five or ten minutes into siesta of that first day I heard it.

"Man in the end cell with broken arm, listen up!"

I pressed against the steel doors of my cell, forcing open a small vertical crack where they met.

"I hear you. Go ahead!"

"We are Marine Lieutenant Harley Chapman and Navy Lieutenant JG Phil Butler. I'm Chapman standing on Butler's shoulders."

He was talking through a high air vent in the end of the closest building to the north. I could just make out his face back in the shadows of his cell. I introduced myself, asked about Hanson, told them I'd been in touch with Risner, gave them Crayton and Spencer's names, and asked them how they were clearing.

"We talk freely every day during siesta. The roving guards on siesta duty always stay together. We have comm with every other building, and we know where they are all the time. But one cough means danger."

After assuring themselves that I knew tap code and inquiring about Risner's condition—it was clear they too revered his leadership—they filled me in on the Zoo.

"The building you're in is called the Barn. It has seven cells. You're in seven. We're in the Office. The building due west of you next to the main gate and south of the pool is the Garage. The building due north of the office is the Pig Sty. Just north of the pool is the Pool Hall. Just west of the Pool Hall and still north of the pool is the Auditorium. It is a real auditorium, with two punishment cells on either side. In the northwest corner of the complex—all across the west side—are admin offices, quiz rooms, guards' quarters, kitchen, and storage room."

I couldn't but chuckle to myself. Damn! These guys were so well organized. Immediately I was thrilled and proud to be a part of them. Harley continued:

"Commander Jerry Denton is the SRO [senior officer]. His standing order is to obey the Code of Conduct. So far there's been no torture here. They take men back to Hoa Lo for that. There are forty-four of us. You make forty-five. We're living in singles and doubles. About half of us have cellmates. You'll find the food about the same as Hoa Lo with a banana thrown in once in a while. You get three cigs a day, whether you need 'em or not, unless you're on the bad guy list. You should take them. It gives the gooks something to take away from you. Welcome aboard, Jerry. Sorry to have you with us, but it's better than being dead . . . so far!"

The next few days Harley and Phil picked my brain for news for themselves and to pass to the others: political news, news of the war, sports news, anything significant that might have transpired since November of '65. I had considered myself fairly well informed but in trying to satisfy their hunger for information, I felt woefully inadequate, as if I'd been a hermit during the last six months of my freedom. I gave them an optimistic assessment of the war, reckoning that we would be home sometime by fall.

On the bittersweet side, one day during that first week Harley said, "Hey, Jerry, some of your Vigi friends are here. Jim Bell, Duffy Hutton, and Glenn Daigle all say hi. We're afraid Max Lukenbach didn't make it. He's not been seen or heard from. Duffy also said to remember: 'Win fairly if you can, but win.' "

I was saddened by the news of Max but it was good to hear from those guys. I laughed at Duffy's reminder. It had been our tongue-in-cheek slogan back in recon attack Wing Three in Sanford, Florida, during the annual bombing recon derbies. The competition between squadrons was always fierce. I pondered its relevance in this new form of competition: me against the enemy—a survival derby. I would win, by God, I would win.

Sometime in May '66 I was moved across the central courtyard to the back side of the Pool Hall. It was a daylight move and for some reason they didn't blindfold me. I shuffled along with my roll under my arm as slowly as possible, breathing in deeply the fresh spring air. It was scented by a huge jacaranda spreading over part of the pool and a few prolific rose bushes that had flourished in spite of revolutionary indifference. Ducks, geese, and chickens were scratching and poking everywhere. I'd spent enough time on the farm to appreciate that aspect of the fragrance as well. I was reminded again as I traversed this spa-turned-barnyard that I was living in a country of incredible incongruity.

Here and there soldiers were digging foxholes, each lined with a single large section of concrete pipe about two feet in diameter. They must be expecting an escalation, I thought. So far there had been only low-level pilotless recon drone flights overhead, all of which had drawn fire from several heavy guns in the area, but still no bombing. Usually the drone would streak overhead, draw a few desperation shots, and be gone. Then the air raid sirens would sound. We loved it, but what we really wanted to see was bombing.

As I was led along the narrow asphalt road that surrounded the courtyard and separated it from the various buildings, I thought what a luxury it was to be carrying my roll under my right arm, to have two usable arms again. The cast had been cut off two weeks earlier by Ben Casey, the camp medic. He had oohed and aahed about how great my arm had healed, but I was shocked. It was black and scaly, and my elbow was all gnarled. It would barely open out beyond ninety degrees, and I could see myself going through life as a semicripple.

The arm had responded well to my therapy, however. I massaged it at least an hour each day—carried a bucket full of water at my side as I paced (a new program at the Zoo provided a pail of water in each cell for spit bathing in lieu of being allowed to bathe or wash clothes more than twice a week in a bath area). I did several sets of arm curls with the bucket each day as well, and finally the arm began to straighten and strengthen. Frequently, I'd stand with the side of my arm against the wall and scribe a mark denoting the maximum extension at the elbow. Gradually the angle of the marks began to open up until for three days the mark was in the same place. And that was it. I would live the rest of my life with my right elbow flexed about thirty degrees. But it would not keep me from doing anything I wanted to do.

A bent arm, a screwed-up shoulder, a squiggly ugly finger, and a broken front tooth: I decided that I hadn't come out so badly—especially when compared to the injuries and associated medical horror stories I would soon learn of.

This move from the Barn on one side of the Zoo to the Pool Hall on the other was only one of dozens that I would make within and between the prisons of North Vietnam. I had lived in four different cells back in Hoa Lo and would live in several different cells and buildings here at the Zoo. I would be back and forth to Hoa Lo again and to other makeshift prisons around Hanoi.

Most of the time there seemed to be no particular reason or pattern for the occasional shuffling of prisoners. But we speculated that from our captors' point of view more frequent changes would disrupt our communications and clearing systems, complicate any escape plans, and destabilize our chain of command. The moves did cause problems for us, but only minimally. New communications systems and command structures could be established almost immediately. New escape plans—individual or collective—would be formulated for the new circumstances.

There was no question that each move could be scary. I'd be jerked from familiar surroundings, routine, neighbors—sometimes cellmates—at a sinister hour. My stomach would churn and my heart would pound as again I faced the uncertain prospect of ending up in even more abysmal circumstances, perhaps even totally isolated from others.

The flip side was more positive: Frequent moves more often meant ending up in contact with different, possibly new, POWs. It could mean getting fresh news from home, news from other prisons (essential policy from our leadership), and making new friends. I also looked at every move as a new possibility to track down Bob Hanson. I kept hoping that someday in some new cell I'd tap "shave and a haircut" and say "Who U?" and the long-awaited answer would be "BH!"

Pool Hall cell eight was about ten feet square. The floor was rough concrete, left when the tile had been removed. There were two wooden pallets elevated about eighteen inches and located at the back corner of the cell, the heads against the long center wall that ran the length of the rectangular building. The floor plan was like an egg crate, with five cells on each side. The doors were wooden and had peepholes big enough to pass a liter jug of water through. There were no windows—only four vent holes about ten feet high near the ceiling.

Communication was easy on the back side of the Pool Hall because the long access yard could be entered only through the gates at each end, and the spaces beneath the doors were ample for clearing.

Air Force Captain Bob ("Percy") Purcell was on my left in cell nine. Air Force Captain Norlan Daughtrey and Navy Lieutenant Commander Ray Vohden were on the right side in cell seven. Percy had been thought dead by his squadron mates. His Thunder Chief had disintegrated in a fiery explosion at low level, and no chute had been seen.

"Man, I was so low I had to come back up out of the rice paddy for my chute to open."

Percy was a pistol. He had ideas on everything, from how to make my soap ration last as long as possible—"Keep it away from water!"—to how to pull the core out of a boil—"Pick off the scab, then trap the mucus between two pieces of thread pulled taut. Slowly twirl the threads wrapping the mucus around them. The mucus, being an extension of the core, gets thicker and more solid until it *is* the core. When the mucus is wound tight to the core, pull on the threads—the core pops out!" This would become an invaluable little operation, as the boils were just beginning to show up on my butt.

Percy was perhaps most famous for his relief mission on behalf of squadron mate Captain John Reynolds, who was held in cell five, almost diagonally opposite Percy's. When John was being denied food and tied to his pallet in leg irons as punishment, Percy pried up his wooden pallet, used it as a ladder to the attic access in the ceiling, crawled across the rafters, and dropped his own food into John's cell through the attic access hole.

"Reynolds, you poor little earthbound sonovabitch, here's Percy to the rescue! Chow down, buddy!"

John couldn't even describe his amazement upon seeing Percy's grubby face peering down at him. They both got so tickled that Percy nearly stuck an arm or a leg through the ceiling as he scurried back like a rat on a rafter. He made it without being detected.

"Hi, I'm Larry Spencer!"

"I couldn't believe it. We were pumping each other's hands like long-lost friends. He was the first American I'd seen in almost four months. (Schwinman didn't count.)

Spot had brought us together in his interrogation room and cautioned us to "strictly obey the camp's regulations, otherwise the privilege of having a roommate will be forbidden."

With his own gear rolled up under his arm, we were taken back to cell eight where my stuff was already set up from the previous two weeks. Risking a few taps on the wall without clearing because of the darkness outside (so much for Spot's warning), we passed the word to the men on each side that Spencer was on board.

"Hey, BP, MB [maybe] it's cellmate season. Bet V HS [*has*] sum 1 lined up 4 U."

Percy had been solo much longer than I and was as lonely as anyone could be, but he celebrated for us too. That night Larry Spencer and I talked long into the night—as would be the case with any new cellmate after a period of solitary—and I began my friendship with one of the most principled, loyal young officers and friends I would ever be privileged to know.

Twenty-six years old, Larry was from the tiny town of Earlham, Iowa, just west of Des Moines, and had graduated as a math major from an obscure college in southeastern Iowa. Although raised in a sheltered environment, he was very bright and had always measured his success in terms of intellectual and academic achievement. He took extreme and justifiable pride in wearing the gold wings of a Navy Flight Officer flying in the hottest carrier-based jets. He was indeed Earlham's finest.

Unlike many of his red-hot, macho, bachelor contemporaries ("Hi, Sweetie, I fly jets. How do you like me so far?"), Larry's idea of a big Saturday night in San Diego was lounging in his BOQ (Bachelor Officers' Quarters) room; eating popcorn and polishing his brass (uniform accessories) while listening to a major-league baseball game. He acknowledged that his experience was limited and although there was an age difference of only six years between us, he was regaled by my stories of fraternity life at UCLA, my own operational experiences in the Crusader and Vigilante, and accounts of liberty in some of the finest ports on the Mediterranean.

Actually, I was pretty much a small-town straight arrow myself (especially by California standards), but from Larry's frame of reference I was a cross between Don Juan and Attila the Hun. Larry had me on Hong Kong, though: He had pulled liberty there and I hadn't, and we both enjoyed immensely his reliving the finest nooks and crannies of dining and shopping on both sides of the harbor.

For a month we lived there on the back side of the Pool Hall, relatively free from hassle by our captors. We called our jailer "Happy" because he was a decent sort who, like Sarge at Hoa Lo, approached his caretaking tasks matter-of-factly. He whistled a lot and was quick to joke and poke with the husky trio of water girls who filled our jugs twice a day. He was probably the most handsome, clean-cut young V soldier I would ever know.

Larry and I spent hours each day tapping with Percy, entertaining him and challenging his imagination. Commander Jerry Denton—still the SRO—was in cell one. Through Purcell, he was able to pass on his guidance and keep track of everything going on in all the buildings of the Zoo. Through our high air vents the men here on the back side of the Pool Hall could flash tap code visually to the Stable and the Pig Sty. The Pig Sty was in touch with the Office and the Office with the Barn. Men in the front side of the Pool Hall could flash clear across the center courtyard to the guys in the Garage. We might as well have had phones from building to building!

The closeness that Larry and I began to develop was reflected in our daily routine. We exercised together, holding each other's feet down for situps. We consoled one another—ministered to one another's boils, especially the ones we couldn't see or that were hard to reach. One day I squeezed a boil on his back that was so festered and swollen that huge globs of blood and pus hit the ceiling when it let go. We cleared for one another to converse on the wall with our neighbors. We took turns saying grace over our meals and then entertained—or tormented—one another with down-home food fantasies as we consumed our rice and pumpkin soup, with deliberate leisure, meal after meal, day after day.

"All right, Coffee, this is not pumpkin soup, it's my mom's homemade meat loaf with just a little celery and onion inside. The top is browned perfectly crisp with her catsup-and-mustard basting, and you can smell its moist, meaty aroma as it comes slice by slice from the pan. And this isn't rice, either. It's creamy mashed potatoes with butter and brown gravy. And we have succulent Iowa sweet corn on the cob fresh from our garden out back, all doctored up with butter, salt, and pepper. And this isn't hot water, it's cold milk and it never runs out. And in the oven we can smell the peach cobbler baking. It will be served hot with a big slab of rock salt–turn-the-crank homemade ice cream."

And we continually reassured each other that we'd be home easily by this time next year.

It was always party time there in the Pool Hall. We celebrated every man's birthday, his wedding anniversary, and sometimes even his shoot-down anniversary, the latter—in retrospect—being a dubious occasion for celebration. When a party was coming up, every man would be assigned responsibility for a certain aspect: food, location, music, trans-portation, gifts, entertainment, special effects. On the big day all the details would come flowing through the walls from cell to cell to the honoree. If a phase of the celebration came in from one end of the cell block—food, music, gifts, etc.—it would be repeated on to the opposite end so everyone could enjoy each detail of the party. We threw lavish bashes at the Palace in Monte Carlo, the Metropolitan Opera House, the Astro Dome. Once we rented Yosemite Valley for a birthday party. Transportation included round trips on the Concorde, white stretch limos with full party stock, elephants, and plush sedan chairs tended by voluptuous harem girls. Food ran the gamut from caviar and crispy catfish to pink, juicy prime rib and lobster tails with crab-mushroom sauce. There was all the exotic food you could imagine, but the basics were never neglected: barrels of hot fudge sundaes, plates stacked with hot fresh brownies, and gallons of cold milk right out of the cow. The gifts were usually personalized to the specific interests of the honoree: gleaming chrome Harley Davidson motorcycles with all the latest gadgets, custom-made airplanes, mega-stereo outfits, diamond-studded watches, state-of-the-art fishing gear, yachts crewed by past Miss Americas. Most of the music and entertainment would have put Las Vegas to shame. Once we had the Radio City Music Hall Rockettes, all nude, bursting out of a huge cake and doing their kick step to the combined jazz of Pete Fountain, Herb Alpert, and Satchmo. As a finale, someone would always come up with a post-party set up for the guy and his wife or girlfriend, always super romantic and low-key. There were quiet rendezvous in ski chalets in front of a crackling fire on thick bearskin rugs, with hot buttered rum to the side. There were penthouses overlooking Manhattan, silk sheets, champagne and violins. Actually, each man had already conjured up such fantasies to be implemented with his wife or sweetheart upon our return.

My fingers curled around the vertical bars automatically, much as a baby's instinctively curl around his daddy's finger as he tugs gently, testing the strength of tiny hands and arms. I had spent hours here at the barred window watching the animal life in the exercise yard between the covered walkway around the back side of the Pig Sty and the eight-foot wall that formed the northern perimeter of the Zoo. Chickens and a few scraggly turkeys scratched out their mindless existence here. Quick little sparrows and linnets flitted from the wall to the eaves, and to the hard dirt on the ground, scavenging for remnants from the scratchings of the larger birds.

Just over the wall was a pastoral landscape: clusters of farm buildings, paddies, irrigation ditches. I had seen it all through the ventilation holes high in the wall while standing on Spencer's shoulders. We had been moved here from the Pool Hall about the middle of June. The paddies and ditches were alive with frogs that would chirp through most of the night. Sometimes I'd lay awake listening to the chirping, actually deciphering letters and even a word here and there: Chirp-chirp—chirp-chirp-chirp, chirp-chirp, chirp . . . Could there be a CIA guy out there trying to reach us? God, the fantasies!

The man in the back corner cell next to us was despondent. But although we couldn't see each other, we could whisper through our adjacent windows when necessary. It was risky, though, because he couldn't clear to his left around the corner like we could to our right. Nevertheless, he needed encouragement and the companionship of conversation, so Larry and I spent a lot of time at the window with him.

One day my mental calculation of the rate of movement of the mid-morning shadows across the face of the wall was interrupted by his deep sigh and dejected comment.

"Shit! Sometimes I think we'll never go home!" He had been there a few months longer than I had and was around the fortieth man shot down. I was the sixty-fifth. No one could have convinced us we would number closer to six hundred by the time we did go home.

"Hang in there, Bill. Johnson apparently committed another hundred thousand troops in the South. The new RVN government under Nguyen Cao Ky will rally their army to a more efficient force. Hell, he's a general. He ought to have the right attitude for fighting the VC. I think things are lookin' up. We'll be outa here for football season! Who's your favorite college team?"

His words were still more of a sigh than a response: "Southern Cal."

Silence. Then he went on: "You know, we haven't heard any bombing activity around here for a long time. I'd just feel better if there was more action. We have to hurt these little bastards right here at home before they're gonna give up. I just don't like all this crap about bombing pauses and safe areas and off-limit areas and no-bomb areas. It just pisses me off and prolongs our stay here."

He was right and we all shared his frustration. I myself had passed the word about the bombing pause through last January, and newer men had told us of the various subsequent bombing restrictions imposed by Washington. Aside from the occasional reconnaissance drones passing over, drawing horrendous barrages of antiaircraft fire, there had been no action. Indeed, it was frustrating as hell.

"Hey, man, they know what they're doing. Johnson and Ho Chi Minh are probably exchanging diplomatic notes right now outlining the details of our release." (In actuality, President Johnson would be sending a note to Ho warning him not to try U.S. POWs as war criminals, as he had been threatening to do.) "We'll probably go outa here on a hospital ship from Haiphong Harbor. Say, did you know I'm a Bruin? How'd a guy smart enough to fly Navy jets get hooked on S.C.? Shit, no wonder you're pessimistic. All Trojans are. They can't beat UCLA, they can't win a Rose Bowl . . ."

"Bullshit, Coffee!"

He'd risen for the bait and had perked up considerably.

"Bullshit! I'll see you at the Coliseum this fall and bet you a hundred bucks on the big game. S.C. will clobber . . ."

We both saw them at the same time. At first just a silver glint in the blue distance. Then another, and another, and a fourth. A division of Air Force F-105s was streaking upward right to left. They were approaching the peak of their pitch-up before rolling one after another into their precision-dive bombing run. They were about to nail some target off to the Northwest.

We held our breath, transfixed, as the roar of their engines in afterburner—like thunder—finally reached the Zoo. Thunder Chief, I thought. No wonder they call them that.

The lead plane had rolled in on his run before the first white puffs of flak began tracing where the planes had been. The next puffs seemed to bracket planes three and four as two began his dive. Now the thunder of the dive bombers was matched by the roar of dozens, perhaps hundreds, of antiaircraft guns—37mm, 57mm, and heavier stuff. A surface-to-air missile, like a roman candle the size of a telephone pole, shot past the remaining plane. He seemed to hover there, so vulnerable, at the top of his pull-up just before rolling into his dive.

"Come on, Baby! Come on! Push on over!" Another SAM was coming up.

I could hear Bill pounding on the bars of his window.

"Way to go, guys, way to go! Goddamn, what a beautiful sight!"

Number four had rolled in, pulled through, and leveled his wings in his dive when the second SAM arced to intercept, then exploded just behind him. A thin wisp of vapor began trailing from his tail area, thickened rapidly, and became smoke. Still he pressed on with his bombing run, disappearing where the others had, behind the jagged outline of the huge bamboo clump outside the west wall.

In the meantime, the air raid warning sirens had begun to wail and the guards, shouting vindictive words to each American in each window, ran down the walkway slamming closed the shutters to each Pig Sty window. The distinct rumble and concussion of bomb blasts emerged through the din of antiaircraft guns slamming their fused projectiles into the Hanoi sky. The last preshutter image I had of the sky was of almost complete saturation by the gray and black flak bursts and the crisscrossed con trails of SAMs.

For the next fifteen minutes there was no respite from the roar of Air Force and Navy bombers climbing and then screaming down toward their targets. Bomb blasts and triple-A fire blended into a constant rumbling so intense that we could feel it throughout our bodies. Twice aircraft roared low over the Zoo, so low the entire Pig Sty shook from the shock waves. We knew, had we been outside, we would have seen the Thunder Chief or Phantom jet bank sharply, our comrade look down, and give us a thumbs-up.

Late that afternoon a huge billowing plume of smoke still occupied most of the sky to the northwest. First jet-black, it surged and boiled into lead-colored shades of gray as it rose in a giant column. We watched it climb even higher until the top of the column began to topple over in the jet stream—forty or fifty thousand feet—forming a long clawlike finger pointing out to the Gulf. I recalled the pictures of the volcano Krakatoa belching its clouds of steam and smoke almost into space. This was an equally incredible sight. No question about it, not only had we shit-canned the restricted bombing policy, we had scored big right off the bat. From the color and density of that ominous-looking cloud, a hell of a lot of petroleum product was going up in smoke. Perhaps this 26th of June, 1966, will be the turning point, I thought. God, I pray it will make a difference. Thank you, God, for the enlightenment of our leadership. Please give them the wisdom now to keep up the pressure.

Just before dark a guard we called Ichabod—he was tall and stringy, especially for a V—came around on his normal rounds. He stopped by our window, made airplane motions with his hands, and crashed them into the ornate concrete railing at the edge of the walkway. I looked into his eyes and said to him—loud enough for Bill next door to hear— "Eight airplanes down, you say! You're so full of shit, Ich. No way did you assholes bag eight. A couple maybe, but not eight." I smiled while I said it so Ichabod thought I believed him.

I had learned from comparing our known losses when I was shot down with the tally they fed their own people, plus inputs from the new guys, that they lied to the order of about three or four to one. Hell, at this point in mid-'66 by their count they would already have wiped out three aircraft carrier air groups—losses that, if real, would have been so staggering the president would have been impeached.

During the next week the VOV (Voice of Vietnam) radio propaganda broadcasts and our bullshit quizzes were focusing on an ominous theme: war crimes trials for the captured American pilots "shot down on the spot and captured red-handed in their heinous crimes against the Vietnamese people."

The big raid on their petroleum facilities was a significant departure from the U.S.'s previous policy of restraint and incremental escalation.

It had hurt them and they were pissed. The only way they could save face was to extract restitution from the perpetrators of their embarrassment, we the captured American pilots.

On the evening of July 6th we heard their trucks rumbling into the courtyard around the pool. The sound of trucks was always unnerving because it meant there was going to be a change. As dismal as my circumstances might be, change always meant facing the unknown again, and there could easily be worse places than I had yet seen.

Soon the Zoo was crawling with guards. We were ordered to dress in our prison khakis, and our rubber tire sandals were tied on tighter with ankle straps made of hemp twine. Apparently we would be doing some walking. That turned out to be the understatement of the night.

We were blindfolded and led one by one to the trucks. By feel we each climbed over the lowered tailgates and settled in next to one another, sitting directly on the truck beds. We weren't allowed to talk but communicated anyway with tap code nudges of knee, elbow, or foot against the next man. If one wasn't touching another he coughed out his initials, and soon we all knew who was aboard. Then the debate as to our destination commenced.

The optimists were guessing we were on our way to the airport. The big raid had made the difference and the Commies were throwing in the towel. This, in spite of the tough rhetoric about war crimes trials. We had all learned, even at this early stage, that in the case of Communists, that which is public is just propaganda and that which is secret is serious.

The pessimists—like my Trojan neighbor—figured: Airport, bullshit! They're taking us to torture sessions, or at best to those frickin' war crimes trials they've been crowing about. What could make better propaganda?

None of us knew, of course, that President Johnson had conveyed to Ho Chi Minh a strong warning that if captured American POWs were subjected to show tribunals on so-called war crimes, there would be no more peace overtures, and he would indeed follow General Curtis LeMay's advice to "bomb the North Vietnamese back to the Stone Age." But since Ho had promised his people public trials, he had to come up with a face-saver.

The trucks left the Zoo, and it was apparent early on that we were heading toward Hanoi. The trucks were covered with canvas, but soon the sounds of horns and bicycle bells indicated we were in downtown traffic. At the Zoo I had peeked around and seen three other trucks. That would make us about forty or fifty POWs.

Suddenly, the trucks slowed, bumped over a curb, and came to a stop. Tailgates clanged open and we disembarked gingerly, still by feel. When the blindfolds came off we squinted around and found ourselves in a small park.

The latter stages of dusk revealed our motley bunch: uncut and disheveled hair, sallow, gaunt faces, broken teeth, all compounded by the looks of uncertainty and anxiety concerning what was about to befall us. I looked from face to face hoping against hope to see Bob Hanson. There had been no evidence so far that he had reached Hanoi with me, much less been in the Zoo. But with so many of us here in sight of one another, to locate him was my foremost thought. It occurred to me, however, that no matter how awful we looked as a group, it was a beautiful sight anyway, to acutally see so many of us together.

The grass beneath our feet was lush, but we weren't allowed to sit in it. The park was no more than a large diamond-shaped island, about fifty yards long, in the middle of a large major intersection. The air was warm and fragrant from the flowers in the trees above us. I was reminded, briefly, of the big city park in downtown Modesto where we had our summer family reunions. I could almost smell the potluck dishes spread out on Grandma's checkered tablecloth, the one she always used on summer evenings in the park.

The prison officials and guards began to pair us off at random, it seemed. Rabbit appeared from a group of staff officers and began the usual harangue: "You must obey all orders. You must show courtesy. You must be careful. You must bow your heads. Otherwise it could be very dangerous for you."

I found myself next to Air Force Sergeant Art Cormier. He had been a medic on a rescue helicopter that had been shot down during the attempted rescue of a downed pilot. I already knew from our comm system that Art was from New Jersey and that his wife and two daughters waited for him there. We greeted each other warmly as our wrists were cuffed together and we were positioned in about the middle of a long line of two men abreast, each pair connected with cuffs.

Rabbit continued with a battery-powered megaphone: "You must remember that you are all criminals and that tonight you are being taken to your public interrogations so that all the world will know your terrible crimes!"

Guards in spanking new uniforms were positioned alongside each man on the two sides of the column, rifles with fixed bayonets held rigidly across their chests. They were all young and seemed almost as unsure about what was to happen as we were. Even though this was the first opportunity for several of us to see and talk to others we'd known only through prison walls, the conversations were subdued. We sensed that something highly unusual was about to take place, and the implications were scary as hell.

With a great deal of jabbering from the authorities in charge, the men at the head of the column were ordered to move out into the intersection and down the center of the boulevard angling to the left. As soon as the entire column of about twenty-five pairs of POWs plus an equal number of flanking guards was into the boulevard, the floodlights came on. A long flatbed truck that had been poised just out of sight of the little park began moving along ahead of us but off to the side nearer the curb. It was jammed with floodlights, movie and TV cameras, and all the associated cameramen and technicians, most apparently Vietnamese, but many obviously foreign. The gas-powered engine of a heavy electrical generator growled from somewhere within the tangle of tripods, lightpoles, reflectors, and people. By now the sky showed no trace of daylight, but it could just as well have been high noon there on the street. We were illuminated by huge floods, flashbulbs, and strobes.

At the first intersection crowds began to emerge from behind the glare. The sides of the street and sidewalks were jammed with shouting and chanting people, some even in a section of bleachers like a reviewing stand. The first members of the crowd chanted sort of halfheartedly, seemingly more preoccupied with the bizarre nature of what was happening. In their faces was a mixture of curiosity and shock. Here for the first time they were actually seeing the "American air pirates" who were wreaking such havoc on their country, only a few days ago the destruction of thirty percent of their country's POL reserve. Of course, there's no way that detail would actually have been told to them, but they too had seen the monstrous mushroom cloud of smoke that fed itself greedily for three days, dominating the entire northern horizon of the city.

Political cadres, the specialists in educating the masses in right thinking, were positioned in front of the people and were exhorting them to chant "*Kowtow, kowtow!*" ("Bow your heads! Bow your heads!") Here and there were clusters of foreign photographers and journalists, their non-Asian features and clothing contrasting sharply with those of the Vietnamese.

Gradually the cadres began to break through the curiosity and disbelief of the people and generated some semblance of the hate and intensity they obviously sought for the cameras, the hatred the world's media was anticipating, I was sure, from their premarch briefings. Indeed, the intensity of the chanting began to compound from section to section, and the people began to respond, caught up in waves of emotion. There were no more bleachers, and the throngs began to spill out closer to us. "Bow your heads! Bow your heads! Bow your heads!"

Rabbit, Spot, and other English-speaking officers began hurrying among our ranks, putting their hands on top of our heads to force us to bow to them. Spot clasped both hands across the top of the head of the POW in front of me, Lieutenant JG Dick Ratzlaff, and lifted both his feet off the ground, bobbing along for several paces as Dick kept his head erect, neck muscles bulging. The people were shouting louder and louder, waving their arms in rhythm with their chanting.

At the next intersection a foreign—maybe Scandinavian—photographer with shaggy blond hair and beard was standing on a makeshift platform of oil drums. He jumped down and began hurrying along with us. As I made eye contact with him he seemed to focus his vindictiveness on me. "Yankee criminal sonovabitch! Killer, murderer!" he shouted at me over and over. His eyes looked crazy, and he shook his fists as his cameras dangled around his neck.

What an asshole, I thought, knowing he'd try to kill me right now if he could.

As the screaming foreigner faded back along the column focusing his wrath on someone else, I became even more aware of details in the crowd. There were large clumps of people dressed alike, in dark blue coveralls. Probably most were entire factory and public works shifts brought out en masse. Most women wore the uniform of their gender: loose, traditional white blouses and black pants. The traditional and more genteel *au dai*—the V kimono—would have been totally out of character for the occasion, and I didn't see a single one. The faces of the people ran the entire gamut in age with the exception of young men, who seemed to be sparse. Visually it was a terribly drab-looking mob, but they were starting to make up for it in other ways. They were becoming ever more agitated and the individual faces more emotional, more hateful. The crowd control was also breaking down. They pressed closer and closer, reaching out to grab a shirtsleeve or a handful of hair or to slug us anywhere they could land a blow.

Art and I had said very little to each other but now we realized almost simultaneously that things could get worse.

"Holy shit! Can you believe this!"

"This is incredible, man." His New Jersey accent grew more pronounced as he made his simple observation.

"Let's take good care of each other. Hang on tight. It may be the only way we're gonna survive this thing."

I couldn't possibly know how cardinal would become that simple rule, not just for the occasion at hand but for the next several years as well: Take good care of each other. Hang on tight. It may be the only way we'll survive.

Now garbage and rocks began flying from the crowd as the chants became more intense; the people were frenzied. Curiosity was turning to chaos. Still the cadres egged them on. The young guards in their spiffy uniforms and shiny bayonets were uncertain what to do. Their role was obviously symbolic. They were supposed to guard the people from the wicked war criminals, not the other way around.

The shouting and chanting from both sides of the street collided right there among our ranks. It was deafening. I flashed back to old World War II documentaries showing a million people in the Nuremberg Stadium: *Sieg Heil! Sieg Heil!* There were thousands of angry V surging in around us now. A wooden clog flew through the air, thunked off Art's head, and clattered onto the street.

"Goddamn sonovabitch!" He rubbed his head with his free hand. A woman, her face twisted in hate and excitement, rushed forward and grabbed the arm of a man ahead, pulling him off balance. Another followed her, slugging the man's partner in the belly. An older man edged closer, his eyes wide, a thick bamboo pole at the ready. As we passed he swung between the guards and slammed a blow across the shoulder and neck of the man in front of Art. A husky young gal in a khaki tunic and black pants rushed by me to the left and socked the guy behind me. An old woman pulled off her conical straw hat and was swatting us with the pointed top as we went by. I warded off her blows with my free arm. Her efforts were almost comical except that she had tears in her eyes.

The guards continued to watch in confusion and uncertainty. None of this had been in their script. Someone else on Art's side had grabbed him and was pulling him back and down. Two or three people were holding his arm and the collar of his shirt. I turned toward him as I kept moving along, grasping his arm with both hands, pulling him up and free from the pair who were pummeling him. As I turned back forward, I found myself staring into the face of a wiry little V guy. He was crouched slightly and his backhand fist was already on its way up from his ankles. It caught me right in the mouth before I could dodge or put up my hand. He hit me so hard that both my upper and lower lips split open. Blood began pouring down my chin and onto my shirt. The image of his contorted face stayed with me for several seconds: his eyes had been two shiny black marbles of hate.

The crowd grew uglier by the minute. Here they were with a carte-blanche offer to focus all the pent-up frustration of their miserable war-torn lives upon those supposedly responsible. They had very little food; it must go to "support the soldiers fighting the U.S. aggressors." They had no vacation time; they must "double their production efforts in order to defeat the U.S. and their lackeys." They had no freedom; it must be "sacrificed for the wartime security of the state in thwarting the heinous schemes of Johnson, Rusk, and McNamara." Here at last the people of Hanoi had a tangible enemy; and, all the better, an enemy directly at their mercy.

Now all the pretense of control by the authorities was gone. The best they could do was to link hands—the prison guards, the cadres, and a few responsible functionaries—to walk along beside us as a human barrier to the wild-eyed people. Rocks and garbage and sticks now hit prisoner and guard alike. The young show guards never did pick up on the obvious need to keep the crowds from us, even as their superiors were frantically demonstrating that it was the desirable thing to do. The English speakers who had exhorted us to bow our heads now shouted the more urgent "Walk quigly, quigly! Hurry on! You must hurry on!"

Ahead loomed a large structure, and from its appearance I decided it was the downtown sports stadium. We angled off the main street, and the entire column began jogging through the crowd toward an opening in the wall. By now I had lost both sandals, and the sharp gravel cut my feet in spite of the thick calluses I had already built up from pacing in my cell.

There seemed to be a blockage up ahead. Our column stalled and the hostile crowd regrouped around us. We were being pummeled with fists and sandals, spat upon, pushed and shoved from one side to the

other. The din from the angry shouts and curses was all the more unnerving because we couldn't understand a word. Some women and girls
were crying from the intense emotion that had been elicited from the
cheering cadres and also, I thought, because of the frightening spectacle
they found themselves caught up in.

The doors of the stadium—of rickety metal, like old-fashioned garage
doors—were kept closed by the press of the crowd. Finally the guards
pried them open about a foot. I saw Sarge straining and sweating to
hold them. The POWs started slipping through a pair at a time between
surges. The guards were striking out at their own people now to get
them off the doors. It was complete chaos. Art's face was bloody, his
shirt torn half off. Mine was too. Our comrades in front and behind us
had fared no better, and still the spitting and shrieking went on. What
was to have been a propaganda feast had turned into a feeding frenzy
and we were the main course. The truck with the lights and cameras
and reporters had remained on the street, but they weren't recording
any of this for posterity.

About the time Art and I had worked our way to within two or three
pairs from the doors, there was another tremendous surge of the crowd.
It gasped as much as roared, women and children shrieked and cried in
fear. The doors bowed inward and the metal hinges splintered the wood
jambs to which they were attached. Chunks of wood exploded into the
crowd as the doors imploded, exposing the tunnel beneath the seats of
the stadium.

As in a classic soccer stadium stampede, we were swept forward in a
torrent of fear and fury. Some of the show guards' rifles clattered to the
ground. Others managed to hold their rifles vertically. If no one was
stabbed by one of their fixed bayonets, it was a miracle. Their eyes were
as wide as anyone's. Art and I locked hands tightly to augment the
strength of the cuffs that linked us. As the wave of faces, arms, and
bodies seethed forward, children were lifted off their feet, bobbing
momentarily, then disappearing with a scream. As we pushed into the
tunnel a young girl went down in front of us. Art steadied me as I
reached down and grabbed her arm, dragging her along for a couple of
steps and back up to her feet, only to see her scraped away somewhere
to the rear against the wall of the tunnel.

Now, concentrated in the narrow tunnel, the guards behind us were
able to stand their ground and hold the crowd back. As they shoved
against the howling mass they filtered out the last few GIs in the column.

The poor bastards in the rear had gotten the worst of it. As I glanced back, I marveled in relief that they all seemed to have made it through.

Art and I hurried on into the stadium and followed the pair ahead of us down an oval running track. After a couple dozen yards, well away from the entry tunnel, we were seated on the track, still in column. All of us were ministering to one another, checking the severity of gashes and bruises, assessing the physical damage. Some blotted their partners' face cuts. Our clothes were bloodied and torn and sopped with sweat.

Although we could still hear the din in the background, it was fading, and the relative quiet of the big old French-built stadium was astonishing. The rows stretched silently up into the darkness and became part of the sky. It was as if the stars and moon were a part of the stadium too. For a few moments, the whole stellar universe seemed to be focused on this little band of throbbing, bleeding men. Like some of the others, I lay back on the cinder track, exhausted, appreciating the sudden peacefulness of the sky and the stars, and the thin sliver of new moon curving quietly among them. Here the air was fresh and gentle and quiet. It fluttered soothingly across my face. There was no talking, not even from the Vietnamese officers and guards.

I closed my eyes and thought, God, what am I doing here lying in the middle of a running track bruised and bloodied by a throng of Southeast Asians? How could my life have taken such a bizarre turn?

Strangely, my mind now focused upon a black and white photograph in my Navy scrapbook: There I was in sport coat and tie, right hand raised in the oath of enlistment administered by a uniformed lieutenant commander, his name long forgotten. I had just graduated from UCLA, having crammed the usual four years of study into five. My college deferment was over, my predraft physical notice received, and I had wanted more control over my immediate future, so I had looked at alternatives. Ironically, three years earlier, I had been attracted by Marine aviation recruiters on the Modesto Junior College campus. But I had flunked their cursory eye test administered in Mrs. Leach's history classroom with alternate strips of sun and shadow from the venetian blinds texturing the eye chart they'd stuck onto the blackboard. A subsequent exam by an optometrist showed my vision to be perfect.

So in the summer of '57, with the prospect of two years in the Army and no driving desire to jump into the world of advertising art—my college major—Naval aviation looked pretty exciting to me. And, having spent much of my time at Westwood playing two-man volleyball on the beaches of Santa Monica, I found the beaches of Pensacola inviting too. Therefore, I went Naval Air.

The sense of fulfillment of duty to country never really hit home until I left the narrow world of campus life and became more aware of the unique and fragile qualities of our freedoms and democratic process. The responsibilities of a commissioned officer had further heightened my appreciation for my country. I had come full circle: art major turned jet jock turned punching bag! How incredible!

About a half-hour later, as we gathered to reboard the trucks and before the blindfolds were in place, I was still mopping the blood dripping from my lips. Everyone had huge welts and cuts. We had been beaten, pelted with rocks and sticks, spat upon, and jerked around unmercifully. And then, inevitably, in words audible only to us, someone started in: "Shit, Cormier, you look better now than when we started!" . . ."Sure, man, walking is good for your health!" . . . "Hey, Denton, that should have sucked up your hemmies for a long, long time!" . . . "Hell, Bill, you must have thought you were back walkin' through Watts on your way to the campus at S.C., right?" And finally, "You guys think we might have won the Grand Marshal's Award for the most disciplined marching unit?"

The ride back to the Zoo was more subdued. Again we weren't allowed to talk, and most of us were pensive anyway, as the reality of the event began to sink in: They had had their big propaganda parade in lieu of actual war crimes trials. The people had supposedly been appeased for it was "the people" who were supposedly demanding the trials—as if the people in any Communist state could demand anything. But the whole event backfired. We would find out from new prisoners that when the stories and footage hit the U.S., the American people were outraged. Even the antiwar senators and congressmen were incensed and united with our president in demanding no more screwing around with POWs. I was never able to imgine what must have gone through Bea's mind, the minds of all our families, when they read about the march and saw the frightening pictures of it.

That night back at the Zoo they tied us to trees in the center courtyard, locked us in the tiny pitch-black cells of the Auditorium, and conducted a few brief quizzes. "Now you have seen for yourself, firsthand, the fierce determination of the Vietnamese people. What did you think?"

"Your government has made a very serious mistake. If you show the pictures of what you did tonight the American people will be very angry.

Even those who may be against the war will condemn what you did tonight. The whole world will see how barbaric you are and how you ignore the rules of the Geneva Convention."

Any other time our responses would have resulted in more beatings, but tonight the V seemed to honestly want our opinions. They must have been disappointed. Later, in a moment of candor, a senior staff officer would admit to Jim Stockdale that the whole idea had been a mistake, that the military had been against it but had been overruled by the politicos.

The next morning I ended up in cell number eight in the back of the Pool Hall, where I'd been a few months earlier; no gear, no bucket, no water. As I lay on the bare wooden planks absorbing, digesting, and ultimately understanding that the past twenty-four hours had really happened and weren't just a bizarre nightmare, I heard a soft tap on the side wall opposite my head. "Tap-tap-tap tap-tap." I responded with "tap-tap."

"I BP, U?"

Hell, Percy's back in his old cell! I responded with "JC, U OK?"

He said yes and asked if I was too. Then he tapped out very thoughtfully the following: "I hope this doesn't sound too presumptuous, but after last night, I think I almost—up to a point—know how Christ must have felt."

I hadn't thought of it in those terms, but we had certainly learned what it was to be scourged. And each of us had carried and been carried by the other. We had been each other's cross.

11

Jerry, Jr.

As much as we may depend upon the technology that would "bind" us to others, or the symbols and rituals that "connect" us to God, they are still but reminders. A letter, a phone call, a prayer, or an altar are only reminders of the deeper spiritual ties that bind us regardless of physical presence. How little of our human reality is physical as opposed to the spiritual we are willing to acknowledge and allow.

April 2nd, 1967

Dear Jerry,

The weather here for early spring has been beautiful. The flowers have been blooming already and we're looking forward to Easter.

We miss you all the more when we're at the lake, sometimes with friends and sometimes just as a family. The kids are all doing great. Kim skis all the way around the lake now. The boys swim and dive off the dock and little Jerry splashes around with a little bubble on his back. . . .

Little Jerry!

I stopped reading because my eyes were filling with tears. I clutched the handwritten letter to my chest and looked up toward the tiny air vent that barely allowed sufficient light to read the words from Bea.

Little Jerry! Who's little Jerry? My voice cracked as I realized, of course, who Jerry was—my third son. Yes, if his name is Jerry he must be a boy, and if he can splash around in the water on his own he must be healthy. He must have been born okay. Everything must have gone all right for Bea. God, I couldn't believe I actually had a letter from her. She had no way to know that I had never received any of her previous letters so this one was written very matter-of-factly, but to me it was like poetry.

I reread the text several times, my mind jammed with visions of the reality of her words. She said all of our family was fine. She and the kids probably would go to California for the summer again. The kids are all sweet and happy and helpful and doing fine in school. And "Jerry is such a sweet, cute, special little guy. Everyone just loves him so much. The other kids are so cute with him."

Oh, God, thank you for my new son.

I thought about his name. We had never talked about naming a son after me, but I guess under the circumstances Bea felt it was appropriate. I thought of the poor little guy having to go through his life as a Gerald Leonard Coffee, Jr., just because his old man was on ice somewhere in a strange land when he was born. "Gerald Leonard Coffee, Jr.," I repeated, shaking my head slowly and smiling and licking the tears from my lips. I was so pleased. And I was so relieved and gratified to finally know the outcome of Bea's pregnancy, that all had apparently gone well with both her and the baby. Finally my prayers were answered.

The letter concluded:

> All of us, plus so many others, are praying for your safety and return soon. But we're all fine, so don't worry about us. Our family and friends have been so helpful and loving.
> You take good care of yourself, Honey. I miss you and love you.
>
> Bea

I sat there in the gloom so full of emotions: relief and thanksgiving for finally knowing; sorrow for missing out on Jerry's entire first year; joy for being the father of—in my context at least—a new baby boy; but mostly gratitude for the blessing of my family—my beautiful children and my wife in whom I had so much confidence and faith. And gratitude for the blessing of simply being alive at this point and for the hope of being reunited with them all again soon. I thought of them and prayed for several hours.

From the beginning, my daily routine had included prayers and actually saying a daily Mass. As I went through the Mass I always visualized it being celebrated by our priest at Lake Mary Parish back in Florida. Each day I visualized arriving at the church, greeting friends, sitting in the same pew, the kids separated in varying ways by Bea and me. I would visualize the various parts of the Mass and recite the parts I could recall: "*In nomine Patris et Filii et Spiritus Sancti . . . mea culpa, mea culpa, mea maxima culpa . . . Kyrie eleison . . .*" When possible, I would save a bit of rice or bread to take as communion during my Mass. The beauty was that now I could visualize the scene with Jerry included, holding him on my knee when he got a little restless, patting Kimmie on the knee near the lacy hem of her church dress, pressing Steve's cowlick down into place, or winking at Dave's happy face as he pretended to read the hymnal and glanced my way for approval. The picture of my family was now complete. Now I could visualize them all in the present and plan for our future accurately. My plans would provide one of the most bountiful sources of hope and strength in the years to come.

I had by now decided the only thing predictable about the V was their unpredictability. I had resigned myself to never receiving any of the letters I knew Bea was writing, so this letter had caught me totally by surprise. Happy, our daily turnkey here in the Pool Hall, had simply stepped into my cell very unceremoniously, waited for my bow, handed me the letter, and left. He could have required another bow as he left, but he had undoubtedly noticed my look of disbelief as I stared at the envelope, recognizing Bea's handwriting. He probably realized I was instantly twelve thousand miles from the tiny cell we were both standing in.

A few days after he had delivered the letter, I had been the last to set out my dishes and ended up washing them for the whole cell block. As I reentered my cell, Happy dispensed with the bow, pointed at me, then pointed over my shoulder toward the east and said, *"My,"* the Vietnamese word for America, then defined with both hands the curve of a woman's body. Does Coffee have a woman? I smiled and nodded in the affirmative, duplicating his sign for a woman's body but perhaps accentuating the curves a little more. Then he did the stairstep routine with his hand: Kids? Again I nodded, held up four fingers and did the stairstep from the bottom up, pausing to tell him their ages—*mot, bon, sau, thom*; one, four, six, and eight.

He acknowledged the information with a trace of a smile. "You?" I pointed to him and traced the shape of a woman with my hands. This time he smiled, stepped back so he could glance out the door in both directions to make sure no one was approaching, then fished out his wallet and produced a picture of his girl under clear plastic.

She was pretty but could have been any one of the hundreds I'd seen in the street that first morning en route to Hoa Lo. I oohed and aahed and smiled and pointed to my wedding-ring finger then to him and her and looked at him questioningly. "Married?" He shook his head with a look of disgust, swept his arm around over his head, generally indicating the whole damn war situation as the reason they weren't married.

Over the years I would have similar conversations with other guards who were eager to exchange such personal information. But they did so with considerable circumspection. To be caught by a superior would likely lead to immediate reassignment to the front. And by comparison, prison guard duty in Hanoi was a very good deal.

After receiving the letter from Bea, I frequently recalled the night I had returned to the Zoo from Hoa Lo after a few days of interrogation there following the Hanoi March. The warm night air seemed to have been infused with the yellow light of the full moon directly overhead. It illuminated the several low buildings of the Zoo with a soft glow that belied the misery and despair within them. The silvery silhouettes of trees softened the lines of all the structures, and I could even distinguish the colors—lavender and peach—of their various blossoms. Their fragrance sweetened the air.

As if this wasn't startling enough, the cool fragrant air carried—of all things—the breathy voice of Julie London singing "Love Letters." The evening English-language broadcast of the VOV was coming through the speakers in each cell and out through the air vents and louvers, so that it seemed to be coming from no specific source but from everywhere:

> "Love letters straight from your heart
> Keep us so near though apart;
> I'm not alone in the night
> When I can have all the love you write.
> I memorize every line
> Then kiss the name that you sign.
> Then, darling, once again I read right from the start
> Love letters straight from your heart."

I read and reread my letter from Bea several times a day. Next to my prayers for her and the children's happiness and well-being, the last thing I would do each night before going to sleep would be to reread her letter. Under the semidarkness of my mosquito net I couldn't really see the words but I soon had them memorized. I would trace my finger lightly across the lines she had actually penned and I would feel closer to her. And finally, I would kiss the name she had signed.

*   *   *

Sometimes I felt uneasy that I had been allowed to write home and receive a letter when so many other POWs had not. By now, I had written three letters, the one supposedly delivered by Schwinman, one at Easter of '66, and one at Christmas of '66. "In accordance with the humane and lenient policy of the government and people of the Democratic Republic of Vietnam and on the occasion of your religious holiday, you are allowed to write a letter to your family."

It had become apparent, however, that, as with most of their policies, there was an underlying motive for their letter policy. If a man's shoot-down and capture had been exploited for propaganda, thereby making him a known POW, he was generally allowed to write and receive mail—when any was being written and received at all. The V published pictures of just enough men and excerpts from statements extracted from them as a result of torture to lend a semblance of credibility to their outlandish claims of planes shot down and pilots captured. In my case, having been the first American captured after the Christmas cease-fire of December '65 they had been anxious to capitalize on me. It had been a long dry spell, and with my capture they could resume their flag-waving about the "superhuman accuracy" of their gunners and the "terrible toll" they were exacting on "the U.S. war machine." So, men who were known to be POWs because of the propaganda focused upon them were "letter writers."

On the other hand, if, for whatever reason, a man's picture, name, or statements were not exploited, he could be interrogated, tortured for military information and a statement of "surrender," and shuttled on into the prison system with his fate unknown to his family and our government. On some occasions, such as the day in fall of '67, we would call Black Tuesday, there would be several major air strikes and seven or eight planes would be lost with several men captured, only one or two being identified as POWs and the fate of the rest withheld.

The policy was clear: Through propaganda photos and statements, allow the fate of just enough Americans to be known to give a semblance of credibility to their claims and to provide a resource pool for continued exploitation. To permit these same men to write home, then, was just a necessary evil, a facade to demonstrate their civility, an issue to which—ironically—they were very sensitive.

The other half, or actually about two-thirds, of the policy was to withhold information on the fate of as many men as possible. In the first place, they figured it gave them leverage with the men themselves— "Your government and family don't even know that you are alive. We can either kill you or keep you here forever and no one will ever know the difference!" Secondly, they believed that the more uncertainty in the minds of men's families and friends in America, the more likely they would be to press our government to end the war on any terms. If a man inquired as to why he wasn't allowed to receive a letter from his family, he was told: "No mail has come for you. If we receive, you will get." This was supposed to contribute to a man's sense of isolation and abandonment, thereby making him more anxious for the war to end and to contribute to that by agreeing to make propaganda statements. Most men, of course, realized their wives and families were sending mail, but even an iota of uncertainty combined with the misery of the situation could sometimes make it all the more difficult to keep faith. It was a cruel policy in any case, and of dubious effectiveness.

So, there were letter writers and non-letter writers, and most men understood that they had ended up in one status or the other mostly through circumstance. Every writer could have refused to write—and some did—until we all were allowed to write. Article III of the Code of Conduct reminded us: "I will accept neither parole nor special favors from the enemy." Even though the Geneva Convention on POW treatment specifies that POWs will be allowed to correspond with their families, in our situation here, to write could have been construed as a special favor. In any case, a sensible policy evolved as an operational consideration, and was formalized by the senior officers. It was highly unlikely, at least early on, that through the writers' refusing to write, the V could be coerced into allowing all our men to write. Therefore, among ourselves we believed it was more useful for some to write than for none to write. I emphasize the word *useful*.

Every letter writer assumed a sacred obligation to get out the names of the men not allowed to write. It was the first priority. In any given communications network each writer was assigned specific non-writer names to get out so no one would be missed. This was usually accomplished through word associations. In my Easter letter, for example, I included Larry Spencer's name. In my letter to Bea I had said—referring to a lady we frequently played tennis with at home—"I sure miss all those dinners we used to eat at Emma's, especially all that corn on the cob. Please tell her I'm fine." Well, the point was that Emma's last name was Spencer and we had never had dinner at her place. Bea would point this out to her Casualty Assistance Officer (an officer specifically assigned to facilitate all her liaison with the Navy and the government), who would pass it on to the Office of Naval Intelligence. They would associate Emma Spencer with Larry Spencer, still listed as missing in action, the corn on the cob with Iowa, and the "her" in "Tell her I'm fine" was referring to his mother. She was a widow.

In my Christmas letter I included the name of a young Navy radar intercept officer, Ensign Dave Rehmann, with whom I would live in the future. I said to my son, "Stevie, I often picture you playing with those little space figures you loved. There was Superman, Batman, and Rayman. As I recall, Rayman was your favorite, right?" In this case, Steve had never played with any little space figures so that called attention to something. Then when I emphasized "Rayman," ONI would check their MIA list, and there would be the name Rehmann. The conclusion would be that Coffee must be in touch with Spencer and Rehmann, so they were both probably alive. And the men's families were notified that, although it could not be confirmed, there was a good reason to believe that their sons were alive and were POWs.

These letters were welcome news, of course, and brought hope to many families. Ultimately the names we got out would be used by our government to demand an accounting of men known to be alive. Once the Communists realized that the U.S. government knew the names of all the men in the Hanoi prison system, they gave up on any idea they might have had of not releasing all the men. Unfortunately, it would later become apparent that not all the men shot down in Southeast Asia would necessarily end up in the Hanoi prison system. Those shot down in Laos and Cambodia would be held in those countries. Since we in Hanoi would have no contact with them, we would not be able to confirm their existence and release later.

There was one very innovative prisoner who managed to make the letter he was writing accessible to several others who were not writing. The others pressed their thumbprints onto the margins of the letter. Then in the text of his letter, the writer alluded to prints in some way; our people at home picked up on it, and the men were identified in this way.

Sometimes an outgoing letter would be so crammed with word associations to ensure that men's names got out that it might make very little actual sense at all to a man's wife or parents. I'm sure that on some occasions there at home the happiness of receiving word from one of us was somewhat tempered by the bizarre subjects and syntax. Of course, this was of secondary concern to the writers. The primary mission was to communicate names. It was consolation enough to simply write to one's loved ones and say "I'm fine, and I love and miss you," especially when the man in the next cell or even your cellmate had not been allowed to write at all.

Ultimately, almost every man was allowed to write and receive mail, albeit some just a few months before our release. The V figured that way no one could go home and say they had never been allowed to write or receive letters from home—just another face-saving maneuver to confirm their "humane and lenient policy."

The Communists' policy of withholding mail in both directions was largely ineffective in enticing men to conform or cooperate with them for the promise of corresponding with their families. But we realized that with such limited contact with loved ones, our prospects for maintaining enduring relationships and marriage were seriously undermined.

Most young married officers in their mid to late twenties had been married only a few years, some only a few months, before their capture. In hardly no time, it seemed, their separation from their wives was becoming longer than the time they had spent together before. Soon men would have spent more time with cellmates than with wives, and intellectually and even emotionally might even know a cellmate better than they had known their wives.

We all considered Ev Alvarez's plight. He had been married for less than a year when he left on his fateful WESTPAC deployment, and now had been here for three years. Even with the benefit of some correspondence, it was going to take an extraordinary commitment on the part of his attractive young wife to stick with him. I, like the rest, began to develop as realistic an attitude as possible toward my own marriage. In my heart I kept faith in Bea, in her love and her dedication to our marriage—especially with my love continually expressed to her through our children. But as the years apart began to multiply, the loneliness and retrospection began to magnify each small conflicting incident or circumstance in our marriage. I began to develop—almost subconsciously—an intellectual hedge in preparation for the worst.

There was no question that the policy of denied correspondence, the perpetuation of the uncertainty of a loved one's fate, the withholding of tender words of love and encouragement—all magnified by the awesomeness of the long years apart—would erode some marriages beyond the point of reclamation. I tried never to even verbalize the question: Would mine be one of them? I held tight to Bea's letter and the hope it symbolized for my return home to loving arms.

12
Embracing the Good Fairy

How much we take for granted the power of physical contact with those in our lives who love and care. A consoling caress, a passionate embrace, or an affectionate pat on the head: They all nourish the emotional hunger within. Never assume they will always be there to give or accept, but instead build up a store from which to draw sustenance should there be winters of loneliness ahead.

My heaving chest and stomach were splattered with the warm, sticky stuff. The volume and force had surprised the hell out of me. It had almost reached my chin. The release had been incredible.

I lay there quietly for another full minute absorbing its significance. I had been missing Bea and human warmth and an affectionate touch more than usual this night. I had felt so depressed, so near tears.

Without ever realizing it I had sought out my genitals with my hand, like a teary-eyed little boy clutching his wee wee just for something to hang on to. I was holding on against a wave of despair when I began to feel the warm, sweet stirrings, like the beginning of a wet dream. I had helped it along until the release came from the tips of my toes and the top of my head. Three years of pent-up desire, longing, and frustration exploded across my bare torso as ecstasy—half moan, half sob—burst from my throat.

I lay still, mind and body drained, then replayed it all again in my mind's eye. My breathing was approaching normal now and my body lay flaccid, seeming to have melted into the pores of my frayed bamboo mat. The release of tension had left me as limp as the thin, dingy towel hanging over one of my net strings. I almost chuckled as I reached for the towel from beneath the furls of the net. . . .

*   *   *

I had been about eight years old when Travis Evans and I were riding our bikes down the hot country lane, heading for the culvert on the irrigation ditch where we could trap frogs. He'd been telling me about catching his younger stepbrother jacking off.

"What do you mean, jacking off?" I had asked.

His laugh was kind of high and silly and even had some of the same lazy Okie drawl that his words had.

"Well, ya dum lil' shit! Ya duneven know what jackin' off is?" He laughed kinda silly again as he guided his rickety bike around a deep pothole with a squashed, dry toad frog in it.

Travis and his dad and stepmother and little stepbrother were Okies, or Arkies, I wasn't sure which—and it didn't matter because they both talked the same. They both came to the San Joaquin Valley every summer to pick fruit. Grandpa had cleaned up a place behind the shed for their tents and dilapidated house trailers, run in a water pipe, and set up a two-hole privy under the big fig tree that was the best climbing tree on the ranch. The Okies or Arkies—all us Californians called them that—had replaced the itinerant Mexicans who used to pick our peaches. I didn't know the reason for the change, but I missed the Mexicans. Old Manuel, their foreman, had taken a shine to me and taught me how to speak Spanish when I was little: *Cómo está usted, amigo?* Grandpa had given me a job: to count the full peach boxes stacked in the orchard before they were lifted onto the flatbed truck for the cannery. I'd record the numbers in a little book Grandpa had also provided, solemnly double-checking my addition at the end of each day, thinking the whole operation would fall apart if my tallies were wrong. Grandpa and Manuel got a kick out of all this, but they were teaching me responsibility at an early age.

Anyway, after a hot day in the orchard, Travis and I had been heading down the road this summer evening to catch frogs and to swim in the irrigation ditch to rinse off the itchy peach fuzz. Grandma would have whaled into me if she'd known we swam.

"Jerry, don't you kids swim in the ditches and canals! That's where farmers throw all their dead animals and you'll get Infantile Paralysis." That's what we called polio in those days, and it was fairly common, but in my eight years I'd never known anyone to get it from an irrigation ditch. Besides, how else was a hard-workin' kid supposed to get off the peach fuzz?

Travis kidded me on.

"Hell, e'vybody with a pecker knows what jackin' off is. Ain't you got no pecker?" Silly laugh again.

I'd heard some big kids talking about jacking off coming out of the matinee one Saturday, and I guess I sort of knew what it was all about.

Travis gave me kind of a folksy version of masturbation, and said he did it all the time, and it was better than candied apples at the carnival.

Well, it was a revelation to me at the time, but for some reason I never felt any compulsion to run right home and try it. In fact, I never did masturbate all through my youth and teen years. I never had any particular moral aversion to it, though, and was convinced that warts on your hands came only from playing with frogs. I suppose that as a kid I had enough to keep me busy and to work off any sexual energy— varsity football, swimming and diving, student government, drama, always a part-time summer job. I had a healthy liking for girls, and it was my discovery of girls that probably distracted me from scouting before becoming an Eagle Scout—possibly the only regret in my life up to February of 1966.

I had never been sexually active in high school or college—this was the early '50s—though there was lots of making out and some heavy petting but never all the way. In fact, there had been occasions when, with some lame excuse or fumbling inefficiency, I backed away from back-seat passion when the girl had finally said, "Okay, let's do it!"

My memories of some of those girls and occasions—the steamed-up windows and the panting and the grappling with twisted clothes and the swearing at brassière fasteners that worked like a Chinese puzzle—all coursed through my mind as warmly as the seed that had just coursed from my body.

A lot of the guys here, especially the bachelors or those who had been bachelors a long time, regaled the rest of us with their sexual exploits. We were all so horny it was nothing to spend an hour on the wall just for a sex story, or maybe a sexual fantasy that had accompanied a wet dream. We'd never say "I had a wet dream last night." It was always "Hey, I had a visit by the Good Fairy last night!" And the other guy would tap back in his most devilish knuckle-tone: "Yeah, but I'll bet you gave her a hand, right?" I hadn't much to add. A guy didn't tell stories about his wife, and I practically had been a virgin when we were married. . . .

I laughed softly to myself as I replayed "practically a virgin." I re-

membered back to the fall of 1953. Two of my best friends, Joe and
Russ, and I were cruising Modesto's main drag one Friday night in Joe's
car. I was in the back seat, my leg out straight and lightly bandaged
from groin to ankle just to keep the burn ointment off my Levi's. One
night the previous week I had been burned slightly while guarding the
traditional Modesto J.C. homecoming rally bonfire we had built during
the day. Sure enough—as was the custom—someone had tried to ignite
it prematurely. They had spread gasoline and tossed a flaming broom
after it. As I had raced over and stooped to grab the broom, the gas
ignited with a whoosh, inflicting minor burns on my face and leg. It
wasn't at all serious but, of course, my poor mom flipped when I came
home from the County Hospital at 3 A.M. looking like a mummy. But
I was fine now and this last bandage would soon be off.

Anyway we were dragging Tenth Street; this was *the* town and *the*
drag from which George Lucas would create *American Graffiti*.

"Hey there, where you chicks from?" Russ was hustling the girls in
the next car.

"Turlock."

"Turlock! G'wan! Nobody's from Turlock!"

They all giggled and roared off with the green light. Well, things
stayed kinda slow on Tenth Street and somehow the subject of Yosemite
Junction came up. Yosemite Junction was supposed to be a whorehouse
east of town about twenty-five miles. Russ and I expressed doubt that
it really existed but Joe said, "Hey, no way! Chester Smith took me
and his brother up there last month. It's real, and by God we oughtta
go out there tonight."

"Hell, yes," Russ chimed in. "I'm game."

"Me too," I said on cue.

We determined that we all had five bucks and enough extra to give to
some old bum in Riverbank to buy us a pint of Old Crow whiskey plus
a half pint for himself. And Joe was already heading east out of town.

Yosemite Junction was a road junction with a small store and a gas
pump. Keep going straight past the store and you wind up on Sonora
Pass over the Sierra Nevada. Turn south there and eventually you enter
Yosemite Valley on the Tioga Pass Road. Behind the store a couple of
hundred yards and up on a rise among some oak trees sat a plain-looking
ranch-style house. It didn't look much like a whorehouse, but Joe assured us most whorehouses didn't. Russ took his last swig of Old Crow
and handed me the bottle to kill. "Right, I'm sure you've seen lots
of 'em."

"You guys will see," he said as he wheeled his '49 Chevy up the dirt lane that curved around behind the house.

"It doesn't look like anyone is there," I said, trying to conceal the hope in my voice. I gulped as we made the curve in the lane. Shit, the back porch light was red.

Well, we got out and did this kind of whiskey swagger up to the door with Joe in the lead, his finger outstretched to press the doorbell.

An older, buxom woman—maybe in her forties—answered the door and looked at us skeptically. "What do you boys think you want here?"

Joe said, "You know what we want. You open for business tonight or what?"

"Yeh, come on in here and let me take a look at you." Then she said with a hint of a smile. "Hell, you guys don't even look old enough to get a hard-on."

I walked in, stifled my shock at a lady saying "hard-on," and mumbled something about having been around plenty.

She showed us into the parlor, and if the outside didn't look like a brothel, the parlor sure did. It had fringed lamp shades, velvet curtains, velvet upholstery on the furniture, and suggestive little knickknacks around on the tables and walls. We all sat on the velvet couch and she made small talk for a minute or two, mostly checking that we had money—five dollars apiece of which she relieved us. Then she turned toward a lurid-looking hallway that had a beaded curtain and said, "Okay girls, come on out."

Three girls kind of swished out with their hands on their hips, wearing skimpy little corsetlike things and high-heeled shoes. I couldn't believe my eyes or even that this was happening. Was I about to get laid?

"Boys, this is Sherry, Martha, and Carmen." Sherry had auburn hair and a peachlike complexion. Joe said, "I'll take Sherry." Martha was not bad looking—just a little plump—but had huge knockers. Russ said, "I'll take Martha." The smart ass; how was he keeping his cool? How'd he know what we were supposed to do? Carmen, who was Mexican, stood by herself in the middle of the room. She was skinny, had long black hair, and a sweet face and dark, sympathetic eyes that couldn't have missed my uncertainty. "I'll . . . I'll . . . I'll take Carmen."

"Come on, Honey." She led me by the hand through the beaded curtain, down the hallway, and into her room. With no preliminaries, she turned toward me and flicked a zipper somewhere and her whole little corset deal just opened up and fell to the floor, and she was right in front of me, naked as anything.

"Okay, Honey, get undressed." So I did. "Is this your first time?" Her accent was heavy. "Oh no, no." As I removed my pants revealing the bandage she gasped, "Oh, *qué pasa*? Your leg!" Damn! I'd forgotten all about the stupid bandage. "Oh, it's a . . . a wound from Korea. I've only been home two or three weeks and I was wounded over there."

How I came up with that I'll never know. She showed real concern. "Oh well, maybe is some way I can make it easier? I can be on top or something?" "No, no, just the regular way will be fine!"

She led me to the wash basin, knelt down in front of me, and started washing me up, and said, "Well, if your leg is okay maybe you like better half and half or regular?" "Regular. Regular will be fine!" I guessed half and half must be half regular sex and half blow job.

She pulled me onto the bed and started rubbing me all over but I just wasn't getting hard. The washing didn't do it, and all her playing around wasn't doing it. "That's okay, Honey, it will get bigger." She pulled me on to her and tried to tuck me in, but I just wasn't hard. We struggled and rolled around and she played and stroked and kissed. Nothing happened.

Then, after the quickest fifteen minutes of my life, going through the motions like I knew what I was doin', the madam came by and knocked on the door. "Okay, Carmen."

Instantly she stopped moving and looked up at me with those big, deep eyes and said, "Honey, that's finish. You know, time's up. *Muy triste. No sé que decir!*" She said the latter almost as an afterthought.

I said stoically, "Well, that's okay. The doctors said I might expect some problems like this for a while."

I dressed twice as fast as I'd undressed while she sat naked on the edge of the bed just watching me, a sad expression on her face. "*Muy triste, muchachito!*"

Joe and Russ were waiting in the parlor with big grins on their faces. We walked out the back door and I glanced back. Carmen's head and one shoulder were sticking through the beaded curtain; she was following me with her sad eyes and shaking her head slowly. "*Muy triste, muy triste!*"

We bounded out to the car laughing and hooting. "Wow, that was fantastic!" said Joe. "Man, Martha's tits are great!" Russ added. "Hey, Coffee, how was your Mexican food?" They both laughed and snorted and slapped their knees, Joe barely able to negotiate the turn at the bottom of the lane. "Hot tamale!" I said enthusiastically. "Hot tamale!"

*   *   *

As the years in prison wore on, I became acutely aware of the importance of the physical touch of human warmth and love. How I missed physical affection now. I continued to give the Good Fairy a hand off and on, not only to release the tension but also to maintain the function. I speculated—with some trepidation—about my future sexual prowess after so long a layoff. Rim fire is a gunnery term that means for a piece of ammunition to go off prematurely for some reason. I fantasized frequently about my reunion with Bea and our first lovemaking and hoped my first look at her or our first sexual encounter would not be the cause of a rim fire.

In spite of living in a vacuum of physical touch and warmth, I never knew of any instance of homosexuality among the POWs. Even though I had cellmates at times and saw many instances of two men living together in a tiny cell for months—never really out of reach of one another—homosexuality just wasn't an option. Physical touch was very guarded. We were all products of a military community in which homosexuality was flat-out illegal, punishable by court-martial.

On the other hand, if a cellmate was ill or had a terrible headache or was injured from a torture session, a head or shoulder massage would be acceptable.

When a man was badly wounded, perhaps both arms broken, and unable to care for himself, the Vietnamese would usually—not always— give him a cellmate to help him out. Some men cared for others totally, fed them, bathed them, dressed them, helped them with their toilet functions. Generally, though, we were all very wary of excessive touching—even though we may have longed for it—because of what it could conceivably lead to in such emotionally harrowing circumstances.

When Dave Rehmann and I shared a cell in late '69 and early '70, he suffered interminably from asthma attacks. His pain and anxiety over his badly disfigured arm which had been shattered on ejection would have been enough, but the asthma exacted an even higher toll. He sat up sometimes through entire nights sucking for air, muscles exhausted and sweating profusely. There was little that could be done without medication, but frequently I'd massage his neck and shoulders to relieve the tenseness, to help him relax, and perhaps at least to doze. I had felt no qualms about this tenderness toward my cellmate.

As relaxed and mellow as I was after that first release, I never slept the rest of the night. My mind raced with the implications of it all.

The next morning I was tapping on the wall to my neighbor. "Howie,

the Good Fairy paid me a hell of a visit last night." And then, before
he could add it himself, I said, "But I sort of gave her a hand."

Later that day, my preoccupation with sex caused me to recall the
funniest story I'd heard in prison.

Air Force Major Tom Storey and I lived across from each other in
the Stardust the previous year. We had both lost our cellmates, and our
doors were the only ones in the cell block that were juxtaposed. We
spent hours on the floor, our cheeks pressed down against the concrete
so we could see the space beneath each other's door. We were there
like that for months and I got to know and love Tom. He was the father
of two, a boy and a girl about the ages of my Kimmie and Steve. We
talked of places we'd been with our families and places we'd go. It was
as if we'd known each other and our families for years. But all I could
ever see of him was the tip of his nose and one eye. Tom could see a
guard's shadow as he might step into the entryway next to my cell, so
we were lucky to be able to clear and to talk as much as we did.

Once we had been talking about how great a *hotsi* bath and a massage
were going to feel when we got out. I had told Tom about my last (and
only) *hotsi* bath in Atsugi, Japan, before flying out to the *Kitty Hawk*.

"Sounds great," he had said. "Back at Tak Li in Thailand we had a
massage setup at the O Club. Great way to end a sweaty two-and-a-
half-hour, ball-bustin' mission over the North or even a shorter, hairy
Alpha Strike. We'd grab a hot shower and a beer and a massage for an
hour and it almost made the whole day worthwhile. The best ones were
in Bangkok, though. Man, those little Thai massage gals were great.
They'd give you a long, slow, sensual kind of massage, then finish up
with a wax job. You ever have a wax job at Atsugi?"

"A wax job? Hell no, man, I was lucky just to get one *hotsi* bath.
My sum total of liberty for this indefinitely extended cruise is three days
in Japan. What the hell's a wax job anyway?"

I couldn't tell how cool he was playing it. He was hoping I would ask.

"Well, in these classy massage places in Bangkok, these girls give you
a nice hot bath and a fantastic massage. Then toward the end of the
massage, when you're really limp and relaxed, she starts messing around
with you until you get hard. Then she keeps it up, you know, slow and
easy. She can tell when you're about to come and she eases off a little,
keeps you right on edge. Then when you just can't stand any more and
you start this horrendous, heavenly come, she presses her thumb over
the end of your weenie and it blows all the wax out of your ears!"

Tom had a great sense of humor. One day, recalling how every military operation, training course, or exercise was always followed up by a critique for future improvement, Tom said in his gravelly whisper, "You know, when we get out of here and they ask us to fill out our critique sheets, I'm gonna tell 'em the exercise had plenty of realism, but the bugger just lasted too long!" Years later we would recall that we hadn't even been halfway through our imprisonment at that point.

13
Unity over Self

The strongest bonds of camaraderie and friendship are born and nurtured in shared adversity. Sadly, it seems that only through adversity do we acquire understanding, acceptance, and forgiveness of self, and then are able to apply them to others as well. The connections between us are solidified when we are willing to share without censure our own fear and weakness, courage and strength, and ultimately the joy of mutual triumph.

Not long after receiving Bea's letter back at the Zoo, I was returned to the Little Vegas section of Hoa Lo. At first I lived in Stardust number three with Air Force Captain Larry Chesley. It was a total surprise to be moved in with another man again.

Larry Chesley was a man of strong personal and religious convictions. Raised in a Mormon family and community in Burley, Idaho, he knew his religion with the admirable missionary zeal of most Latter-day Saints members I had known. He taught me the history of his church, the Book of Mormon, and about the Mormon church in general. When called upon to defend or clarify the tenets of my own religion, I felt inadequate by comparison. Larry's example—and pressure—caused me to delve into my own beliefs and spirituality much deeper than I otherwise would have. In some ways, Larry and I shared the same values, especially love of family and a propensity to question and debate. In other ways, however, we were very different and probably wouldn't have been close friends on the outside. Sometimes we argued like a couple of hungry lawyers, causing the roving guard to slam open the peephole, make us bow, and reprimand us sternly for making noise that could be heard outside the cell.

"Shhhh! Kip shilent!" This would be followed by a long glare, through which we could hardly keep a straight face as we heard our neighbors across the passageway laughing their asses off at our intensity.

The next day while comming with them from beneath the doors, they would inquire in a sarcastic whisper, "Did you guys . . . uh . . . reach any decisions last night?"

And one of us with face pressed to the space beneath our own door would usually reply, "No, but I bet him I was right. That's about eighteen thousand bucks this knothead is gonna owe me when we get outa here."

It was true. About the only way to "settle" an argument without reference material was to simply declare a "POW fact" (I know it's true; I can't prove it, but I just know it's true) and make a bet. That would at least end the discussion with each guy smug in the certainty he'd won the bet.

Larry had a remarkable physical attribute that came in very handy. He had this precision bite with his front teeth. He could crunch off a fingernail as crisply as the sharpest nail clippers. I had been filing my nails down on the rough concrete of a slab or the pitted iron of the stocks. It was a tedious process. But with Chesley, after he had done his own nails, I could wash my hands and let him go through my ten fingernails in less than a minute. I never asked him to do my toenails, however, and he never offered.

Chesley had an interesting philosophy about dealing with the V in interrogations. Most of us felt that a strict military bearing—straight and proper—was the most effective way to deal with an interrogator, to at least elicit his respect as a fellow military officer. Chesley, on the other hand, consciously tried to present himself as the most pitiful, disheveled, unpromising resource for Communist exploitation that he possibly could. Relatively slight of build and with thinning hair, he'd shuffle off to be quizzed in rumpled clothes as if he were about to collapse in a heap. He didn't escape the torture any more than the rest of us, but the V probably enjoyed hammering him less than those of us who puffed out our chests from the quiz stool. We all had to be actors at one time or another, and this was Larry's act. Of all the mice in this cat-and-mouse game, he may have been among the cleverest. Beneath the surface of our differing styles and our bullheaded debates, we grew to love and appreciate each other immensely.

In growing close as cellmates, our unexpected moves and separations were all the more wrenching. I would live in a tiny space with another man for a year or more, get to know him—in many ways—better than his own wife knew him. Then suddenly, as part of their inscrutable plan, the guard would slam open the door in the middle of the night, tell one or the other to roll up his gear, and then within minutes each would again be alone.

So it was on a restless June night that I was snatched apart from Larry in Stardust cell three, blindfolded, and shuffled circuitously through the Little Vegas complex ending up in Mint number two.

After the guard removed the rag from my eyes, Nasty, the officer supervising the move (someone had named him Nasty because that's what he was), snarled with the curling lip that was his trademark, "Co, too many times you show bad attitude. So now you will live here for some time. You must not talk with the others." With that he moved his eyes from cell one to cell three, and I was immediately heartened. As bad as this all might be, at least I wasn't isolated, alone.

The Mint consisted of three cells, more tiny even than my original cell in New Guy Village. It was the same setup: concrete slab, stocks, open bucket, but with less space between the slab and the wall. My pacing in this ten-inch slot had to be more crablike, contorted really. But I soon developed a kind of leaning, shuffling three-step-and-turn rhythm by which I covered several miles each day.

The large barred windows at the narrow end of each cell opened to the east and would have been a blessing if not for the pigs. The V had chosen this corner of the alleyway between the cell block and the perimeter wall to locate the prison pig sty. The nearly constant din of squealing, snorting, rooting hogs was bearable, but the odor was eye-watering, worse even than the lidless toilet buckets I'd suffered in previous cells. The lowest point was during the twice-weekly slaughters: With maximum shouting and extraneous supervision, a butcher would wrestle out a shrieking pig, clout it in the head with something, and bleed and gut it right under my window. There is no adequate description for the combined stench of pig shit, garbage, steaming blood, intestines, and fat. If I'd never really appreciated the mundane convenience of fresh, tightly packaged spare ribs from my refrigerator at home before, I certainly did after this summer of '67.

To my left, in cell three, was Navy Commander Howie Rutledge. He was a tough, stringy little Okie who, along with a few other senior officers, had a reputation as a "strong resistor." For a situation that may call for a "thank you" to a guard or jailer, Howie was as likely to say "fuck you"—as if the V didn't know the difference. Problem was, that same guard might be on your next torture team, or have the authority to summon a doctor. He would remember who had said "fuck you" and who had said "thank you."

Since he'd been downed in November of '65, Howie had been plagued by more boils than the average guy. I figured it was his bitterness coming out. They had really enjoyed torturing him.

Seven years earlier, Howie and I had known better times together. He had been one of my flight instructors in the Crusader training squadron in Jacksonville, Florida. He was a happy, hard-partying, hard-playing, "don't give a shit" guy who loved to dog fight. Hasseling in and out of afterburner and making curly white contrails in the blue Florida sky was what Howie lived for. He considered himself—and was—the consummate fighter pilot.

On the other side of me, in cell one, was Navy Lieutenant Commander Nels Tanner. He was a Phantom pilot; an easygoing, cherubic kind of man from Covington, Tennessee. Early on in the extortion of his "concrete act of repentence," Nels had been tortured to write a statement about how pilots on his ship—because of their supposed disenchantment with the war—had refused to fly anymore. Finally, Nels had to acquiesce. Mustering up his last-ditch creativity, he had scrawled something like "Things is so bad on our boat, ain't nobody wanna fly no more. Our CO, Commander Clark Kent, said he ain't gonna fly no more, and our operations officer, Lieutenant Commander Ben Casey, said he ain't gonna participate in operations no more neither."

The Vietnamese made him clean up the grammar and syntax, but left in Kent and Casey. They were so pleased with the statement, they printed it in one of their propaganda magazines that goes out in several languages to their brotherly socialist partners around the world. Somewhere along the way (we suspected it was someone in a visiting peace delegation), it was pointed out that Nels had socked it to 'em, that Clark Kent was the comic book character Superman, and that Ben Casey was a TV actor playing a doctor.

Nels was immediately tortured, forced to write an apology, and was then slapped into the stocks in the Mint. He had been here now for nearly six months and would ultimately spend nearly two years in stocks or leg irons.

Nels related to me—through the wall, of course—a quiz he'd had the previous month with a senior general staff officer who had apparently just wanted to see the man who had tricked his extortioners. After listening to his harangue, Nels had asked, "How long are you going to punish me for this? As you can see, my ankles are swollen and raw from the stocks. They are badly infected. I have written an apology. What more do you want?"

The staff officer exploded. "Apology! Apology! You have embarrassed my government so much, there is no apology enough, and there is no punishment enough for you!"

"I tell you, Jerry, as I hobbled back across the courtyard to the Mint here, I held my head a li'l higher. The asshole couldn't have paid me a nicer compliment."

Taking advantage of the increased light here in the Mint, I reread Bea's letter frequently, translating each phrase into a vivid real-life image.

One day I noticed the dot. I stared to make sure. Yes, there tucked up into the crotch of a lowercase letter "l" was a tiny dot. A fly speck? Quickly I scanned along the same line and then the next one. Yes, another dot, no fly speck. This one was nestled beneath a "d" where the tail trailed off. God, it had worked!

My spine tingled as I stared at the minuscule dots beneath several letters, and my mind raced back to reconstruct the scene I'd almost forgotten, when I had read about Everett Alvarez's shootdown and a statement from his wife about a letter he had written. I remember telling Bea that if that ever happened to me I'd put little dots under certain letters to spell out my secret messages to her. She had acted as if this was another of her youthful husband's hotshot pilot fantasies.

In my Easter letter I had used an old-fashioned dip pen. The point was sharp, but I sharpened it more by scraping it on my concrete slab. I placed the tiny dots carefully using whatever letters were available in my word associations: "Forget B.S. in first letter. This camp in Hanoi. Torture." I'd added the names of other men from my wing in Florida who were live POWs. I also included in the text the following word association: "David, I can just see you playing with your little connect-the-dot books to get the big picture."

I had initially scanned Bea's letter for dots when I'd received it three months earlier, but my cell back at the Zoo was so dark I hadn't been able to see them. Now, my heart pumping with excitement, I deciphered her message! "Send names and locations. Hang on."

Although I was elated to realize my dot message had been received and now answered, I was struck by what was, to me at least, the rhetorical encouragement. "Hang on!" I'd been hangin' on for two years now!

I was never able to use the dots again because all subsequent letters were written in the presence of a V officer, and would soon become just postcards with six lines to write on. Even those would be censored. They were suspicious of any reference to weather or health. I learned to plan my six lines very carefully, making some short comment about health or weather; they'd do their censor trick on it and leave the rest of the text alone.

Days passed fast in the Mint. Howie was hurting more than usual and was in and out of stocks just on general principle. With Nels in stocks too, I spent a lot of time communicating with them and passing information from one to the other, all to help make their days pass faster and to take their minds off their misery. Sometimes with all the tapping and clearing, along with my own prayer and exercise time, working on my French vocabulary, POW roster and other memory lists, memorizing and composing poetry, and planning projects for the future at home again, I'd frequently go to sleep at night thinking, Hell, I didn't get done everything I'd wanted to do today. I was learning that routine gave me a sense of control and accomplishment. I was also beginning to realize the significance of the experience I was enduring, that God wasn't laying all this on me for nothing. He was preparing me for something. I would use the insights I was gaining to accomplish or contribute something unique.

In that spirit, I was beginning to embrace—probably more than I realized—each day, if not eagerly, then purposefully. And each night I would console myself with "Okay, Babe, that's another day closer to home . . . whenever it may be."

I realized that my purpose there in the Mint between these other two "incorrigible criminals"—one resisting through creativity, the other through stoicism—was to comfort and encourage them.

Howie Rutledge was a compulsive communicator. Once he had me clear the small storage room on which the three Mint cells opened so he could stand on his bucket on top of his slab and talk out his window to the guys down the alleyway in the end cell of the Desert Inn. I'd thought he was crazy, but by golly it worked, and helped us to stay in touch with the rest of Little Vegas.

During siesta time, Howie would communicate constantly. We could both lay on our slabs and tap softly, but it still required a watchful eye for shadows beneath the door. One time a guard we called Squeaky (because of his high-pitched voice) became suspicious. As he lurked outside my door, I could see the sole of his sandal partly exposed from behind the door jamb. I thumped softly on the wall three times: danger, danger, danger! Still Howie tapped. I thumped again, louder. He kept tapping. Squeaky caught me in the third series of thumps. Howie and I both spent the next week in the leg stocks. With all three of us immobilized, communication was reduced considerably. I could still stretch and twist my body to tap essentials, but recreational comm stopped.

During that time in stocks I focused on poetry each day for several hours. Back at the Zoo an Air Force Captain named Norm Wells had taught me "High Flight," the incredibly descriptive poem by a young Royal Canadian Air Force pilot named John Gillespie McGee. He had been killed during the battle of Britain, but he left a legacy to which all pilots could relate. McGee spoke of "slipping the surly bonds of earth" and dancing "the skies on laughter's silvered wings." I could not help but focus upon the poignancy of those lines now as these surly bonds of iron clamped me tightly to the earth.

The poetry had become so important to me as a source of beauty, strength, and inspiration. As I had learned later, Norm had been forced by his mom each year of his boyhood to learn a new poem to recite at their annual Thanksgiving family reunion. He inspired the rest of us to go back into our own youth, to resurrect the poetry we had been forced to learn by some "mean ol' English teacher" or wise parent along the way, none of whom could convince us at the time that it was a worthy endeavor.

Poetry provided countless hours of escape from our grim reality. The poems of Robert Service and of Rudyard Kipling had appealed especially to our sense of adventure and individualism, but to our sense of duty to others as well. We had really locked on to Kipling's poem "If," in which he gives advice to his son, but especially the one verse that reminded all of us through the years:

> If you can force your heart and nerve, and sinew
> To serve their term long after they are gone
> When there is nothing left within you
> Except the will that says to them, Hold on!

God, I was holding on. Sometimes I thought that's really all that was left in me; the will that keeps saying "Hold on! Hold on!"

I decided one day to compose a poem about food to entertain Howie and Nels. We had received bread a couple of times in lieu of the usual rice. It usually came in a small roll about six inches long, and it was apparent that wherever they kept the flour for this bread—somewhere in the dungeonlike kitchens of Hoa Lo—there were plenty of bugs and weevils and roaches and flies. But at least, I reasoned, they were protein supplements. Anyway, the next time we received bread, I was immediately inspired to compose my poem after taking the first bite:

> Little Weevil in my bread
>   I think I just bit off your head.
> I see the place where you have bled
>   The dough around it is all red.
> But that's okay, for now instead
>   I know for sure you're really dead.
>
> I wonder if your name was Fred.

Well, when I passed it to Nels the next day, he got so tickled after the first two lines, he was bangin' and scratchin' and scrapin' his laugh on the wall to me, and then I started laughin' and I never did get the rest of the poem to him. I allowed later as how after those first two lines, things did sorta go downhill.

In a corner of the storeroom outside the Mint, the V had piled several weeks' worth of pumpkins for the twice-daily soup. The pile was so big the weight crushed the softer pumpkins on the bottom, most of which began to rot and turn green with mold. From beneath my door while clearing, I'd watch rats assemble in the pumpkin slop, gorging themselves to a waddle. They made almost as much noise slurping and squealing as did the pigs behind me. At least we never had to deal with the smell of rotting pumpkins—it was always subsumed by the heavy odor of the pigs.

One day while clearing under my door and tapping with Nels to help distract him from the pain in his swollen ankles, now squeezed tightly by the rough stocks, a grayish blur suddenly filled my entire field of view. A rat hit me going full tilt. His snout smacked into the bridge of my nose and slid upward to wedge momentarily between my cheek and the bottom of the door. By the time I'd realized what had happened and recoiled, he had already disengaged and was out the rat hole on the other side of Nels's cell. He had come tearing out from under Nels's door, turned the corner into my cell just as he'd done uneventfully many times before—only this time my face had blocked his way. I could hear Nels laughing uproariously. That bastard, how could he even know what happened, let alone think it funny?

I repositioned myself on the floor to clear and tapped a "C" (the all-clear) to Nels, who was still giggling.

"I bet that one got you head-on, didn't he? I saw him go zooming out of my cell. He'd turned just enough so I knew he was gonna go right around the corner and into your cell where you were clearing. And when you stopped tapping, I knew he'd nailed you right in the kisser. Thanks to the both of you for a great laugh!"

A few days later in the shadows of late afternoon, I was in the same clearing/tapping position passing to Nels Howie's advice on how he should approach his next quiz in order to get out of the stocks. Of course, none of us could know Nels would spend the next sixteen months in leg irons, his quiz tactics be damned.

"Howie thinks you should remind them of their responsibilities under the Geneva Convention on POW treatment. He says it probably won't do any good, but it's your duty to remind them any . . ."

Again my view was suddenly obscured by a huge brownish, fuzzy face. I yelped and sprang back against the back wall of the cell. The image pursued me. Large black nose. Black eyes that seemed to engulf me with their bright intensity. Pink tongue between sharp, white teeth. My heart was pounding as I tried to fathom the size of such a rat.

Rat? My body slumped in relief as I began to realize that it wasn't a rat. I was chuckling aloud as I returned to the floor. Sure enough, foraging among the pumpkins was one of the prison puppies. He had slipped in through the rat hole out of my view to the right, had been intrigued by the tip of my nose almost protruding to his side of the door, and pounced upon it in mock attack. He was a cute little ball of fur about two months old. He only had a few weeks more to live. In another month or so he and the rest of his litter would be chased down by a band of whooping guards, clubbed to death, cooked, and eaten.

At least Nels and Howie had had another good laugh as I explained to them about the commotion in Mint two.

In mid-July, the V seemed especially uptight. Nasty was slapping men into stocks and withholding rations at what appeared to be his whim. But we knew better: He didn't have that authority, so it was probably part of an approved purge. Word came from the Desert Inn that both Risner and Stockdale, the senior Air Force and Navy POWs at the time, were under a lot of pressure. Others were being tortured to get them to indict the senior men for their leadership, to reveal their orders and policies, and how they were being passed on. Upon my arrival in the Mint, I had passed to Howie and Nels the orders and encouragement we in Stardust had received from Risner and Stockdale. Tenuous communication links had been established to both of them separately. Again the prison authorities thought they had isolated them from any contact, but again they had underestimated our perseverance and creativity.

One night just before midnight, Nasty and some guards took Nels from his cell. There had been a lot of shouting of orders and clanking of locks and iron bolts. I heard the abuse, the punches and kicks, the shoving against the walls, and the grunts and groans of pain. During the next three days Howie and I prayed for Nels and kept each other company.

At nearly midnight of the third day, Nels was returned quietly. No sooner had the guard left and the space outside was quiet than I heard his soft but urgent call-up: Tap-tap-tap tap-tap.

I emerged quickly from my net and hit the floor to clear and tap.

Nels tapped rapidly and I could actually sense the anguish and torment in his tapping. "Jerry, I'm sorry. They worked me over with ropes. Made me say how I knew Stockdale's policies. I told 'em from you. They're probably gonna come for you. I'm so very sorry. They took me to be in a propaganda movie, too. Shumaker and Harris were there. They had been through it all, too. They've got a real purge goin'. I'm so sorry, Jerry! I wish I could have been stronger."

I knew he was hurting more now for implicating and condemning me than during the entire time he'd been in leg irons and cuffs. I tried to return an upbeat reply but without much conviction.

"No sweat, Nels. I know how it was. We can only do our best. Please, don't feel badly about it."

He acknowledged but tapped no further.

I knew it was only a matter of time before I found myself facing the same kind of session that had left Nels so low. Still, I put all my heart into my sign-off to him: "GN, GB."

One thing was certain. We were all in touch with our humanness— our strengths and our weaknesses. There was no bravado here. And in acknowledging our weaknesses and finally forgiving ourselves and one another for them, we were learning both humility and compassion.

The next morning Nasty snarled an order for me to dress in long sleeves and trousers, slapped me into the ankle stocks, and cuffed my hands behind my back. In a few days, the heat rash on the small of my back began to turn to boils. After about two weeks, I could count by feel over twenty of them. On the fifteenth day, I was taken out and tortured with the ropes. Nothing had changed.

The sudden resurgence of memories of previous sessions came back with a rush. The searing pain seemed to take up exactly where it had left off the last time. I lied and cried and cursed until they gagged me with a wad of rag wrapped around the end of a piece of rope. Finally I acknowledged that I knew Stockdale's policies, but by agreeing to be in the damn movie I was able to evade telling them how we had reached him. Then they put me on a stool with my ankles cuffed to the rungs. After two and a half days with no sleep, I wrote an apology for my "bad attitude" and promised never to communicate again.

On the eighteenth day I was taken back to cell number two in the Mint. After another snarling admonishment, the jailer pointed to the paper on the wall with the camp regulations and closed and locked the door. Instantly I was at the base of the door to clear: Tap-tap-tap tap-tap.

Tap-tap came the immediate response.

"I J C U?"

From my left came "H R." I smiled.

And from my right came "N T. Welcome back!"

14

Hanoi Moon

Life sometimes passes ever so slowly. We are frequently led to believe that stability is stagnancy, that sameness is deadly. Yet beneath the surface of calm acceptance an inexorable current is moving us forward. Perhaps only from that place of feeling trapped do we stop to integrate the truths by which we flow with the process and allow ourselves to move on.

Keys! The jingling of keys in the night; in the night when they shouldn't have been there.

I stopped pacing and listened. I had learned that sometimes the guards did it just because they knew the terrorizing effect it had on each man in each stifling cell. I listened and watched the half-inch crack beneath the door of my cell for the first sign of trouble.

It was clear now, the sound of key on key, keys on ring.

In the normal routine and in their proper context, the sound of the keys had become almost like an old friend, a measure of time passing— so slowly, but passing nonetheless. In the morning: keys . . . door open . . . empty bucket. Midmorning: keys . . . pick up food . . . eat . . . keys . . . set out dishes . . . fill water jug. And so, another day closer to home, whenever it might be.

Nothing could happen, time couldn't pass without the keys. At night, however, the keys were wrong and my heart pounded harder as I saw through my door-bottom "window" the dark form of rubber-tire sandals on brown feet.

Suddenly the random jingling stopped and was replaced by the sinister little clink-clink of selection. He was picking out my key. That was the sound, the one night sound, that had come to make the time stand still.

Instinctively I glanced around for anything out of place in my cell. It was one of only seven here at a grubby little prison fashioned from an old maintenance building next to the Hanoi power plant. It was even more filthy than Hoa Lo, so we had dubbed the place Dirty Bird.

As I stood before the door, the lock creaked in the eye of the hasp. I was sweating. Several drops broke free from my bare chest, joined, and coursed their little zigzag route down my torso, pooling at my navel, then broke free again and melted into the waist of my loose-fitting shorts, already soaked.

The bolt of the door slammed open, echoing through every wall in the building. The night swung in, revealing Swish and Mouth. Swish held a small flashlight, but the unfrosted 60-watt bulb on the wall above me diminished its beam. By habit, he shined it in my face anyway. Swish was just the usual gunguard. He was named Swish because he walked like a prissy girl. Though the custom of men walking arm in arm or embracing was very common to the V, hundreds of combined man-hours of crack- and peephole watching had revealed to us that Swish seemed to relish this affectionate custom with more than comradely interest. I think he knew we knew, but that didn't seem to make him any more of a bastard than he already was.

There he stood, half a step behind Mouth, with his small Czech-made grease-gun automatic cradled in his arm.

"Bow! Bow!"

With a brief but by now well-grooved rhythm, I nodded my head and rolled my shoulders slightly forward, then straightened again. A drop of sweat, rolling down my nose, landed on the black rubber strap of my left sandal. His keys clutched tightly in his hand, Mouth just stood there, in the jaundice of my 60 watts, considering the shabbiness of my bow.

Standing there, waiting for what was sure to come, I thought of the men in the other cells, especially my two buddies on either side. All had heard the keys. All had heard the bolt. All had heard the "Bow!" Interrupted from their plans, their dreams, their prayers, or their pacing and memory work, they waited, hardly breathing, straining to hear some clue of who or why. It made little difference where the keys stopped. As often as not, the first stop only portended the next, and the next. And besides, if it's "him" it's almost the same as if it were "me." We suffered the same pains, as if all were joined to the same nerve fiber stretched taut from one end of the cell block to the other. We all felt the same anxious knot in our middle, knowing that the temporary security that develops from being in a familiar cell, with an established routine and a good comm system, was about to be jerked from beneath us again.

I knew my buddy on one side had his tin cup against the wall, his ear pressed tightly against the bottom, listening for an order from Mouth or some signal from me. I knew the one on the other side was watching my door, his sticky face pressed against the tiny nail hole running obliquely through the inside corner of his door, his body stretched across the doorway to keep both feet behind the edge of the door jamb, thus avoiding the costly betrayal of a shadow beneath the door. Should I disappear that night, just drop out of sight, my friends would know—unless, of course, we should *all* drop out of sight.

Our experience thus far had given us reason for serious concern. Just as I had reported the delirium and death of my anonymous friend that night in New Guy Village, others had told me of instances when men would be taken out for what would seem to be a routine quiz and simply never return. A guard would be seen retrieving their gear from the empty cell later on. Some would reappear eventually in a different prison, but others would never be seen again.

Mouth made the crisp, chopping motion with one hand across the outstretched wrist of his other, meaning "put on your long-sleeved shirt and long trousers." By this I knew I was about to go to a quiz, or my cell was about to be inspected for unauthorized items, or I was being taken out. To be taken out after "office hours," as the V themselves called the time from 5 P.M. to 7 A.M., implied ominous things.

But Mouth wasn't finished. He rotated his hands, one over the other in the paddlewheel motion. "Roll up your belongings, you're moving out."

Then, to punctuate his little charadelike performance, he barked, "Quigly!"

So, I was moving. Where to? Perhaps just down the passageway in a routine switch to keep us off balance. It had become fairly routine to do this periodically to keep us from getting well organized in communication and clearing procedures, or escape coordination, or whatever "diabolical plots" of which we were regularly accused.

As I slipped into my trousers, I listened for other keys, for other locks to open, other activity out in the open-air passageway. I could hear nothing but my own heart beating. The outside silence meant I would be traveling alone.

I knew that wherever I was going, I must get out a signal . . . soon. If I coughed an "M," my comrades would know I was moving. A "Q" would indicate a quiz. They would pick it up as instinctively as a night creature reads the enveloping darkness. The ears of each prisoner had become so finely tuned to all sounds in relation to our tap code that they would easily perceive my sign.

I approached the familiar task of packing my belongings into my blanket roll so that no matter how much it might get banged around, all would be secure. The loss of anything—my cup, my toothbrush, or even my sliver of lye soap—could be a disaster. When one had so little, so little meant so much. Strangely enough, I had even come to appreciate how little I really needed to subsist—an insight that would never have been accessible otherwise. I surveyed my meager inventory gathered neatly on my rice straw mat. It provided the only clean place on the pitted cement floor. Recalling the proper place for each item in my bundle, I gingerly set my tin cup and a one-liter water jug aside to accommodate my unfolded blanket.

"No! No!"

Mouth shook his head.

"Man, I just don't read you. What the hell do you want me to do?"

He smacked me on the ear with the heel of his hand. I knew my buddies heard it.

Swish, slouching in the doorway, interjected a few words and poked his weapon toward my mat.

Mouth grunted an answer, then squatted down. With a great show of distaste, like a girl picking up a dead mouse by the tail, he lifted the corner of my mat. I comprehended the action but not the meaning. He wants me to roll up my mat and nothing else. This is a new one.

Under their satisfied scrutiny, I complied. Then as I stood before the two of them, dressed in my faded khaki "longs," still stained from the bloody parade over a year ago, and with my mysteriously empty mat rolled neatly under my arm, I just didn't know whether to cough "M" or "Q."

Stepping down the two steps from the cell to the passageway, I understood why Mouth was more disagreeable than usual. The night was hot and sticky, bad enough to give even the V a good case of heat rash. Even so, it was better than the superheated atmosphere of my cell. In fact, it was like stepping out into an ocean breeze—at least ten degrees of relief.

With his flashlight, Swish pointed to the spot where I was to stand while Mouth closed and locked the door. That's it, don't let any fresh air get in there, whatever you do.

At the far end of the passage, I could discern a small cluster of figures, two wearing pith helmets and with shoulder-slung weapons, and one with a flashlight. The helmetless one, with the flashlight, shorter than his two comrades, was Louie the Rat. He liked to fancy himself the camp commander. He had been assigned as a sort of officer-in-charge of this "camp" but he was obviously supervised closely. He and the others were given very little latitude in dealing with us—to our benefit.

I moved along the walkway with Swish following. The passageway, formed by the cells on my right and the roofless shell of the warehouse on my left, was fairly wide. Cough, cough, cough, cough-cough! Surely my rasping "Q" would be recognized instantly. On the other side of the doors, the thought would be: What the hell is that going to be about? Hang in there, Babe. God bless. And a short prayer would be breathed.

Louie said in his whiny voice, "Tonight you will go someplace. Wait some minutes."

Within the next few minutes, I found myself blindfolded and handcuffed in the back of a beat-up ambulance-type vehicle, seated on the floor between what must have been litter attachment brackets. As I leaned back against the side of the vehicle, I appreciated that Louie had left the cuffs fairly loose. The chatter between Swish and the driver was relaxed. With this, I relaxed a little myself. We had all learned that when the mission is really serious and they're uptight about getting something from you, the hostility in their handling and speaking comes through clearly.

Looking down, beneath the blindfold, I saw the little Czech-made machine gun in Swish's lap. As deadly a weapon as it could undoubtedly be, we had come to belittle it: You can tell; it's swell; it's Mattel.

Outside, someone cranked the engine into action; actually cranked it by hand, like an old Model-T Ford. It died and was recranked; died and was recranked twice more. In the name of frugality, they usually set their carburetors so lean that the drivers had to use more gas just revving the engine to keep it running at idle. As we jostled out of the power-plant yard, the springless beast bounced me on and off the brackets on the floor. I tried to use this movement to disguise my hand sweeping up, almost imperceptibly, pushing my blindfold up a little more.

"Isssh!" The muzzle of the toy gun slapped reprovingly at my hand. "Co! Tsk, tsk, tsk!"

Down the ramp and onto the street we went. I counted the passing of blocks by the drainage dips at each intersection. Three blocks, four . . . at five we made a sharp right that caused me to brace my feet against the other side. The driver jammed the reluctant gears into reverse, then backed in a ninety-degree arc to the left and stopped. The gears whined again; we turned right and were on our way. The driver, now less casual, had barked and bitched at the pedestrians and cyclists throughout the maneuver, the sum total of which was another left turn.

At rare times like that, when I seemed to be so close to the everyday people of Hanoi, I wondered what they were thinking; why they were out on that particular street, going in that particular direction. And I wondered what they would have thought had they known that only inches away from their war- and work-weary bodies sat a captured American pilot, that curious, impersonal entity found only within the clichéd context of "U.S. war of aggression," "U.S. ruling clique," and "Saigon puppets." I wondered if, somehow, through the callus of indoctrination, they could possibly think of me as just another human being, just as they seemed so human to me at this moment. We're really looking for the same thing in life, Lord. Why can't we make it? Why must it come to this?

Slowing down . . . left turn.

About four or five blocks after our last turn we slowed again. The conversation, which I wasn't understanding, took on a more purposeful tone. Halfway through another left, we stopped. An order was passed to the outside and I heard the dull clunk of wood on wood. Suddenly, the scene outside was clear: It was the sound made by the street guard raising the crude, counter-weighted barrier blocking the entry to Pham Hong Thai Street—the street that passes right in front of Dirty Bird and the Annex, and then, a few feet farther down, along the south side of the power plant.

For the past few months (squinting through the cracks in the boards, battens, and tin that had been a window), I had watched the guards admit army vehicles and dump trucks that were hauling debris from around the power plant. I had watched them deny access to others, surmising that the restriction was to protect the power plant from sabotage and keep the curious neighbors away from the prison.

We were rolling again; down Pham Hong Thai Street, past my unsuspecting comrades in their 60-watt ovens, past the point where Ninh Binh Street butts in from the south. I could visualize the heart of the power-plant district outside.

The plant had been attacked several times. Some of the damage had been inflicted by a sophisticated weapon we called the Wall-Eye. It homed into its target on a TV-type sensitivity to dark and light contrast.

To thwart this contrast-sensitive eye of the wall-eye missile, the entire power plant and surrounding neighborhood—roofs, walls, sidewalks— had been painted gray. The people there endured a threefold environmental oppression. First, like the power-plant district in most large cities, the air was always choked with coal dust, so thick that it collected on bare shoulders like black dandruff. Second, the streets and buildings there, like the rest of the city, assumed that all-pervasive drabness of any society where freedom of expression is stifled. And finally now, nothing was left to inspire imagination. There was no dark, no light, no sense of contrast anywhere in the entire neighborhood.

Suddenly we jerked to a stop, jerked forward a few more feet, and then again to a stop as the engine expired. After all the driving, we were scarcely fifty yards down the street from my cell.

Outside, Louie's voice snapped officiously. I heard the broken panes in the window of the ambulance's door shift against themselves as it swung open and banged against its hinges. Swish moved past me and grabbed my sleeve.

"Co! Come down."

As I stood on the curb with my rolled-up mat in hand, Mouth removed my towel and dropped it to my feet.

The power-plant Annex, as we had dubbed it, was a line of about eight two-room apartments that had been abandoned as living quarters after the first raid. Each faced onto the street. A common corridor in the rear, much like the passageway at Dirty Bird, joined them all together in a communal entity. Each two apartments shared a common kitchen and wash area along the corridor. Being one of the newer and more substantial buildings in the area, these accommodations had probably been quite choice. It was likely, though, that two or three families had been quartered in each, thereby reducing them to the crowded shabbiness of the surrounding bomb-shaken structures.

Louie was more officious than usual. There were orders and acknowledgments over and over. The driver slammed and reslammed the weary door. The whole damned neighborhood would be roused from its drab and uneasy sleep, people peeking furtively through the straw-mat screens of the tiny apartments and rooms to which they'd been assigned, all watching this Chaplinesque drama in the grubby yellow circle of the lone street light.

To any who might witness my arrival, I would appear to be a new prisoner to the Annex. The more "going and coming fire drills" staged by the authorities, the more obvious it would be that Americans were being imprisoned here. That was the purpose of this exercise: Word would get around and leaks would filter through to our government, if not by covert means, then surely through the myriad of foreign journalists and "investigators of U.S. war crimes." Schwinman had told me he had been given a complete tour of the city. I felt certain that this whole routine was just the beginning and that others would soon follow in that junky old ambulance.

I was led into the only lighted room in the Annex and seated on a low wooden stool. The walls, though freshly whitewashed, were bare, except for the omnipresent red-framed photo of Ho Chi Minh over the door to the back corridor. The red-tiled floor was still wet from a half-assed splashdown and the air was warm and moist, almost steamy. Before me was a massive wooden table with ornate floral carvings on the apron and legs, all now chipped and scarred. One of the castors was bent almost to the side of its little ceramic wheel, a cultural vestige possibly left by some French-favored mandarin, now contemptuously misused in the service of the People's Army. Had Zhivago returned to find his old boyhood furniture-friends so treated?

Louie sat across from me, his finger tracing a deep gouge in that formerly splendid mahogany plane. As usual, the relative heights of his chair and my stool ensured him a downward perspective, even though I sat as erect as possible.

"Co, tonight I ask you some question."

I said nothing.

"How do you think about this camp?"

I wondered what he was probing for. Or was he just killing time? "I think it is illegal for your government to keep POWs in a known target area. The Geneva agreements on POW treatment specifically forbid this."

"Why you think this is a target? What is target?" He shrugged. "You can see. Many, many people live here." He made an indifferent little wave toward the street.

"This power plant supplies electricity to most of Hanoi. Your air defense system and most of your local industry would be hurt very much if it might be destroyed." We had learned to structure our own sentences for their ease of comprehension.

Louie widened his eyes in sham surprise. "Hanoi? Hanoi? Why you think this is Hanoi?"

"I saw the road signs that said Hanoi the first morning I arrived in the city. The guards kept saying Hanoi this and Hanoi that." I paused. "And the water girls wear football jerseys that say Hanoi High on the front." Surely Louie isn't really so naive as to think I don't know where I am, I thought, but he persisted in this futile effort to keep me from knowing where I was and that I was only one of many other American POWs.

My sarcasm met a blank expression as he pondered the more immediate problem of my knowing exactly where I was within Hanoi. "And besides," he meowed, "why you think this power plant?"

My smile was as condescending as I could make it. "Because it looks like one, and it sounds like one, and it smells like one, and there are a lot of electric wires going from it in many directions." And besides, I thought to myself, my neighbor *told* me it was a power plant the morning after I'd moved in.

"Nah!" Louie grunted, warding off my words with half a head-shake. "You make mistake; you make many, many mistake. How do you think about the food in this camp?"

I realized now he was just killing time.

"It is not enough and it is dirty and it makes my stomach hurt and makes me have diarrhea."

I didn't even get into my intestinal parasites, the rash of boils I had already endured, or the body weight that had disappeared. On the one hand, it had been a scary thing to see myself deteriorate like this physically, but on the other hand, I continually marveled at my physical and emotional resilience. I had shit spaghettilike worms into my bucket and was revulsed at the thought of passing them out through my throat while asleep, as had happened to at least one man so far. I had stoically outwaited festering boils in my nose, my ears, and the crack of my ass, knowing there would be no relief until they were ripe enough to depressurize by squeezing out the core—the self-infliction of intense short-term pain for the prospect of long-term relief—perhaps several times on the same boil. In a year and a half, my weight had gone from 165 to an estimated 130, and I knew the spiral wasn't over.

Louie repeated his Catch–22 answer more emphatically: "You should remember the war. Food is very difficult. Even so, your ration is bigger than the armymen's, and much bigger than the people's in the villages."

After a long politically inspired monologue in that whine I'd learned to hate, Louie must have made his main points to his own satisfaction. He paused, apparently to assess the effect it had had on me, but was really just sopping up the long night, to make my recent "arrival" look legitimate. The charade would never work if, within only a few minutes, I went traipsing back down the street to where I really lived.

At last he said, with more than just official interest, "Do you think your government will bomb the power plant if you live here?" This was the first question of the evening for which he really wanted an answer.

Without hesitation I said, "Of course, and in fact, they already have."

"You see! Your government does not care about your life! Johnson will kill you himself!" He slapped the table, leaned back, and crossed his legs, satisfied with himself.

"Not so," I countered. "You can remember in the last raid the power plant was hit but our cells were not hit. Our pilots are always very, very accurate." I lied. In the lethal crossfire of SAM 2s plus triple-A and light arms fire that saturates the sky over this entire end of the city, in spite of their intentions the guys were doing damn well just to hit the city block that the power plant was on, let alone to miss our little prison enclave. That put us well within the "circular error probable." We had been lucky so far.

"I think you will die here no matter if bomb kill you or not," he snapped from his chair and strode toward the door to the street. At the doorway he paused and spoke to Swish at the other door. I recognized the Vietnamese words *Mot mot gios*: eleven o'clock. It had been 9:30 a few minutes earlier when Louie's watch was accompanying his finger through the air as he dramatized his monologue. Swish replied with something affirmative as Louie disappeared into the moonlit street.

For the next hour at Swish's direction I sat on the cool tiles of the floor, meticulously scraping dried drops of whitewash from the tiles around the edges of the room with a piece of broken glass. After scraping each tile, I splashed away the loose flakes of lime with a full bucket of water. An overkill, of course, but the puddles of excess water were cooler to sit in.

Mouth was in and out. He and Swish joked as they watched me wallowing there in the thin pools of water, probably comparing my relative bliss to that of the tender-skinned buffaloes they had both tended as boys in the verdant countryside. On my way north I had seen those gentle, plodding beasts that could slog a plow through several kilometers of paddy each searing day. I had even seen one lolling in a huge bomb crater filled with seepage, with his own little master lounging easily on his shoulder and cooing into his ear. It was a scene dear to all V hearts—

North and South. To them, this image of the little boys and their buffaloes heading for the water as the sun dipped below the peaks of the Truong Son range imparted a feeling that all was well, a sense of peace and serenity. This was the Vietnam of other days.

"Co, wash."

I could see from the shower behind apartment number one that several of the other rooms down the line were lighted. I coughed my initials twice as I removed my shorts and turned the water on. Strain as I might, I could hear no double-cough reply from down the corridor.

Swish and Mouth smoked unconcernedly, hardly paying attention to either my cough or the sound of the running water. But to me, the sound of that water spurting from the open end of the rusty pipe and beating on the slimy concrete slab was like a chorus from heaven. And of all the good fortune, there, wedged between the pipe and the peeling wall, was a piece of soap, a little smaller than a motel-sized bar. I washed and rinsed, washed and rinsed again, and then again.

I rinsed and rubbed the sweat and grime from my shorts and then from that offensive rag of a towel. And then I just stood there, my hands extended overhead, gripping the curved pipe just above where the nozzle might have been. With my weary body dropping limply from the leaden spout, the joy of the cool water was indescribable. I swayed slowly from side to side, playing the water down over each part of my body. With an almost sensual satisfaction, I could feel the welts from heat rash receding inward; each tiny blister shriveling back into its respective pore. God, it felt good to cool down! I missed hot water in the cold of winter, but this moment now was worth the promise of hot water year-round. I knew that if I could chill my skin sufficiently, I might get through an entire night without being awakened by rivulets of sweat trickling from my groin, waist, and inside my upper arms.

I dried the lower half of my body gingerly, wringing the towel two or three times to insure that my genitals and the surrounding area were as dry as possible. The stars in the southern sky were softly bright. The night seemed to take on a new and welcome dimension as a light breeze cooled the droplets from my chest, back, and arms. My closely clipped hair dried fast and I had only to pat the water from my eyes. I let the breeze do the rest.

It had been several months since I had even seen the stars. The Arch of Capella stretched from the right: Perseus and Pleiades, the Seven Sisters; then bright, beautiful Aries, the eternal beacon to all men in uncharted seas; Orion, the triad of his belt perfectly parallel with the ridge pole of the tile roof before me; and lastly fiery orange Betelgeuse. I could barely see Polaris above and behind me, but the shower roof blacked out its eternal pendulum, the Big Dipper.

As I craned my head toward the sky and glanced from roof to roof, my two guardians probably suspected I was sizing up the area for the implementation of some dark scheme. Their suspicion roused them from their flat-heeled squat as they smoked and chatted, perhaps about how lonely it got for Mouth between his wife's semiannual visits from their native village.

Obeying Mouth's slightly impatient motion, I stepped through the front door and onto the sidewalk, then hesitated there, for I was unprepared for the sight that greeted me.

The moon was full, suspended in the eastern sky, halfway between the terracotta roofs of Hanoi and the sparkling zenith of the night. All of its light seemed to be focused onto this short strip of weed-cracked asphalt and, incongruous as it seemed, Pham Hong Thai Street was magnificent.

The daytime drabness of those gray walls and roofs was transformed into a cloak of black velvet that appeared to cover it all like the soft, luscious moss of a shaded brookside glen. Each corner, each edge, each windowsill and doorway reflected the moonlight with a luminous, ghostly sheen, like freshly fallen black snow.

As I stepped out into the deserted street, the moonlight felt like it was in the air itself, lingering on my arms and shoulders like frost, flowing ankle-deep from curb to curb, rising up onto the cement walks and walls with a phosphorescent sigh.

As I waded on, I looked up at that shining face. Well, 'ole moon, beautiful . . . gorgeous . . . splendid moon . . . you've just been shining down on my beloved Antipodes. Did you see my love tonight? . . . Did she see you? . . . Did she think of me? . . . My love . . .

But I was now abreast of the Dirty Bird gate, and in a few seconds, Mouth would order me to go inside. He would then jingle his keys and single out mine, the one that would re-seal me into my steamy cell with its dreary 60-watter. This night would be left outside, out here in the center of Pham Hong Thai Street, in the center of Hanoi, North Vietnam, on the wrong side of the world.

I must have stopped walking.

"Co!"

The moon was misty now.

15
God = Strength

Fear for our survival is a sure sign we're trusting only in our own strength. However we may be in touch with our God, there is great strength in knowing we are never alone. Once that is internalized, every thought, act, concern, project, or challenge has a spiritual dimension. Unlike formal religion, which as often as not divides us, this spiritual dimension connects us with all things.

After I was returned to the Little Vegas complex of Hoa Lo, the routine seemed to stabilize. There had been no moves for a while; clearing with communications systems and a chain of command had been established and were refined.

One afternoon I was locked in an interrogation room at Little Vegas, left alone "to ponder my crimes." This was one of our favorite quiz rooms, if there could be such a thing, because some GI, while left alone, had used a piece of charcoal to write in huge script on the back wall PHUC HO. Either because the lettering was so fine, or because the words were so huge, it was hardly noticeable. But sitting there on the stool during quiz we each felt very smug as this great insult to their president stood scrawled across the wall behind the interrogator. No one knew— nor cared—what "Phuc" meant in Vietnamese, but the phonetic meaning served us well.

Anyway, the door to this room had louvers that allowed me to look down, but not straight out. Unexpectedly another POW's feet and legs appeared. I could see no sign of a guard so I whispered loudly, "Pssst! Hey, what's your name?"

The guy came right up and said, "Hi. I'm Navy Lieutenant Ed Miller. Who are you?"

"Navy Lieutenant Jerry Coffee." We didn't have his name on our list in the Stardust, so I figured Miller must be a new POW.

"Hey, Ed, you got any news from home?"

"Yeah! It might be news to you that we landed a couple of men on the moon last August. Three astronauts; two went to the surface of the moon and the third remained in orbit around it."

"Sonovabitch! Ed, that's fantastic. That's great! We didn't know that. Thanks a lot. I'll pass . . ."

His cough barely preceded the return of the guard who took him on to the bath area.

We put men on the moon! Everyone was elated when I passed the news on. The next time I was outside and saw the moon in the daylight, I looked at that beautiful bear with such pride. We'd put men on the moon—so surely we could trounce the VC. I'd be out of here before Christmas.

"On this occasion of your Christmas holiday the camp authorities invite you here to this Christmas Room on Christmas Eve so you may enjoy the Christmas tree and receive gifts. And tomorrow you will have a special dinner," said the prison official we called Cat.

The tree in the corner of the room was kind of scraggly, but it was colorful. About six regular light bulbs had been painted blue, red, and green and were hanging on various sagging limbs. The bulbs dwarfed the tree, and a tangle of dark extension cords pulled the top down to one side. There were a few homemade tinfoil ornaments, and under it were some oranges, tangerines, and bananas clustered on a bed of white cotton.

"Receive gifts? Gifts from home, from my family?"

"No, these gifts here are for you," said Cat as if to say, You fool, what do you think this is, Christmas? He nodded to a basket of candy and fruit on the table between us.

"Go ahead, you may take some."

I took an orange, two tangerines, a banana, and a handful of candy wrapped in paper. I immediately started eating one banana and set another one out.

"Would you like tea, a cigarette?" Again Cat nodded to the table: a teapot and cups and a pack of Truong Sons.

"Just tea."

"This is the birthday of your God, Jesus Christ. Will you be praying to him for peace tonight?"

The guards heard many of us desperately invoke the name of God and of Christ in this very interrogation room during torture sessions. We had prayed intensely for deliverance from our predicaments. I recalled painfully, "Father, if it be thy will, take this cup from my lips; but in any case, thy will be done."

"I will be praying tonight as I do every night, for peace, for my family, for my fellow prisoners here, and for the Vietnamese people."

"I pray for peace. I pray that the Vietnamese people in the South will be able to protect their freedom, and that the Vietnamese here in the North will one day know freedom."

They talked rapidly between them, laughing and shaking their heads in pity of my erroneous thinking.

"Co, you always say wrong. In the Democratic Republic of Vietnam we already have freedom—the freedom to defend our country, the freedom to work hard, freedom to work for the good of the revolution! We have freedom from exploitation as well, freedom from capitalist profitmongering."

"Well, I'll still pray for you tonight."

"Don't you want to kneel in front of the Christmas tree to pray?" He was serious. I shook my head.

"No, I'll pray back in my cell." I downed my tea and gathered my fruit and candy, indicating I was ready to go. They didn't like to be preempted in deciding when a session was over.

"Go back to your room now!"

My room, I thought. My room, indeed!

The turnkey returned me to my cell, and before the jailer closed the door he handed me three candy bars wrapped in red foil. "Socola," he said. Chocolate, I figured. He seemed pleased to have been the bearer of gifts, so I said *Cam Ud* as I bowed barely. I figured I could get away with it since he was in a holiday mood. He never looked twice, closed the door, and turned to the task of opening Tom Storey's door across the passageway to take him to the Christmas Room.

The December air was cold so I kept on all the clothes I had worn to the quiz, including Old Blue. I threw my blanket around my shoulders and sat cross-legged on my slab, leaning against the wall. Thoughtfully I peeled the orange, carefully separated the sections, then ate each one slowly.

Funny thing how these people go to extremes, I thought. One week they've got a purge on, torturing every man to make him write some damn statement, or a biography, or a request for amnesty. Then when it's Tet, or Easter, or Christmas, they put on their happy faces and wish us well. Truly an Alice in Wonderland environment!

My first "holiday Q" had been at Easter, only a few months after I'd been shot down. Sarge had rattled his keys outside my door at the wrong time of the night, made the little chopping motion across the wrist meaning "long sleeves" and trousers. He led me into a quiz room off the entry courtyard near the gate.

As we entered the room, I saw a table covered with a clean blue cloth, on which were a teapot and tea cups, a dish of cookies, and a bowl of flowers—gladiolas. Rabbit, a photographer, and other officers were gathered off to one side. Waiting for me across the table was a very old and obviously venerable V priest. I didn't know then what a dying breed he was. As time went on, there also would be fewer and fewer churches and temples and shrines and fewer and fewer worshipers. Within Indochina there had been all the traditional Oriental religions: Buddhism, Confucianism, and so on. The French, like all colonialists— ostensibly to justify their colonialism—brought Christianity as well, and the missionaries had established Catholicism which, until the Communist takeover, had thrived. With the initial loss of over a million Catholics migrating to the South before the country was partitioned, the church now was stagnant, and dwindling rapidly as the older generation died off. Rather than go through the messy and potentially unpopular persecution of clergy and closing of churches and temples, the regime— with dialectic patience—would simply "educate" the younger generations away from religion. It would be characterized as the opiate of the masses, the means by which the oppressor causes the oppressed to simply endure their plight.

The wizened little priest introduced himself in broken English with a French accent as Father Jean Baptiste Ho Tam Dien. He offered me confession and holy communion. I accepted both, although I mumbled a very generic confession, nothing about "bombing women, children, and old folks in the DRV." I'm sure it was a disappointment to Rabbit and the other prison officials attending.

Before I left him, the priest passed to me, almost furtively, a plastic rosary, beads and all. I took it back to my cell with me and recited the Rosary daily along with my other prayers.

Every Sunday the senior officer in each cell block would pass a certain signal on the wall—the church call—and wait a few minutes while it circulated. Then every man stood up in his cell—if he was able—and at least in some semblance of togetherness we would all recite the Pledge of Allegiance to our flag, the Lord's Prayer, and frequently the Twenty-third Psalm, focusing on the part that says "Thou preparest a table before me in the presence of mine enemies. Thou anointest my head with oil. My cup runneth over."

Every time I thought of this I realized that in spite of the fact that I was incarcerated here in this terrible place, I was blessed. Because I maintained faith that some day, *how*ever, *when*ever, I *would* return to a beautiful and free country. But the V around me would never know anything else; it was *my* cup that runneth over.

I also derived a great deal of physical comfort from the Rosary. When I had been in the Mint the previous summer and was being punished with my legs in the stocks and both hands cuffed tightly behind me, and I'd been that way for a couple or three weeks and didn't even know how I'd get through another night or day, I found I could grind a little notch in the crucifix of that Rosary, use it as a key, and open almost any set of cuffs they could find to put on me. In the middle of the night, Howie Rutledge—in the cell closest to the entry to the Mint—would stay cramped down on hands and knees, peeking under the crack to warn me if a guard approached while I was able to release a cuff, put my arms in front to rest my shoulders, and sometimes lie back and get a little sleep. When a guard approached, Howie would warn me with a "danger" thump on the wall.

Then the next week I'd been down on my knees clearing to enable him to get out of his cuffs when he was being punished.

Shortly after that the Rosary had been taken away.

I opened one of the candy bars left by the jailer. After the first bite, I realized that aside from appearance, any similarity to actual chocolate was purely coincidental. I spit out the first bite, which tasted like bitter sawdust, and consigned my candy bars to the rats.

The foil caught my eye, however. It was red on the outside and silver on the inside. I spread it out carefully and flattened it and began folding it into an origami bird, a swan. As I folded, my mind wandered back to the Christmas Room. Would I like to get down on my knees and pray in front of the Christmas tree! If I had learned anything thus far it was certainly that I didn't have to get down on my knees to pray. I did at first, I suppose out of desperation. I had felt so helpless that I guess I had wanted to maximize my supplication in God's eyes. But I had realized my need was so constant I couldn't spend all my time on my knees. Besides, I was already spending a lot of time on my knees clearing and in interrogation rooms.

"On your knees, hands over your head! You will stay there until you repent your crimes!" One of their favorite "nonviolent" mini-tortures.

Anyway, I said my daily Mass and frequently recited the Rosary sitting or sometimes pacing. I was beginning to realize that God was always with me because He was within me. Howie Rutledge had shared his favorite passage from the Bible when we were in the Mint together: "I lift mine eyes unto the hills from whence cometh my help. My help cometh from the Lord my God." My help had indeed come from the Lord.

I held up the little red and silver swan, smoothing the creases in each fold. By holding it at arm's length out from beneath the upper bunk, I found that the yellow light of the bulb enhanced its charm. I smiled as I recalled the *hotsi* bath in Japan, and how the little masseuse with the incredibly strong hands and feet had giggled as she'd shown me how to fold a swan.

Strong hands. Strength. What was that little formula that Risner had scratched into the wall of that cell in New Guy Village? Two words with an equal sign between them: God = strength. God equals strength! I was finding it to be so true. In these abysmal circumstances I realized that I had never yet been totally alone. And I had always been able to find just a little more strength when I'd needed it. I recalled Risner's words during one of our early sessions in Heartbreak Hotel: "Remember, Jerry, our Lord will never ask us to endure more than we are able to endure." By now we had all seen the truth in that.

I flattened out the second piece of candy foil and began folding it into crisp little pleats, not sure where I was heading with it. I thought, what a weird way to spend Christmas Eve.

I had spent the last one at the Zoo, in a cell with Larry Spencer. We had had a great Christmas party throughout the Pool Hall that day, with everyone passing the details of his assigned specialty—food, entertainment, music, whatever—to everyone else, sort of round-robin style. We had limited the exchange of our imaginary gifts to those for comrades in immediately adjoining cells. We didn't want it to get out of hand! That night Spence and I had entertained ourselves telling about our respective family Christmas traditions, then by playing "basketball"—tossing a little ball of wadded-up paper into each other's cups and keeping score. He had won the swisher competition but I outscored him on banked shots off the wall.

With a piece of thread, I now tied the length of pleated foil in the center, then fanned out the edges and attached the corners so I had a pleated rosette to go with my swan.

All through this Christmas Eve the guards had been on holiday routine as well. The turnkey's family had come into the prison to spend his duty day with him. Most of the day I could hear them not far from my window talking and laughing. His little boy—probably about three or four—apparently had a toy car, and I could hear him revving and honking just as I had heard my own little boys in past Christmases.

"Vroom, vroom, vroom! Toot, toot! Toot, toot! Vroom, vroom! Toot, toot!"

I also heard him giggling with delight at something funny his daddy had done. And I heard him cry when he hurt himself some way. And I heard my own children laughing and crying . . . I was suddenly struck by how laughing and crying transcend race or class. How hunger, pain, joy, delight know no boundaries of skin color, shape of eyes, language, or ideology. That day, especially, I had realized that we are all so much alike in our humanness. And if I were to emerge from this place with any hatred or bitterness, it would not be toward the Vietnamese people.

Little Toot outside my window had caused me to think of and miss my own family all the more throughout that day. Still freshest in my mind was the memory of that last Christmas at home when the kids had received their puppy. What shrieks of delight.

We had been apart other Christmases. Both of my Mediterranean deployments had been winter cruises. Both times the ship had spent the holidays anchored in the harbor at Cannes, France, and I had had the watch. The Christmas lights and decorations had made the nighttime panorama from the ship all the more sparkling, but it was still a lonely way to spend Christmas. I hadn't even known then what real loneliness could be.

I started folding the third piece of foil, again not really knowing what would emerge. I began wondering what would be included in tomorrow's "special meal."

As it turned out, there was more than a special meal the next day. Christmas night several of us were taken from Hoa Lo and combined with others from the Zoo at the huge old French-built cathedral in downtown Hanoi. About thirty Americans gathered for Mass, celebrated by old Father Ho. The photographer had a field day as we listened to the homily about the Christ Child weeping "because of the napalm being dropped on the people of Vietnam by the cruel U.S. air criminals."

At least the Mass itself was celebrated in Latin and couldn't very well be bastardized. The propaganda photographers swarmed around us as we knelt at the communion rail. We lingered there, kneeling close to one another and trading news from the two prisons and passing on all the new POW names that had been accumulated. At least the service was a communications boon. Rabbit and the others kept trying to shush us up with mean-eyed threats, but to no avail.

Later on I heard that the Protestant prisoners also had a service at which communication had been greatly facilitated. In comparing notes, we decided the main difference between the Catholic and Protestant services was that the priest condemned us for dropping napalm but the Protestant minister harangued his audience more on cluster bombs and white phosphorus. Both services had been propaganda shows.

As I finished folding the third piece of candy foil a star emerged, without any premeditation on my part. How appropriate, I thought: my Star of Bethlehem. The star for the top of my tree. I pulled three of the stiffest straws from the little hand broom in the corner of my cell and attached the ornaments to them with thread from my blanket. Then I jammed the other ends of the straws into a crack in the front edge of the upper bunk so they protruded out in three directions, the swan and the rosette and the star dangling before me just above eye level. In the yellow light my little ornaments glowed and twinkled softly as they bobbed and rotated slowly in the chilly air. And I was immediately struck by the satisfying simplicity of my Christmas.

I thought more about the birth of the Christ Child and the simplicity of the Nativity. There was nothing to distract me from the pure awesomeness of the story of Christ's birth—no materialism, commercialism, no food, presents, or glitz. Just me and that little baby.

Finally I thought intensely of Bea and the children and of their own Christmas Eve activities, close unto themselves certainly, but perhaps now with friends and family celebrating the occasion in all the usual ways. I prayed for them and for their joy and peace and well-being. And I knew there were many prayers and toasts for me. I felt them all.

I was beginning to realize and appreciate my own spirituality because I had been stripped of everything else. Everything by which I had measured my identity was denied: my rank, my title, uniform, clothes, money, car, the trappings of my religion. It was just *me* left—my flesh, bones, intellect, and soul.

And where was I now finding answers and sustenance? Where was I finding strength? From within. It had been there all the time. And as I had gone deeper within myself with God, I began to realize and see more clearly all my connections to everyone and everything else. To go within and to know myself was the key to understanding everything outside, my relationship with God, with the man in the next cell, with the geckos on the wall, with my family on the other side of the world, and with all elements of nature.

But for the moment I had God, myself, and my rosette and my swan and my star. I realized that although I was hurting and lonely and scared, this might be the most significant Christmas Eve of my life. The circumstances of this night were helping me to crystallize my understanding of my journey within to find God there, and thereby to see Him everywhere.

16

Peepholes and Cracks

In our human family, the color of our skin and the shape of our eyes or the sounds of our language count for so little. We all laugh and cry, hunger and thirst, celebrate and mourn in the same ways. We all take pride in our national cultures and heritage. With the realization of kinship in the true sense comes an understanding and empathy that leaves no place for hatred and bitterness.

One, two, three, four; yep, four pairs of pastel-colored panties hanging on the line. Pink, blue, yellow, and green; each pair had white lace around the edges. Who would have thought Snow White wore pastel-colored bikini panties with lace? I wondered what color she was wearing today. Geez! They were sexy there just hangin' on the line with two bras and a white blouse and a pair of black pajama trousers.

I could see the clothesline at the far left side of the horizontal crack between the boards that had been nailed across my window. Fortunately they had been in a hurry when they converted this old maintenance and repair building of the power plant complex into the single cell block prison we called Dirty Bird. I had seen the boarded-up window the night I'd been moved here from the Mint. I had been discouraged by the prospect of no air circulation and no visibility. The planks had appeared to be flush against one another. From the inside, however, with the eye up close, the cracks were a veritable window onto Pham Hong Thai Street.

Snow White was an attractive, if husky, girl of about twenty who lived across the street and to the left. She lived with a couple a little older than she, perhaps her older sister or brother, and their baby—not quite a toddler. Their abode was the only low single-story building on that side of the street. Snow White seemed to have a daily job somewhere, but always returned home earlier with the baby, and cared for him on weekends.

I called her Snow White because of her long black hair, but mostly because each morning about five thirty, it was she who led her neighbors in calisthenics.

"Mot, hai, ba, bon! Mot, hai, ba, bon!" the loudspeakers on the street corner blared each morning with a woman bubbling out instructions and encouragement between exercises, as martial music played in the background. There was usually an uneven line of seven or eight sleepy, bored men out in the street each morning dutifully following Snow White's bobs and stretches. That's why I called them the Seven Dwarfs.

It was a pathetic sight each dreary morning. Although she seemed to be fired up by her sense of responsibility—it could have been the most meaningful thing she did each day—the dwarfs seemed to resent having to be out in the street at that hour, let alone put up with her youthful, revolutionary zeal for toe touches and side-straddle hops. In any case, they all seemed resigned to the fact that they had to be out there. It was apparent that someone would be taking down names if they weren't. After each session they would all blend back into the dull gray buildings across the street and around the corner for whatever breakfast might be available that day. The whole routine each morning was a great theatrical testimony to "the happy, healthy, working people's zest for life and fitness in support of their revolution."

Separating Snow White's house from the three-story building directly across from my vantage point was an alleyway. Just inside the alley protruding from the wall of the bigger building was a faucet, the only source of fresh water on the block. That's where Snow White had just washed her clothes in a small tub. The parade of people to and from the water tap in the morning and evening was a unique source of entertainment. I constantly had to be careful, though, that the guards didn't catch me from behind peeking out, or they would have nailed another board across my crack, closing off a great source of both entertainment and insight into the daily grass roots microdrama of the revolution.

The ground floor of the building directly across was an old storefront with big windows on both sides, miraculously still unbroken. I called the old guy who lived there Doc; he was one of the seven dwarfs. He looked to be about sixty—all bent over from the load of stonemason's tools, buckets, and bricks that he carted off over his shoulder each morning. The next building was on the corner where Bahn Thuy Street dead-ended into Pham Hong Thai Street. An ancient-looking woman lived there with, I guessed, her daughter, who was also old. I had spied on them all during my earlier tour here at Dirty Bird.

At the far right of my horizontal world across Ninh Binh Street was another two-story place, another abandoned store below, and an apartment above. One of the store windows—the one closest to the ruins of the power plant—was boarded up, but the other was covered by a curtain. Here lived a couple with their three children, a delicate little girl of about four, a little boy of two, and a baby about one. I guessed the baby qualified the young mother to stay home each day rather than trudge off to some factory or bureau. Watching the little girl care for the baby, I was reminded of the children I'd seen in the countryside, the smallest of little girls—never boys—with a baby sibling straddling their cocked hips while pursuing other household activities. The babies never had diapers. They'd just let go anywhere while the mother or big sister held them out in midair. "In Vietnam, it is considered good fortune if your firstborn is a daughter so she can help care for the other children." I had been told this by a "good guy" interrogator we called the Soft Soap Fairy back at Little Vegas.

One day I was peeking out during siesta. Except for the little green garter snake I was watching wind its way through the grassy buffer between my building and the curb, the neighborhood was still. Suddenly, the heavy air was pierced by the ominous groan of the air raid warning siren, winding its way laboriously to an even higher pitch. The snake froze in place. The siren peaked and wound down, up again and down, and so on across the city. The shout of sleepy guards roused from their midday naps began to reverberate from the plaster, timber, and corrugated tin of the open air passageway outside my door. The metallic "shick-shick" of their cocking weapons and the sound of their running footsteps blended with the rise and fall of the sirens. Within a few seconds I heard triple-A in the distance. The door of the little family's storefront hovel banged open; the mother, frantic with fear, came running onto the sidewalk. She had the baby clasped in her right arm, held the little boy's hand with her other hand; he was barely a walker. The little girl, absorbing her mommy's fear, was screaming; they were all crying. The triple-A and a few bomb explosions were closer now. The few others in the neighborhood who weren't away at work began shouting and running along too. After a few steps down Ninh Binh Street practically dragging the boy, the mother dipped low and scooped him in her left arm. She disappeared down the street scurrying toward the air raid shelter with a child under each arm and the little girl running along clinging to the tail of her blouse.

I watched it all with such mixed emotions. When the sirens wailed, I was glad because it meant bombing, action, and possibly progress. Long periods without bombing were discouraging. But there I saw the fear and terror in that mother's eyes and my heart just went out to her. The power plant and surrounding neighborhood had really been pounded. She was running for her and her children's lives.

My mind flashed back to the usual strike briefings aboard the *Kitty Hawk*, the wrap-up by the Air Wing Commander: "Okay, guys, that's it; ordnance, rendezvous, navigation, timing, ground and air order of battle, strike tactics, and egress. Emergencies and safe areas. Now, the power plant is heavily defended. Our flak and SAM suppressor flights will do their best to hold it down, but there's likely to be a lot of distractions on your bomb runs. Concentrate. Put your ordnance right on target, right on the power plant. We don't want to have to go back in there and do this again. Any questions? Fine. Good luck to each of you. Let's go!"

Who would ever have thought about the mother and her three children? "Uh, yeah, CAG [Commander Air Group], a question. What about that little family that lives on the corner across the street from the power plant?" How ridiculous! It had all been so impersonal, that destruction from the sky. Under the circumstances, I felt no qualms nor had I misgivings about the bombing, but this scene had introduced a new element into the equation.

Through the years past and yet to come, I would log thousands of hours spying through the tiny cracks of boarded-up windows and transoms, peering stealthily over the tops of high windowsills and through the spaces between doors and floors. I would clear for others to communicate by keeping guard through rat holes at the floor and air vents near the ceiling. It was a constant challenge and struggle to somehow expand my world beyond the confines of whatever hot or cold cubicle in which I found myself. When moved into a new cell or situation, my immediate task was to check out the peepholes, perhaps to enlarge a hole or crack for optimum viewing yet not so it was large enough to attract the attention of the guards during a cell inspection. Luckily, they would never close a cell door while they were inside, so they seldom had a chance to see how porous a door might be. Even to stare through a crack at another wall beyond the one that confined me was better than nothing.

Maybe a bird would fly by, or some ants crawl through, or a leaf flutter down. Perhaps there would be sun, or shadows, or I'd see some rain-drops fall.

I had learned to expand my world by smell and sound as well. I could smell rice and fresh bread five minutes before it arrived in the passage-way outside my cell. I could smell the damp freshness of the first rains and enjoy the memories its aroma conjured up. I could differentiate the smell of the Zoo and of Hoa Lo, and now of Dirty Bird.

I learned to interpret sounds and visualize those interpretations. Once, early on, I passed a long intestinal worm into my bucket. It was about eight inches long and looked like a piece of spaghetti. I had no idea how common they would become and was shocked by it at the time. I called *"Bao Cao!"* a couple of times until the guard on duty opened the peephole. I held the writhing worm up dangling from a stiff broom straw and said *"Bac Si, dao!"* ("Doctor, pain"), all the time rubbing my stomach. He considered the worm for a moment, glanced sideways where the water girls were filling jugs, and motioned me to give him the worm. I passed it through the peephole on the stick, and he slammed the little door shut. The next minute or so was pandemonium out there as he cornered the girls with the worm. They screamed and cursed and knocked over water cans trying to get out of there. I could hear him laughing and yelling at them, probably saying something like "I'm gonna make you eat it! I'm gonna make you eat it!" It was a classic universal scene of boy teasing girl with a worm or a cockroach or a frog. The last of the three girls went shrieking out of the cell block as he roared with laughter and cracked up further telling another guard about it. Somehow he had removed the edge from my own anxiety as I had pictured the whole scene out there and almost laughed along with him. I never did see the *Bac Si* about my worm, or the ones that came after that one.

Every daily activity had its sound as well: the keys at the right time, the giggling of the water girls, the sounds of each guard's voice and of their families on weekends when they came to share the duty hours. The sounds of trucks, of birds, and of ice on mud puddles crunching under feet; the stamping cadence of the guard force during their morning PT; the shrill clang of the various prison gongs measuring out each day; the mind-rending discordance (to my Western ear) of traditional Viet-namese music when piped through the prison PA system; the wrenching screams of a man being tortured, and the sound of my own heart pound-ing when I suspected I'd be next; the faint tapping of a pal next door: GN/GB/GBA—Good Night, God Bless, God Bless America.

One time back at the Zoo I had been clearing for Percy next door so he could comm with Jerry Denton at the end of the building. I was stretched out on the cool tile floor watching from beneath my door. I could see the back walkway all the way to the gate on my right. Clearing here was a pleasant task because it was so easy. I became familiar with all the sparrows in the area as they'd congregate around the grains of spilled rice under the food-serving table just opposite my door. One little guy had only one leg, but he never let it bother him. He was as perky and fat as the rest of them. I called him Ray because Ray Vohden in the next cell could use only one leg. He would use a crutch to walk for almost eight years because the V had so badly fouled up all attempts to repair his wounded leg.

Anyway, I was clearing this day during siesta and suddenly the gate swung wide open. I jumped up to Percy's wall and thumped it hard with my fist. I heard him pass it to Denton as I quickly returned to my position to keep track of our intruder. It was one of the stocky water girls, two five-gallon cans slung over her shoulder on a carrying pole. I could see her only from her knees down, and why she was working during siesta I couldn't figure. She set the cans down hastily a few feet from me, moved near the wall, and thinking she had total privacy unbuckled her belt, took down her khaki trousers, pulled her pink panties down to her ankles—I couldn't believe what I was seeing—squatted against the wall, and started peeing. Even as she squatted I couldn't see above her shoulders, which was just as well because that meant she couldn't see my eye either.

Finally she finished, pulled up her pants, and went on about the business of filling our jugs on each doorstep, humming contentedly all the while. That afternoon every man in the Pool Hall vicariously enjoyed my description of what had happened. Of course, I left out the part about how fat her knees were and made up the part about the sexy lace on her panties. We all broke up in tears when one of the guys down on the end observed, "Boy, Coffee, if she'd known you were watching her take a leak she woulda shit!"

Peepholes and cracks were essential to our communications, if not for direct talking or visual signals, then at least for clearing. I decided they were also essential for my sanity. I was able to stay in touch with nature, of course, and the V-watching was fascinating whether it be a bored sentry clicking the bolt of his weapon open and closed, stopping only to scratch his balls, or watching Snow White hang her pastel panties on the line. And that hadn't been the half of it there on Pham Hong Thai Street.

There was a picket gate that swung across the entrance to the alley with the faucet. On this quiet afternoon, in preparation for her bath, Snow White had closed the gate. There were about three inches between the pickets and she was concerned about being seen by the guards who lived farther down in my building so she adjusted the gate and put a couple of straw mats over it for privacy. This blocked any view from the guards' area, but opened my view from a different angle. So I watched, and she had no idea.

She was very modest. She took off her blouse and bra, but left on her loose black trousers. She poured water from the faucet over herself and down into her black pajama bottoms. She lathered her arms and shoulders and breasts, then rinsed several times. Next, she washed her hair, and it took her about twenty minutes to rinse out all the soap. Watching the movement of her firm wet body, naked from the waist up, was an unforgettably sensual experience. Finally she dried and combed her shiny black hair slowly and deliberately. She dressed and then washed out a few clothes, walked across the street directly toward me, and hung them on the line just to my left. I must have relived every sexual encounter and make-out session of my life during the rest of that day and through the night.

That evening Snow White retrieved her bras, blouse, and trousers, but she left her pastel panties—pink, blue, yellow, and green—on the line for an extra day, just for me.

17

Free to Choose

The pressures and complexities of our lives too often force us into a survival mode where integrity and loyalty are compromised. It's easy to lose sight of the best within us as we expend our energies rationalizing our choices. Yet at heart we know that survival isn't enough. Our lives must reflect a spirit of well-being that comes from planting our feet firmly and finally against a sea of ambiguity and saying once and for all, "This is right and that is wrong and, by God, I know the difference."

"I think you're right, Ed. We have no business being in this war. It's strictly an affair for the Vietnamese to settle among themselves."

"Not only do we have no business here, our interference is illegal. It's an undeclared war of aggression, Bob, and that makes it downright criminal. That makes us criminals."

I looked away from the loudspeaker high up on the wall. I had been staring at it incredulously. "Larry, can you believe that shit?"

Chesley shook his head in disgust. After months of solitary confinement for both of us, we had been reunited in our same old cell in Stardust.

The broadcast continued. "Actually, the Vietnamese government has every right to try us as war criminals. We have forfeited any rights under the Geneva Convention on the treatment of POWs. Ed, even the Code of Conduct has no application here."

They went on about the strength and correctness of the antiwar movement and wished it success. They asserted their decision to not only disregard the Code of Conduct, but to actively cooperate with the prison authorities, and to obey the camp regulations. And so the taped communication between "Bob" and "Ed" continued for nearly an hour: two senior American officers, supposedly having just met, carrying on an antiwar dialogue with sincerity and conviction. Chesley and I looked at each other in disbelief. The early spring had seen a continuation of the crackdown and purge of the previous summer and fall when I had been in the Mint and at Dirty Bird. Communication between cell blocks was tenuous now. The senior officers who had comprised the core of resistance leadership had been removed and were being held elsewhere in a prison they called Alcatraz. During the propaganda mass on Christmas Eve, I had lingered at the communion rail and had made brief contact with Commander Jim Mulligan, who told me about the place. It sounded grim.

Now, here at Vegas, men were being tortured again to write autobiographical statements, statements of "apology for bombing innocent women and children," and statements requesting amnesty—which by definition acknowledged criminal culpability. We were being forced to read news broadcasts and statements on the prison radio—all in contravention of the Code of Conduct and of our Senior Officer, Jim Stockdale's, policies.

Once the V had learned what Stockdale's policies had been, they had tried to undermine them systematically. The radio broadcasts were usually worthless for propaganda value, and most "readers" screwed it up so badly, it was often comical as well as ineffective. But it supposedly undermined our leadership, and that seemed to be the prison authority's primary goal at this time.

The "Bob and Ed Show," as it came to be known, was very different, however.

"Sounds like one is a Marine and one's Navy, but both senior," I said. "They sound like they really believed all the shit they were saying."

Larry voiced both of our major concerns. "Man, junior POWs could buy that shit. A guy who's been kept isolated and isn't aware of how these bastards have treated us. How's that gonna sound to a young guy who has been exposed to antiwar sentiment at home and who may have come with reservations about the whole effort? I mean, statements like this from our senior officers—our own role models—are worse than the crap coming from Fulbright, Morse, McGovern, and all the SDS jerks. This could devastate a new POW's will to resist."

The overall effect of the broadcast upon the men in Stardust was a downer. The consensus was that it was "disappointing, disgusting, and depressing."

Later, we received word from the Desert Inn where Bob and Ed "lived" that they were a Navy Commander and a Marine Lieutenant

Colonel respectively. After the broadcast, they had been put together as cellmates. They not only refused to communicate with the others in the Desert Inn, but had sent terse messages to leave them alone. The two were observed to spend more time outside, and were allowed to eat some of their regular meals at a "picnic table" in the spring sunshine—a "privilege" magnified even more as in the dark, egg-crate cubicles of the Stardust, the spring days seemed to simply pass the rest of us by. Periodically they were joined at these meals by another senior Navy officer whom I will call Gene. Eventually he would join them to make a threesome.

These three POWs each seemed to have their own reason for cooperation. They were different in many ways. While Bob and Ed were cellmates, there were reports of the sounds of their raging arguments. Ed, we would learn, was a bitter opportunist, pissed that he'd been shot down and anxious, it seemed, to do whatever was necessary to shorten his stay here, get home, and get on with his future, a future obviously no longer to be found in the U.S. Marine Corps. Gene, it was said, was a religious man, wracked by the guilt of losing his crewmen when they were downed, and also deeply worried about his physical state, having suffered some kind of stroke or seizure shortly after capture. While he was in solitary, the V had planted many questions in his mind about the morality of the war. The answers he conscientiously sought were the ones the V provided. He came to agree with them that it was his moral duty to help end the war as soon as possible, even if—to him—that meant participating in the Communists' propaganda programs. If Bob ever articulated his motives to anyone, I never heard them, so I never knew what prompted his behavior.

Ultimately, these three would be moved back to the Zoo, and then into the Garage with four junior officers who had been kept out of the mainstream, but who were less than enthusiastic about the war. For several months, they produced antiwar statements and met with visiting peace delegations. Compared to the main body of POWs, their existence was practically idyllic. And that was the impression received by many visiting journalists and delegates: that the treatment of American POWs was indeed "humane and lenient."

There were weeks of mundane routine punctuated by purges and pressures, and at least some startling news now and then. From the Hanoi Radio broadcasts, we heard of President Johnson's decision to not run for a second term. That told us something about the degree of political turmoil at home. From the same mocking source, we heard of Martin Luther King's murder, and then Robert Kennedy's as well. The news hurt to the core and revealed even more about the social turmoil at home. Sometimes I felt terrible about what must be going on with so much dissension and tragedy back in the U.S. It was so frustrating to think our political leadership could not adequately articulate to the American people what needed to be done here, when to me and my comrades experiencing this Communist system firsthand day after day, it was so obvious. How could the American people have any doubts about the insidious terror and brutality of Communist regimes? We knew the people out there in the streets of Hanoi were not much better off than we were here inside Hoa Lo.

The V were on the amnesty kick pretty hard. During one Q, Soft Soap Fairy had said, "In accordance with the government of the Democratic Republic of Vietnam, enlightened policy of V and the prison authorities, some of you may be accorded amnesty. We distinguish between the black-hearted, diehard criminals who challenge the camp authority and refuse to see the error of their ways and the reformed criminal who is contrite and shows his repentance through concrete acts."

Of course, the Code of Conduct reminded us, "I will accept neither parole nor special favors from the enemy." Our senior officer's policy backed this up: "Accept no early release. We will go home sick and wounded first, and then in order of our shootdown." It was further understood, however, that if a man were simply ejected as it were, with no strings attached—no request for amnesty, no statement of gratitude—then he should go. We knew by now, however, that scenario was very unlikely.

Continuing the quiz, Soft Soap Fairy (so named for his effeminate manner and his sympathetic "good guy" role as an interrogator) said, "So, Co, how would you like to go home before the war is over, to rejoin your family? Surely your life must be passing you by. It is your duty to be with your family. I think that would be best for you. What do you think?"

"Of course, I would like to go home. But I will go when the others go."

Soft Soap Fairy frowned, shook his head, and said almost apologetically, "But many will never go home. Many will stubbornly refuse to see this is the only way. Our beloved president Ho Chi Minh is very kind. Only it is necessary to write a letter to him requesting that you

are allowed to go home to your family. He would understand. He too
has a family."

"You mean a letter requesting amnesty, right?"

He shrugged. "Amnesty, kindness, call it what you may. But I think
you should seriously ponder your situation."

Back in my cell I passed on the substance of the quiz to the others,
then dismissed the whole thing. How could they afford to send me home
anyway, brutally tortured, having all the POW names to date memorized, having been held at a military target complex, knowing the location of at least three prisons? No way would they release me. Soft
Soap Fairy must have gotten my name confused with someone else's.

The next day I was taken out of the cell and measured by a tailor. I
couldn't believe it—this little guy with glasses, obviously unfamiliar with
the prison and uncomfortable around a POW. He held a pin in his
mouth like it was a badge of his trade. He never used it. He just flitted
around me with his tape measure alighting cautiously here and there
while his helper wrote down the measurements. God, they were actually
measuring me for special clothes!

A few days later, during my next—and last—quiz with Soft Soap
Fairy, I flatly refused to write a letter requesting amnesty.

"Co, I tell you this: Soon some of you will be released. I think when
this has happened, you will think different."

A month later the prison radio announced the release of three American POWs: a Navy Ensign and a Captain and a Major in the Air Force.
Each had written for amnesty and released statements referring to their
humane treatment, and expressing their gratitude to the V. We listened
to their statements with disappointment, to say the least.

My reflection on that event probably mirrored those of every other
man in Stardust. I envisioned myself going home, the reunion with my
family, and an end to the mental and physical abuse and the mind-
crumbling harassment. Yet we knew these men were disgraced for having disobeyed the Code and their senior officers. And surely no amount
of rationalization on their part could obscure this fact from them. What
bittersweet return awaited them, the boundless joy and relief of reunion
overshadowed by the thoughts of comrades in arms left fermenting in
the Communist prison of North Vietnam. But I might have faced the
choice myself. Had I been standing at the airport in my newly tailored
clothes, suitcase in hand, and certain release waiting with but a signature
on a letter of amnesty to go—literally, perhaps a life-and-death deci-

sion—would I have been able to resist the short-term relief for the long-term peace of mind and self-esteem? I was glad it hadn't come to that. It would have been a different dimension of torture.

The ultimate irony was that the three who were released had less than a year as POWs combined, and some speculated that the Ensign would beat his squadron mates home as they fulfilled the remainder of their WESTPAC deployment aboard their aircraft carrier.

Navy Seaman Apprentice Doug Hegdahl had been blown off the USS *Canberra* by the concussion of its guns during a predawn shore bombardment. He was picked up by North Vietnamese fishermen, turned over to militia, and found himself in Hoa Lo. Truly an ignominious way to become a POW.

The young Dakotan, after warding off weeks of accusations—"Spy! Commando! CIA!"—finally convinced his interrogators of his innocence—not just innocence of the charges, but of adulthood as well. The beefy nineteen-year-old didn't impress the prison authorities with his intellect and was almost disarming in his basic friendliness and lack of guile. But in actuality, Doug Hedgahl was dumb like a fox. He communicated with the others at his first opportunity and rapidly developed bonds of loyalty and friendship. He eagerly acknowledged the Code of Conduct and the authority of his senior officers, and that, of course, was everyone. Nevertheless, the V thought him to be innocuous and assigned him to light upkeep and clean-up details around the Plantation, a new prison complex. Alert and clever, he became a valued reconnaissance asset to his senior officers.

When it became apparent that an early release was possible for some POWs, Hegdahl became a prime candidate, of both the Vs and of our leadership. He had been primed with the names of all the POWs in the system, and had the entire brutal history committed to memory. He missed the February '68 release by a hair. He had refused to write the word "amnesty" in his letter to Ho Chi Minh.

In August of '69, however, still primed and approved for release by the SRO of the Plantation—the downtown camp where he was held—Hegdahl made the cut. He was released with a Navy Lieutenant and an Air Force Captain. They joined the ranks of the three who had accepted early release a year and a half earlier and of three more who would accept release in the future. All of these men knew that, with the exception of Hegdahl, they had acted counter to the SRO's overall policy and the Code of Conduct. Over and above whatever personal feelings of guilt or remorse they may carry into the future with them, they had all exiled themselves from any future formal association with the contemporaries they left behind. As would be the case with Ed and Gene, no official accountability would be imposed. Simply to have to live with their choices—as it is for most of us—would be accountability enough. Five of the six would just drop out of sight; Hegdahl would become an instructor in the Navy's SERE school in California. He and the naval officer did spend the first several weeks back home contacting the families of POWs with whom they had been especially close, an effort truly appreciated by all.

Of course, the V continued to make hay on the fact that all of these men had been released to visiting peace delegations. "You see! These are the American people who really care about you—not Nixon, not Rusk, not McNamara, none of the war criminals in Washington. They will let you rot here."

18

Kinship with All Life

———————————————————•———————————————————

*Life is everywhere, quite apart from the human connections we easily ac-
knowledge through sight and sound. How little we understand through mere
words; how much more is possible through opening all of our senses. Through
an awareness of our kinship with all of life we open new dimensions through
which we behold beauty, experience awe, and express love.*

———————————————————————————————————————

"Cheep-cheep, cheep-cheep, cheep-cheep!" As the Green Hornet
cheeped expectantly through the peephole in my door, he made little
wing-flapping motions with his hands up near his shoulders. Then he
pointed into my cell, barely masking his excitement. I knew he was
looking for Charlie. So, I thought, the word was getting around. Still I
said nothing. Again he cheeped and flapped and leaned closer to the
tiny window in my door so he could inspect the upper reaches of my
cell. Almost without thinking, I pointed to my left down the passageway.
His face lit up as he nodded quickly and slammed the little tin flap shut.

I heard him take off in the direction I had pointed, practically bouncing
off the walls, cheeping and flapping his way from cell to cell in the
inimitable style that had earned him the name the Green Hornet, always
buzzing from cell to cell carrying out his roving guard duties far more
enthusiastically than the others. He appeared to be younger than the
other guards, partly because his head seemed smaller than normal and
whatever kind of hat he might be wearing always rested upon his ears,
barely touching his head. But he could be mean, too, depending upon
his mood.

Today, however, his youthful exuberance and curiosity propelled him
in the direction of the little bird the Americans had captured and were
keeping in their cell. So intent was he on locating Charlie that he didn't

stop to think that I shouldn't even have known in what direction he could find Charlie unless there was a comm link between me and Charlie's cell, which of course there was.

Charlie was a sparrow, rescued from oblivion by the four guys down in cell number two at the opposite end of Stardust. They had watched with fascination as the mother sparrow had labored so diligently to build her nest on a metal brace in the cozy space between the wide eaves of the building and the wall of the building itself, all just above the high wide window of their cell. They had watched her fluff in the final touches, then lay and protect her eggs. Tiny peeping sounds had marked the moment that new, tenuous little lives had commenced, and they cheered the little mama on in her subsequent ceaseless trips to bring food for her ravenous though fragile brood.

We have all watched at some time in our lives the activities of a bird building its nest, marveling at the incredible process of preparing for new life. Then we go on about our business knowing the outcome: eggs, chicks, worms stuffed down throats, attempts to fly, and an occasional scrawny carcass on lawn or pavement—victim by chance of premature exit from the nest and the mother's care. But how often do we witness the entire process with analytical appreciation for that peculiar scheme of life, that incredibly beautiful process, and empathize with the mother bird's struggle to fulfill the demands of her instincts, to fulfill her own sense of duty and purpose? Such had become the bond between the four men in Stardust number two and the noisy little sparrow family that had come in to share their tiny slice of the world.

About this time the prison authorities launched a campaign to clean the overhangs and ledges of years of cobwebs and debris, splashing them down with water, and whitewashing the walls. When they came with their ladder and tore down the nest over Stardust cell number two, cascades of dust, moldering twigs, dead insects, and tiny feathers swirled down, most of it—baby birds, fragments of shell and all—bouncing off the windowsill and onto the walkway outside.

As the guys in the cell watched in sadness and dismay, they were quick to notice that not everything bounced off the sill to the outside. Much of the debris and one of the fledgling birds fell into the cell and the saga of Charlie began.

The tiny bird was just beginning to feather, still wrinkle-pink and all beak, mouth, and noise. He—or she—seemed to have survived the crash to the floor in that miraculous way that tiny helpless things survive such crashes. The men made a nest of shredded toilet paper and then made up for the shortage by tearing the remaining squares in half and using them very carefully. Since the little fellow was still in the head-up, mouth-open mode, they formed tiny "worms" of bread or rice and dropped and poked them down Charlie's gullet. For moisture they tipped water from their jugs into their hands and let the bird peck at the drops slithering down their fingers.

Soon the entire cell block—sixteen to eighteen guys—knew about the bird and a name-the-bird contest commenced. With the creativity sparked by fertile minds eager for challenge, the names began to roll in. Uncle Ho (the sobriquet of the President of the DRV), Killer, Falcon (the USAF Academy mascot), Thud (nickname of the Air Force plane F-105 Thunder Chief, also appropriate for the bird's mode of entry), Dilbert (the fictional Navy pilot who does everything wrong) . . . The guys in cell number one picked the name Charlie and were declared winners by Charlie's folks. Charlie, of course, was the nickname the GIs in South Vietnam used in reference to the Viet Cong, the Communist guerrillas. Since this was a Vietnamese Communist sparrow we were dealing with here, Charlie was indeed an appropriate name.

Charlie became a very important part of our lives. His foster parents began promulgating daily "Charlie reports" detailing his progress. He became a very real part of our prison family. The four men focused upon Charlie their pent-up instincts to nurture and protect. And he was a most willing object of their affection. Soon he wasn't at all happy unless cuddled into a lap or a hand, enjoying the little strokes and nudges as the conversation focused upon his development, or the course of the war, or who had won the '68 World Series. He would sleep in his own cozy nest each night beneath the small basket that was supposed to collect used toilet paper but never did. For all he knew, this was the life of your average sparrow and wasn't he lucky to have been born one.

As Charlie began to feather out, his wing feathers grew asymmetrically, perhaps from some scrape during his free-fall entry. Whatever the reason, he developed in lopsided fashion and his first wobbly flights were in tenuous circles. In one sense this wasn't all bad, since his world precluded much straight-line flight anyway. But as he developed, his own natural-turn radius was a little larger than the dimensions of the cell. He'd take off, do perhaps a quarter circle, bump into the wall, and flutter down to the floor. They'd pick him up, brush him off, and he'd bravely try again.

Most of us could relate to Charlie here because we too had had difficult times at one time or another during our own flight training. All aerodynamic engineers to some extent, we sent messages of encouragement, as well as complex aerodynamic analyses of the problem—and solutions to boot. "Pluck a feather from his strong side and tie it to his weak side." "Tie a little object under the wing pit of his strong side so he can't flap that wing as hard." "Launch him at an angle so he can see what it's like to go straight, then he'll compensate on his own." Or, from a Navy pilot: "Hell, don't worry about it. That's how you AF guys fly all the time anyway, wandering all over the damn sky!"

Charlie was an indomitable little guy and soon became adept at getting where he wanted to be by making little quarter- and half-circle flights from floor to bunk to a shoulder or a head, to the top of the door frame, and back again. He soon became one of the guys, eating whatever was on the menu as well. Rice seemed to be his favorite, but he'd eat anything. However, one of the guys swore Charlie made a sour face one time when gobbling down his little thimble-ration of sewer greens.

Soon the guards and water girls heard about Charlie, and he became quite a celebrity. The Green Hornet visited his cell every day—on duty or not—just to see Charlie. Someone would hold the bird cupped in his palm near the peephole, and the Green Hornet would stick one finger through the small bars to stroke his head and go "cheep-cheep-cheep." Most of the guards were more reserved, however, and after scrutinizing the mandatory bow of the prisoners, would sort of glance around the cell in vague disinterest. But when Charlie was presented, he projected such a cocky and fearless image that the guard's face would crack into a smile, absorbing but not really understanding the incongruity of it all.

The water girls became especially intrigued with Charlie, even though there was normally very little interaction between them and us prisoners. Early in the morning we would set our empty water jugs and our brimming buckets outside the cell. Later the water girls would come around— usually in pairs, sometimes in threes—one with two five-gallon cans of boiled water balanced on a long *chogi* pole over her muscular shoulders, the others ready to ladle water into our waiting jugs. These gals were rarely attractive, or even very feminine.

Now they too checked on Charlie regularly, shy at first but less so as they perceived Charlie's benefactors were not "the worst black-hearted criminals" but just other people trying to ease their boredom and pain by nourishing and loving a plain little sparrow. I would have said the novelty of nourishing and loving, but in reality they were just giving heed to their most natural instincts.

One day the huskiest and least attractive of the water gang talked the guys into letting her hold Charlie. She slipped him through the bars of the peephole carefully, cupped him in her hand, and stroked his head feathers, cooing softly. Suddenly she looked up and, with a devilish twinkle in her eye, opened her mouth wide, moving her face toward Charlie as if to eat him. "Oh no! Please don't eat Charlie!" came the chorus from inside the cell, each man feigning fear and horror. Instantly she showed her feminine innocence, giggling loudly and jabbering to the other girls about how these stupid Americans really believed she was gonna eat this bird. Again and again she pretended to gobble up Charlie, the guys expressing their "fear" and the girls giggling away. Charlie just glanced around perkily, perceiving no danger, and apparently enjoying the unusual view from the outside looking in.

This soon became a routine with the water girls. Sometimes they would pull in a roving guard to witness their teasing ritual, laughing and giggling like bubbling water. Then they would gently push Charlie back through the bars and go on with their drudgery, perhaps considering new perspectives and thoughts about these strange Americans. As for the guys, it brought back memories of more joyful times—playful, teasing times with sweethearts or sisters, and perhaps a more compassionate perspective on the "fullbacks from Hanoi High," as we called them.

The salvation of Charlie and the joy he brought to the entire Stardust seemed like the most natural thing in the world. Every man in the cell block derived vicarious joy from imagining a little feathery being cuddled in his own palm, stroking and scratching, making soft sounds, and exchanging love and tenderness with another living creature.

As I considered this I realized that we pilots—especially jet fighter pilots—are by nature expansive in our view of life, embracing great gobs of sky and earth and wind and sun and clouds at a single sweep. We are open and extroverted, loving and appreciating life in all its forms from the macro to the micro. Surely we were accustomed to living and operating in the former, but now we found ourselves suddenly limited to the latter. In the confines of the various tiny cells I had occupied so far, I had become intensely aware and appreciative of all life that was available to me, anything to which I could relate and connect through observation or play.

Although hardly prone to domestication to the extent Charlie was, the geckos—the little chameleonlike tropical lizards—in my cells provided hours of joy and comfort. In each cell I had become familiar with each one, their own distinct habits and personalities. I watched them hatch from little reptile eggs, perfect miniatures, and observed them grow, hunt, spar, fight, mate, and die. They would spend most of their time hanging around in the vicinity of the light bulb, stalking the bugs and insects it attracted. As cats stalk their prey, they would inch closer in minute increments and finally pounce like lightning when close enough. And I'd cheer, "Yeah! One less bug in this cell!" Once I watched a fairly young gecko stalk and grab a big moth. Its wingspan must have been six inches across. As soon as the gecko grabbed it, it started flapping its wings and I thought they were both going to get airborne. I could see the gecko's little neck tighten and his tiny suction-cup toes hanging onto the wall for dear life. Finally the moth tired and the gecko started maneuvering him toward his hole near the corner at the ceiling. It was about the size of a quarter. As he got the moth to the hole, he arched his neck and started driving him in. The huge moth's wings folded back around the gecko as he poked and punched and squeezed its bulk into the hole ahead of him. Finally they disappeared, and that gecko didn't come out to hunt for over a week.

Sometimes when I'd catch a gecko and stroke his belly, I could see into his stomach through his transparent skin. It was obvious when one had had a good day hunting. "Way to go!" I'd say. "One less hungry person in this cell!"

As the male geckos would spar and fight for a female's favor, they would circle each other menacingly, with tails raised and swishing like fierce dragons. After several thrusts and sometimes debilitating bites, one would retreat and the victor would turn his attention upon the female. She would usually give him as much of a fight as his competitor had, but ultimately she'd give in. He'd grab her by the nape of the neck, nudge her tail aside, and get on with it. And I'd smile and say "Atta boy!" and then go off into my own fantasy.

Sometimes if a gecko was on a flat surface near a ninety-degree edge— a door jamb, for instance—I'd move my finger or a piece of straw or bamboo along the edge so he could just see the tip of whatever was moving. He'd think it was a bug, start swishing his tail, and attack. I'd imagine myself reduced down to his size and doing combat with my broad sword against this huge, ferocious dragon, ultimately considering how many I might yet have to slay. This was also the best way to catch them, luring them close, being careful not to grab a tail or it would instantly slough off and wiggle on its own for a while as its previous owner made a clean—if tailless—getaway.

Once I watched an old scarred gecko die. He didn't move for a long time but got weaker and weaker. Finally he slipped down the wall, caught himself, then sagged again. When he could maintain his hold only with one foot he hung there for a long time, refusing to give up. Ultimately he lost his suction on the last toe, slid down the wall, and plopped onto the floor. He lay there for half an hour, sides moving more and more lightly, till finally his little black eyes—which had scoped out a lifetime of insects, females, and adversaries—just clouded over. The ants had carried him off by morning.

Again, being an observer of their rites of passage and stroking their little heads and bellies provided me with a way to express my own appreciation and affection for other living creatures. It was better than nothing, of course, but I still—perhaps even more than I was consciously aware—longed for some affectionate reciprocation, someone to stroke my head, and maybe even more so, my belly. The prisoners' affinity for these little creatures was so universal that we ultimately adopted them as our official mascots. As a squadron might call itself the Fighting Gamecocks or the Tasmanian Devils, the POW wing as a whole became the Golden Geckos.

I spent hour upon hour studying ants, spiders, and roaches as well. I was always amazed by the sense of community and cooperation that governed the activities of the ants, the ruthlessness of a spider pouncing on a victim in its web. I was always intrigued by how much smaller a cockroach appears dead than alive.

Dog meat being considered a delicacy in much of Vietnam, several adult dogs and at least one litter of puppies usually were running around Hoa Lo. On the rare occasions when I actually saw—and more rarely was able to pet—one of the puppies, I would realize again what I had already known: A puppy is a puppy is a puppy, in the dingy courtyards of Hoa Lo or in the wrapping-littered floor of a living room on Christmas morning.

These dogs were a strain of chow, the adults menacing, but the pups cute little fur balls with tails curving up over their backs. I could always draw comfort and a smile just from the sight of one of the puppies, just from knowing they were there. So it was all the more distasteful when they came of age for slaughter, usually at three to four months. The guards would take sticks and clubs and literally chase a puppy through the prison yard, clubbing and kicking it along to get the adrenaline pumping through its body, apparently making the meat that much more of a delicacy. It was a disgustingly savage thing to hear the yelling and yelping as a cornered puppy was clubbed to death, a strange counterpoint to the gentleness accorded Charlie by the water girls.

Getting back to Charlie: He ultimately learned to arc his way all the way up to the high window ledge. He would survey the strange unknown world outside the bars and inevitably swoop back down inside, landing happily on a shoulder or an extended finger as if to say "I'll take you guys anytime compared to what I might find out there!"

He became so much a part of our routine and was so accepted as one of the guys that he'd walk around the floor and explore on his own, doing his own thing when the guys were going through their morning exercise routine. One morning one of the guys was doing toe raises between the bunks—raising up on tiptoes and down again over and over to strengthen his calves. On one of the down strokes, to his horror, he felt Charlie crunch under his heel and heard an abbreviated little peep. "Oh shit, it's Charlie!" All knew immediately what had happened. They lifted his little broken body and bent feathers into his nest, listened to his shallow breathing, and tried to coax more life out of him, but to no avail.

That night Charlie died while his little head was being lovingly stroked. In the few weeks of his short life—more than his siblings had managed— he had been the object of so much pleasure, and had provided the means for all of us, captives and captors, to show the better sides of our nature. We all missed him terribly. And the little shit never did learn to fly straight.

19

The Voice of Vietnam

Nothing can replace the sheer, exhilarating beauty of the whole picture; a free country in which individual opportunity flourishes and human potential is boundless. We enjoy the unique freedom to strive, to risk, to succeed, and to sometimes fail, but always bounce back and succeed again as many times as we choose. We preserve that freedom by being well informed, by learning from history, by linking cause and effect, and by separating the wheat from the chaff.

By early fall of '70, as our memorized list of POW names approached four hundred, a trend toward communal living began. Ensign Dave Rehmann and I had lived together briefly back in Little Vegas, but now we were reunited back at the Zoo in cell number one of the Barn. He was a radar intercept officer from the backseat of a Phantom jet.

A vivacious young officer from Lancaster, California, Dave was one of the most positive, upbeat men I would know in that negative, downer environment. And this, in spite of a terribly deformed right arm and frequent asthma attacks which caused him to struggle for each breath.

His arm had been badly shattered when he had ejected from his plane, the ulna into four or five pieces. Although the V had applied a cast, the untreated wounds and burns on his arm continued to ooze pus and fluid until the cast became saturated. He'd lived for months with the soggy clump around his arm. The putrid smell was bad enough, but worse yet, the ineffectiveness of the cast had allowed pieces of the ulna to heal off center one from the other, like a crankshaft. The final product was a lumpy, curving forearm to a wrist with little rotation and a curving, clawlike hand. It was still oozing infection after several years.

Together Dave and I developed ideas for profitable business ventures—everything from theme parks to alternate energy, from innovative flight schools to aquaculture, from specialty food franchises to citrus farming. This isn't to say that life was pleasant, but it was life, and planning for the future seemed to engender hope. As a young creative bachelor with an entrepreneurial flair, Dave figured his life in freedom would be a game and money was the best way to keep score.

Although suffering from frequent bouts of asthma, Dave dealt with it stoically and insisted on doing his share of communicating and clearing. We had good comm lines all the way to the far end of the Barn, through seven cells with two to four men in each. One day an inquiry came all the way from cell seven at the other end, passed patiently through the walls by the men in each cell in between.

"Hey, we're interested in growing citrus when we get home. Ask those two fruits from California in cell one if they know anything about that." After Dave and I shrugged to each other acknowledging our ignorance, I saw the gleam in his eye about the same time he saw it in mine.

For the next five days, as the self-styled authorities, we passed on everything we could imagine about "citriculture." We lay awake each night creating the next day's lesson. "The soil has to be rich in the following chemicals." (We picked every fourth one from the Periodic Chart.) "Expect to pay at least $1300 per acre." (Seemed like a knowledgeable input.) "Select seedlings carefully, the tap root of each being the key to its gender. The single root is male and the double root is female. Ensure selection of only one or the other because they bear fruit in opposite years, male even and female odd." (Big hassle to harvest only one or two female trees in a grove of males.) Finally, on the last day, "New technology includes innovative labeling techniques whereby each tree is marked close to the ground with a small Sunkist branding iron. Then ink is added to the irrigation water, and each orange or grapefruit grows out prestamped 'Sunkist.' "

Well, with that last lesson the guys in cell two, who had been dutifully passing on every detail, pounded the wall in the flat, emphatic tone that unmistakably meant, "You sneaky SOBs, you've been putting us all on for an entire frickin' week!" My co-conspirator and I nearly rolled on the floor laughing. Pox, the roving guard, looked in on us and scolded us just on general principle. American "criminals" weren't supposed to be having fun.

Although the Zoo had been expanded to the east—an area we called the Zoo Annex—and some existing administrative facilities in the countryside were being converted to makeshift prisons, the Communists seemed to be running out of space for us. Possibly as a result of the space crunch, Dave and I were moved to a larger cell in the Office, where we were joined by three others: Air Force Captain Mike Lane and Navy Lieutenants Brad Smith and Chuck Zuhoski. This was the precursor of twenty to thirty men living together in the same cell bay.

We and the groups in the other Office cells debated about why there were now several men in a cell. Aside from space considerations, could it mean an actual change in policy? Could this be the first tangible consequence of Ho Chi Minh's death? That had been the most significant event in the modern political history of the country. Surely there would be some policy fallout. We recalled speculating on this a few months earlier.

On the morning of September 1, 1969, the prison had been absolutely quiet: no gongs, no exercise cadence or news through the prison loud-speakers, none of the routine bustle. It was as eerie as if the place had been evacuated in the face of approaching U.S. troops bent on liberating Hanoi. Finally at noon the funeral dirge began to play—deep, plodding chords played by a marching band. It would continue unbroken for three days. Just after noon that first day, the Green Hornet opened our peep-hole and waited solemnly for our bow. He was wearing a black arm band to which he pointed, then said slowly with all reverence, "Ho Chi Minh." He crossed the index fingers of both hands into an X and put them over one eye, then the other—his sign language for "dead." We saw other guards with tears in their eyes.

Ho's death was really no surprise. He had been very frail for the past year, and there had been hints of his possible death in some of the propaganda material. Still, the political significance with relation to Communist military strategy and to policy on POW treatment was so-bering.

We all had mixed emotions about the occasion. Regardless of his original intentions, Ho had presided over the Stalinlike eradication of hundreds of thousands of his own countrymen and imposed a regime of terror and repression over all of North Vietnam. With his power so centralized, he surely must have approved the policy of brutal exploi-tation of POWs. We considered him directly responsible for the deaths of many of our brothers, both in the fields and villages after capture and here in the prisons of Hanoi itself.

On the other hand, we could see that the officers and guards were deeply saddened, for their perspective of "Uncle Ho" was narrower. If

JFK had been "the father of our country" as well as the shining symbol of hope for our nation's future, the grieving of Americans and our collective sense of loss would have been even greater than it was. Such was the case with the North V and Ho's death. In spite of our adversarial relationship with them, it was nevertheless a *human* relationship, and I could not help but empathize with their grief.

On the third day, only blocks away from the Hoa Lo prison, in the huge People's Square, the coffin with Ho's embalmed body, which had been on display, was sealed. The funeral dirge increased in volume and intensity and was accompanied by discordant chants of "Ho Chi Minh, Ho Chi Minh, Ho Chi Minh . . ." The reverberation from the twenty-one-gun salute could be felt in our cells. As multiple flights of MiG fighters thundered their salute low over the city, we riveted our eyes on the small strips of sky to the east between the eaves and the top of the wall. We missed the heart-quickening glimpse of the flashing aircraft we'd sought. They'd flown directly over Hoa Lo.

But the real question in my mind had been how Ho's death might affect the war and our treatment. Were we seeing evidence of this new treatment as the trend toward communal living for prisoners continued?

In the summer of '70 we were shuffled around again. Mike Lane and I were moved to the Pig Sty, which by now had been converted from the several two-man cells I had known in '66 with Larry Spencer to four six-man cells. Lane and I joined four others: Everett Alvarez, my fellow Californian, the first to be held as a POW; Art Cormier, my partner in pain from the Hanoi March; Harry Johnson, whose children were Jet and Jill; and Norm McDaniel, a black officer who could sing like an angel. We all became very close in spite of the compromises necessary for six bodies to coexist in limited space. But the ventilation was good, with large windows at both ends of the cell, and our daily time outside with the other eighteen men in the building was generous compared to previous circumstances. There was so much conversation and getting acquainted I barely had time to miss Dave Rehmann, but I did—just as I had missed Spencer, and Chesley, after living so closely with them.

The practical requirements of a larger group as well as our military orientation made our organization as a "squadron" quite logical. The senior man, hence CO, was Air Force Captain "Pop" Keirn. He enjoyed the dubious distinction of having been a POW in Germany just before the end of World War II. So far he'd been able to keep our captors from knowing this. The second senior man was Operations Officer (called The Executive Officer in Navy organizations), and so on. The senior man in each of the separate cells was a Flight Leader. Each flight had duties and chores for a period of time. Other individuals—according to personal inclination and the CO's choice—were designated as Communications Officer, Security Officer, and Sanitation Officer. McDaniel was Chaplain. I was Flight Leader of Flight Four (our cell number), and together with the other flight leaders comprised an advisory council to the CO and Ops. This would be our basic organization at all prisons for all POWs living communally in large cell bays. It served us well.

After years of solitary and semisolitary confinement, we relished living together. Nevertheless, each man had come to value his solitude. Sometimes the pressures of close communal living could become almost overwhelming. So there developed a practice whereby anytime a man felt the need for solitude he merely draped his towel or a piece of clothing over one shoulder. This meant "Please do not disturb." He could pray, meditate, study, create, dream, or perhaps even cry in "privacy." No one would intrude.

One night in December of '70 an elite, uniquely trained unit of our special forces raided a small prison in the countryside about twenty miles from Hanoi. The place was called Son Tay. They came in low by helicopters, surprised and annihilated the guard force, and looked for the American POWs they were to rescue. But the place was empty. Only by coincidence had the dozen or so GIs being held there been moved the previous week. The raid had been carried off impeccably, V casualties had been significant, American casualties nil, and, had they been there, the POWs would have been home free.

When this happened the V really went to GQ. They conducted a thorough shakedown throughout the prison system, confiscated all contraband collected over the years, i.e., cuff pics, pencil lead, string, wire, needles. They even searched the orifices of our bodies—a task previously considered by them as far too indelicate. As a direct result of Son Tay, all American POWs were consolidated back downtown to Hoa Lo on the 30th of December. We were put into the eleven cell blocks surrounding the huge courtyard in which I had watched the Vietnamese prisoners from over my windowsill in Heartbreak Hotel almost five years earlier. Each of these cell blocks held twenty to forty men. Each comprised a squadron. Each squadron was named after its CO's personal call sign, which he had used while flying tactical missions. "Pop" Keirn was an Ohioan, so our call sign was "Buckeye." We called the new setup Camp Unity. This was consistent with our overall motto, which had been proclaimed by Jim Stockdale years earlier: "Unity over self."

Although the V never told us about the Son Tay raid or why the new security precautions had been implemented, it was clear something truly significant had happened. The VOV propaganda diatribes were particularly venomous and were laced with phrases like "darkest imperialist scheme yet" and "blatant violation of sovereignty" and "commando raids doomed to annihilation." Rabbit put it more succinctly one day while talking to Keirn through the barred door to our cell bay: "If the helicopters come here, they will never take you out alive. You will all be killed first."

Months later, when finally apprised by a new POW of what had happened at Son Tay, we considered the news with mixed emotion. On the one hand, we were proud and encouraged that our government would plan and execute such a risky operation to actually rescue some of us. On the other hand, since such a risk had been considered necessary, it seemed apparent that our government did not foresee our release through diplomatic negotiations or military victory as an early eventuality. That was discouraging.

The raid had caused the V to put us all together for the first time, and Camp Unity would be the final venue for larger and larger groups to live together and mingle in the courtyard. Our senior officers—though still not acknowledged by the prison authorities—were given more say in policy and routine. We had the brave raiders of Son Tay to thank for all of this.

We remained in fairly stable groups all through the spring and summer of '71. Communication between all the cell blocks was established and maintained, thereby facilitating for the first time completely standardized policy from the senior staff. The policies were code-named the "plums," and the first one was "Follow the Code of Conduct."

Through the years, living with and next to many different men, I always inquired about my crewman: Have you ever heard of Lieutenant JG Bob Hanson? Do you have him on your list? Did you ever? Any name close to Hanson? I never received a hopeful reply. In the communal living arrangement we had during that time, I never once encountered a man who knew or had heard of his whereabouts.

I'd had a low-key interrogation in the "Phuc Ho room" with a staff officer I'd never seen before. In impeccable English he had referred to the papers on the desk in front of him.

"Your name is Coffee!"

"Yes, Navy Lieutenant Gerald Coffee."

He was nonplussed by my reference to my rank.

"And your crewman's name was Robert Hanson." They always pronounced it "Hanshun."

"Yes, Robert Hanson. Do you know of his fate?"

The staff officer shook his head as he studied the papers and said, almost absentmindedly, "He is dead. I myself have seen the spot he is buried."

I pressed him.

"I see. Then his grave must be very close to the main north-south road, Highway 1."

I reasoned that if he said yes he was probably lying about Bob, or really didn't know. There would be no reason I could fathom that my captors would have carried Bob across the same paddies I'd traveled just to bury him.

The officer looked up at me. He had a kind and straightforward face.

"No. His grave was very near the sea."

We were able to follow the progress of the war and the peace talks fairly accurately by reading between the lines of the VOV propaganda broadcasts. In fact, although they were intended to demoralize us and shift our thinking, the broadcasts were generally more beneficial than not. Sometimes, though, after five or six years of hearing everything that was bad about my country, about the free enterprise system, and about our cause in Southeast Asia, I had to dig very deeply for the faith that was necessary *not* to change my thinking.

The Communists had been so blatant in their own lies and deceit that their most effective, most damaging propaganda was right out of U.S. newspapers. Early on in indoctrination sessions as well as on the VOV, I realized they lied even when the truth would have served them better. Later, however, they began to realize the higher credibility of Western media and used it extensively.

It was truly demoralizing to hear antiwar statements from certain of our senators—McGovern, Fulbright, McCarthy, and Morse—and congressmen when we were taking torture to keep from making even milder statements. When Jane Fonda and her group came to Hanoi, she received the grand tour of damaged facilities, especially "churches and schools," and pathetic gatherings of civilian casualties, all supposedly "targeted by the U.S. military warmongers." Her eager hosts smiled and danced for her, gave her flowers, and conducted the canned tour designed to reinforce all of her preconceptions of the situation. They allowed her to visit face-to-face with a few of those POWs who had been shot down only recently, had been kept out of contact with others, and had known only the improved treatment, and, most significantly, no torture.

When back home, Fonda extolled the generous and humane treatment of the American POWs at the hands of the North Vietnamese Communists. Ramsey Clark, the former U.S. Attorney General, was duped by the same show. He, too, returned to the U.S. to reaffirm the determination of the Communists but not before recording an interview with Miller and Wilber, the two collaborators, encouraging them and offering his legal expertise should they experience difficulties upon their return. The interview was piped through the prison speaker system.

During Fonda's broadcast to "captured American war criminals" on the prison radio, I had sat there in my cell—lonely, hungry, and prickly with heat rash—listening in disbelief as she called me a "war criminal" and told me I had been "used by our government as a pawn to fight this illegal, immoral war against the peace-loving Vietnamese people." She encouraged me to cooperate with prison authorities to bring the war to an end as soon as possible—on their terms, of course, because it was their cause that was just. They deserved to win. She reproachingly pointed out that since I as a pilot was responsible for the deaths of so many innocent people, I should show my appreciation all the more for my humane treatment.

As I sat there listening, I shook my head slowly in disbelief. I'm not sure I would have been so reserved had I known that upon my eventual return and amid revelations of our abysmal treatment, she would call us "hypocrites" and "liars."

The visiting peace delegations and the antiwar movement in general had a definite impact on our treatment. On several occasions, men had been tortured to get them to meet with "peace" activists and foreign journalists. I had not been tortured to meet with Schwinman back in '66, but the outcome with the letter I was forced to write had been the same. Had I known I was to be tortured so brutally to change my letter to Bea, I would have taken it earlier in refusing to see him altogether. Sometimes after torturing prisoners to agree to see a delegation, even the V could see the incongruity of the situation and the meeting would not take place after all. Most of the time, however, they would proceed as scheduled, usually with a torture guard—arms folded and a coil of rope hitched to his belt—standing in the shadows nearby. Often meetings with peace delegations were reserved to "showcase" certain POWs.

Although he had little control over the situation, Lieutenant Commander John McCain, whose father, Admiral J. S. McCain, Commander of all U.S. forces in the Pacific theater when John was shot down, may owe his life to his father's position. Although he was seriously injured, the Communists kept him alive simply for his potential value as a special "showcase POW." In that regard, however, and to John's credit, they wasted their effort and medicine. It's likely that many men were allowed to die because they didn't have "showcase" potential.

The visits by the antiwar delegations, with their praise and encouragement of the North Vietnamese, had not only impacted our morale and undermined our determination to resist; they also legitimized for them in their own minds their policies of torture, degradation, and exploitation of us. Thinking, actually convincing themselves, that the peace activists who cheered their victories represented the majority of public opinion in the U.S., the Communists were all the more eager to exploit us for supporting propaganda.

I was lucky to have been shot down before any significant antiwar movement had developed. Most of the time I was able to discount it as the ramblings of a few activist kooks. But the men shot down after '68 had seen firsthand the antiwar movement expand in scope and apparent legitimacy. For these latecomers, the conflicting statements and exhortations by generals, congressmen, and peaceniks alike had more connection to the reality they had known and made it that much more difficult to resist the exploitation and to keep the faith, no matter how extensive their internal resources. What did inspire their resistance as much as anything was the saga of resistance by the POWs who had gone before them during the preceding four years.

Later on into 1970, '71, and '72, it became even more difficult for all of us as our frustration grew and the propaganda became more sophisticated and drew more and more from respectable Western sources.

We could see that the same antiwar rhetoric that made it more difficult for us also encouraged the North Vietnamese to believe that what they couldn't achieve on the battlefield they could achieve "in the streets of America." Had they to rely only on their military success and progress in South Vietnam, they would have been likely to throw in the towel after the resounding reversal of their Tet offensive in 1968, especially if we'd followed up with B-52s then.

Interestingly, I had become aware through the years of a change in the thrust of the political indoctrination quizzes. The emphasis swung gradually from "inevitable Communist victory" on the battlefields of South Vietnam to the inevitable victory of "the forces of peace" in the world. We were witnessing firsthand the encouragement and heightened determination of the North Vietnamese brought about by the antiwar movement in America. Even though mostly conscientious and well intentioned, it seemed to be extending the war by years.

From the VOV we could tell the proposals and counterproposals in the Paris peace talks were progressing, albeit at a painfully slow pace. In the spring of '72, the V began to phase out the requirement that we bow to them. There was never any official notification as such; they just stopped enforcing it, so of course, we stopped doing it.

Also during this time, the food improved markedly, outside time was increased, and best of all, we were allowed to mingle freely as one entire group. In late summer we were allowed to play Ping-Pong and volleyball. One day during a closely contested volleyball game, I was struck with the realization of the importance of fun in our lives. Until I began having it again, I hadn't realized how much I had missed just plain fun.

Letters and packages from home began to be distributed more frequently. One day I was called to one of the interrogation shacks that had been erected in lean-to style against the outer walls of the cell blocks. Elf and Dog were paired up as interrogators. Elf was a diminutive man with waxen skin you could see through, like the belly of a gecko. He had been a translator at the Zoo a few years back. Dog had been the commander of the Zoo for a time and had now worked up to commander of Camp Unity. He liked to be around more now, smiling and laughing it up as conditions improved.

"Co, today we have some letters from your family for you. I think you should be very pleased about it." Elf's voice was as little as he was. He always sounded as if his voice was being provided by a ventriloquist somewhere nearby. His pale cheeks and beady little eyes enhanced the gecko image.

He shoved two letters and a photograph across the table. My eyes went immediately to the black and white photo. God, it was precious. All four of the kids were standing on the beach. It appeared to be a couple of years old. Jerry looked to be about four, wearing a little jersey with a big number 16 on it. The older boys looked like they'd been playing hard, bathing suits askew and hair all tousled. Kim looked so demure with one foot in front, toes pointed in a classic little ballet pose. I dwelled on the photo a long time. Actually, the "letters" were six-line cards that had been the regulation now for several years. They were dated May and June of '71, over a year old.

"Will I be allowed to keep these with me?"

"Yes, of course you can keep your letters. They are yours."

During one of the purges of '68, my first letter from Bea had been confiscated. Since then any correspondence from home had to be devoured and savored in only a few minutes, then returned on the spot for "safe keeping."

"Good, then I'll read them later."

"What do you think of the war situation now?" Dog asked. Elf translated with seriousness. It was a question asked frequently at quizzes lately.

"I believe the war is going well for the Americans and South Vietnamese now in the South. If your government really wants to end the suffering of the Vietnamese people, it must negotiate seriously at the peace talks.

Dog's bland, jowly face was even more intent as he asked another question. "What do you think of the election between Nikshun [Nixon] and Magaburn [McGovern]? That would be very bad for you if Magaburn does not win. He has said that if he wins the election, he will come right here in Hanoi on his knees and beg for you."

"I would rather remain here in your prisons for another presidential term of four years than have our president come and beg you for my release," I replied.

Dog listened to my answer intently, and I realized he understood English.

"Humph!" His head bobbed disdainfully as he blurted out, "Probably you will then!"

20
Peace with Honor

The peace process begins with the individual. Our world is a reflection of the struggles, values, commitments, and hopes of each of us. When we honor the principles of freedom and human dignity, boundaries disappear and we are connected to others with love and respect. This is peace with honor.

"Invictus"

Out of the night that covers me,
  Black as the Pit from pole to pole,
I thank whatever gods may be
  For my unconquerable soul.

In the fell clutch of circumstance
  I have not winced nor cried aloud.
Under the bludgeonings of chance
  My head is bloody, but unbowed.

Beyond this place of wrath and tears
  Looms but the horror of the shade,
And yet the menace of the years
  Finds, and shall find me, unafraid.

It matters not how strait the gate,
  How charged with punishments the scroll,
I am the master of my fate:
  I am the captain of my soul.
                    —William Ernest Henley

I was lying on my mat wondering about Henley's background and what might have motivated him to write that poem, when I heard the deep rumble of a bomb explosion, one that would finally change the course of this war—and my life. Even though the noise was in the distance, it shook the buildings of Hoa Lo. There were more explosions in rapid succession, and they kept going. Now there was a deep constant roar that grew in strength: airplanes; big airplanes.

"Gotta be B–52s," someone said.

"Hot damn!"

Several of us were up on an elbow or sitting clear up, listening. Still the roar increased and the explosions continued and our building shuddered. The lights flickered, dimmed for a few seconds, then went out. Blackouts were routine during night raids, but this one appeared to be a result of the raid rather than a precaution.

Finally there was the sound of antiaircraft guns, big ones somewhere very close to the prison. The air raid warning siren began its low growl, rapidly increased in pitch and intensity, and then continued pulsing high and low from there. The explosions continued without pause. No doubt about it: Only B–52s could lay such a long, constant pattern.

"Look at that!"

I turned toward the big open window. What sky I could see was bright orange. I quickly extracted myself from my net, as did the others. Little bits of plaster and dust were falling down around us.

"Holy shit! The sky's on fire!"

The entire southern horizon appeared to be in flames. And still the bombs were exploding, huge vermilion flashes preceding each shuddering shock wave. The flaming exhaust of SAM missiles traced smoky trails through the sky, some silhouetted by the flames in the distance.

"May Bay My! May Bay My!" American aircraft! American aircraft! The public loudspeakers had now begun to blare out the words in conjunction with the wailing siren.

Suddenly there was an explosion high in the sky above the eaves line of the roof. We could see only the instantaneous light, like an orange-blue flash bulb. A SAM had exploded. Huge chunks of flaming airplane began tumbling into view as it plummeted to earth.

"Oh, God, help them to get out, please!" Our prayer was almost in unison.

The bombs continued for a total of about fifteen minutes. Then the aircraft engines faded, and the secondary explosions commenced. The entire southern horizon, at least 150 degrees sector within our view, was in flames.

"Sonovabitch, is this awesome or what!"

"You must keep shilent! You must keep absolutely shilent! You must show good attitude!" A guard stuck his head up to the bars in the cell bay doors and shouted in to us.

"Me, I'm packing my bags, guys, this is it!" someone said, ignoring the guard.

"Finally!"

"Yeah, finally!"

We were all standing up on the sleeping platform, practically mesmerized by the flames in the distant sky and the continuing punctuation of secondaries. We realized we were witnessing an awesome spectacle, and more importantly a change in bombing strategy. It was obvious that a lot of people would be dying out there and an awful lot of material, equipment, and supplies were going up in flames. This would certainly up the ante for the North Vietnamese to maintain their presence in South Vietnam and for their apparent intransigence in Paris.

No sooner had we traded speculations on the circumstances in Paris or in South Vietnam or in the USA which had caused the president to escalate the bombing in such quantum proportions, and had crawled back under our nets when we heard the same droning rumble again and the explosions of bombs, this time somewhere to the north.

"Way to go, guys, give 'em hell!"

"Ooooee! We'll be outa here by January at this rate!"

Again the air raid warning siren cranked up a minute or so after the first bombs hit.

"Man, don't you love their great air defense system? They count on the bombs to be the first warning sign!"

"The system can't be all bad, look where we all are!"

"Lucky!"

"Yeah, a few lucky shots!"

The second raid lasted as long as the first. We knew the destruction had to have been comparable, but we couldn't see anything to the north because of the high windows and the sixteen-foot walls around Hoa Lo.

The third raid was accompanied by night reconnaissance drones buzzing through the Hanoi skies, so this time the guards had something to unload on, but apparently without success. We had learned that every time a plane was hit or brought down over Hanoi, the guards cheered and that caused a churning feeling in the pits of our stomachs. They had cheered, of course, when the fiery chunks of 52 had come tumbling down in the first raid.

Two days later, during the raid on December 12th, the prison buildings shuddered, big chunks of plaster raining down, making huge white clouds when they hit the floor. Dust and debris were rattled loose from trusses across the upper spaces of the cell bay, and the electricity was out until morning.

The B–52s came back again the next night, and the next, and every night for the next two weeks. There was no bombing on Christmas Eve, and included in our Christmas prayers was the hope that the bombing— if it hadn't yet made the desired difference—would resume again after Christmas. It did; and it continued until the 29th of December. And when it stopped again, we prayed that *now* it had made the difference, that the Hanoi government had decided this was too high a price to pay.

"In accordance with the agreements signed this date, January 27th, 1973, by the government of the Democratic Republic of Vietnam and the United States of America, concerning the cease-fire in all of Vietnam, North and South, the disengagement and removal of all foreign military forces from the territory defined as South Vietnam, and the exchange and repatriation of all Prisoners of War on both sides, the following procedures will apply . . ." A young interpreter had first translated Dog's officious speech, then had read the text of the document in his hand.

We stood quietly, hardly breathing, dressed against the chill air and formed in ranks according to our cell blocks. Extra contingency guards were posted on the periphery for the occasion.

The Kid's English was damn good. He was a stranger to us, probably tapped by the general staff for this especially auspicious task. He continued, a little more relaxed, like a performer who's nervous at first, but begins to hit his stride after the ice is broken: "As for the release of American pilots shot down and captured in the Democratic Republic of Vietnam . . ."

A chill ran down my spine as the word "release" reverberated in my mind. Release! Oh, God, let it be true.

". . . their departure shall take place in increments of approximately one hundred and twenty men at two-week intervals. The sick and wounded shall depart in the first increment, followed by the others in the order in which they were captured."

Still we were silent. Dog smiled smugly as the interpreter went on. If he was looking for some sign of jubilation or relief, he had to have been disappointed. By this time, by interpreting almost everything that happened—the mood of a Q, or a change in schedule, or in food as a good or bad sign—we had all been up and down; optimistic and pessimistic and hopeful and disheartened so many times that we just wouldn't believe it until it actually happened. In fact, we had developed a "science" we called "gastropolitics." This meant that when the food was bad, the peace talks weren't going well; when food improved, the peace talks were going better. And our spirits were up and down accordingly.

The young translator read more technical stuff and then lowered the paper to his side, unable to contain the smile that tugged at the corners of his mouth. Still we stood dumbly, each man trying to absorb in his own way the impact of the words we had just heard. ". . . their departure shall take place . . ." Departure? Release?

Now Dog himself continued in English: "In the meantime, you must all continue to show respect and to obey all the orders of the camp officers and guards. If you do not strictly obey all of the camp regulations and show a good attitude, you can still be severely punished."

Then, yielding to the vestiges of habit formed over the previous years, he added, "In fact, if you do not show good attitudes and obey the camp regulations, you may or may not be allowed to return to your country. But, according to you."

He paused for effect and surveyed our military formation, barely masking his disdain. How it must gall him after all these years to have orders from above now to recognize our rank structure and treat us with a semblance of respect.

"Return to your room!"

Colonel Risner was positioned out in front of our individual squadron formation and opposite Dog. He did a smart about-face with all the dignity and military bearing within him.

"Fourth Allied POW Wing, atten-hut!"

We had called ourselves the Fourth Allied POW Wing because in recent American history there were POWs—in World War I and II, in Korea, and now in Vietnam. We were allied because among us were one South Vietnamese officer and three Thai noncoms. These four, though kept separate much of the time, had communicated and worked with us at every opportunity.

Approximately four hundred men had snapped to attention on Risner's command. The thud of eight hundred rubber-tire sandals coming together smartly was awesome and seemed appropriate given the occasion.

Risner continued, "Squadron commanders will meet with me at 1030 hours today just before midday lock-in. Dismiss your men."

The nine squadron commanders returned Risner's salute and did a crisp about-face maneuver to face their men. In unison the squadron commanders dismissed their units. "Squadron, dis . . . missed!" It sounded damned good.

Barely six months earlier such open display of military organization among us would have been met with a company of riot guards brandishing fixed bayonets. Certainly all the signs were right. The kind of conditions and treatment we had anticipated prior to any release were now in effect. As we entered cell block three, some men were exchanging a wink and a smile or a light punch on the shoulders, but most, with minds racing unto themselves, already projected themselves twelve thousand miles away and considered the joyful and spooky prospect of reunions with loved ones.

Our squadron commander Ted Koffman, assembled his flight leaders for a conference. "What do you think, guys? Is this it?"

Lieutenant Commander Jim Pirie, an A-4 Skyhawk pilot from Bessemer, Alabama, had the usual twinkle in his eye. "Hell, man, my bags are packed. If this is some kind of ruse, they've got me sucked in."

Ev Alvarez, with whom I had lived off and on in a variety of circumstances over the past three years, was still skeptical: "You know, I've been up and down so many times over the years that I'm not sure what to think. It looks good, everything seems right, but I'll believe it when I see it. I'm not ready to party it up . . . yet." He emitted a nervous little laugh and looked playfully sideways at each of us. My God, he had been there for almost eight and a half years, the first six months totally alone. By now he had learned from his family that his young, attractive bride of only a few months at the time he was shot down had finally lost hope after three or four years and left. He didn't know if he was divorced or what. Yet he had endured it all, kept faith in his family and in our military effort in Vietnam. He had maintained his sense of duty and purpose—and his sense of humor. He was an inspiration to us all.

Later that afternoon, after our comm session linking all the squadrons with the most senior officers (who were held together in a separate cell block and, as far as the V knew, were out of touch with the rest of us), the consensus was very positive. Orders came down for "no celebrations, no fraternization or friendliness, and no unnecessary confrontation with the prison guards. All conduct will be dignified, professional, and on the guarded assumption that release is imminent. We will operate from a position of cautious optimism." There was no question in my mind, however, that nearly every man in Hoa Lo, if he were as normal as I, was about to burst with joy as the prospect of going home became more tangible.

Within a few days of Dog's announcement, there was a big shakeup in Camp Unity. Everyone, it seemed, was moving somewhere. I practically held my breath as I rolled my gear up in my mat. This move should tell the story, I figured. This would be the key to our immediate future.

They began moving us out selectively. Alvarez and I were led across the courtyard to cell block number seven, the closest one to the entrance to Camp Unity via the drive-through at the end of Heartbreak Hotel. We entered to near chaos. Holy shit! It was true.

There in one huge room were the first eighty or so men shot down from August of '64 to July of '66. There was my first cell mate, Larry Spencer, whom I hadn't seen since early '68. We embraced and clapped each other on the back. There was Render Crayton and Dave Rehmann. We hugged too. There were the most senior officers with whom I had been in contact along the way, all of whom had earned my utmost respect for their positive leadership: Colonel Robbie Risner, who had helped me get off on the right foot, Commander Jim Stockdale, the senior Navy POW, whom—while isolated and alone in the Mint—Air Force Captain Dave Hatcher and I had kept in the comm system with a tricky note-drop in the bath area of Little Vegas. Stockdale, too, had been an inspiring example and would receive the Congressional Medal of Honor for his leadership under extreme duress.

Commander Jim Mulligan shook my hand vociferously, thanking me for bringing him into the comm system back at the Zoo by talking through the wall on our cups. Mine had been the first American voice he had heard in months. We also recalled together our brief morale-boosting exchange at that Christmas Mass back in '68. Commander Jerry Denton was there. He had been our senior officer at the Zoo in mid '68 during a purge in which most were tortured. His leadership and encouragement had been invaluable. All the senior men looked especially haggard and beaten down. The V's focus on them and their refusal to stay down, their determination to exercise command, had taken a visibly heavy toll on them. Phil Butler and Howie Dunn, the first men to contact me at the Zoo, introduced themselves. Commander Howie

Rutledge, with whom I had commiserated in the Mint through the steaming summer of '69; Commander Bill Franke, my pessimistic neighbor in the Pig Sty during the big raid in June of '66, was all smiles; Art Cormier, my partner in the Hanoi march—all were there. Most of these men had survived that infamous trek, now almost blurred away by the passing years.

I was reunited with my friends and neighbors from Sanford, Florida, Lieutenant Commander Jim Bell, Lieutenant Commander Duffy Hutton, and Lieutenant JG Glen "Coon Ass" Daigle. During all of our captivity, I had never seen them until now. We had all deployed from heavy recon Wing Three there in central Florida within six months of each other. Our reunion was raucous.

After the celebration, the contact with the others from Sanford made me recall painfully the sight of Bob Hanson floating in the water closer to shore as the boats had approached. I scanned the room full of men perfunctorily, not really expecting to see Bob, but still clinging to the small ember of hope. Coon Ass and I commiserated with each other on our losses; his pilot and my friend, Max Lukenbach, wasn't there either.

To some extent I had been in touch with all of these men through the years because the V had kept us more or less in grouping according to our shootdown date. But this was the first face-to-face encounter with many of them, so it was a warm and joyful occasion. The joy of our reunion was limited only by a constant, underlying awareness that any number of things could screw up the peace process. We were certain the Communists were as anxious as we to have the whole thing over, especially now that the B-52s had been turned loose on Hanoi, but they were as likely as not to try to capitalize on the euphoria created by the prospect of peace to exact further last-minute concessions. Down deep we knew the process was still probably quite tenuous, but we tried to put that out of our minds.

After organizing our squadron structure, we spent the next several days getting reacquainted. We swapped news from home received primarily through the letters of the past six months. Many of us held pictures of our families we'd just received in small packages the past year. The vitamins, freeze-dried coffee, raisins, and sweat socks had been like manna.

We were allowed open-door privileges throughout much of each day. Out in the courtyard, we mingled with the men from other cell blocks. We could even talk with men who had been downed in B-52s during the Hanoi raids the previous month. Even though there had been many indicators, most of us were stunned to learn that the antiwar movement was now more serious and broad-based than we had imagined.

"People at home are really fed up with the whole damn war," a young B-52 navigator told us. "Many in Congress are now against it. There are demonstrations somewhere almost daily, and riots aren't uncommon. A lot of kids have defected to Canada to keep from being drafted. The shooting of the students at Kent State was a real shocker. It's a damn mess."

Although this news was a downer, life in general in cell block seven those last few weeks in Vietnam was downright pleasant. The days were chilly but full of sunshine and outside exercise. We couldn't get enough news from the B-52 guys. At first they and the few guys shot down in tactical fighter and attack planes in late '72 had all been kept separately in their own cell bay, cell block five. They hadn't been allowed out in the courtyard with the rest of us, but we had pressed around their barred entry door much of the time, and they had crowded around on the inside. I had talked to an eager young navigator shot down on one of the last raids. He hadn't even been there long enough to have a prison haircut and his maroon striped garb was still stiff with newness. "Jesus," I told him, "you guys and your bombers were magnificent, absolutely awesome! After the first raid on the 10th of December, we prayed you'd keep coming back. But with all the SAMs and triple-A fire, it must have been scary as hell."

"You're right, Commander, it was hairy as hell!" He was the first person to call me Commander. I had been promoted two ranks by now, and the title almost went over my head.

"Well, we were down here cheering for you. We're sure you guys have finally made the difference. Thanks a lot, fella."

He seemed incredulous that it was I who had thanked him.

"Sir, it was *you* guys that inspired us! We been keepin' you all in our prayers for years. We been tryin' like hell to get you outa here. Commander Pirie here has been tellin' us what you guys have been through. Man, you guys are on everybody's minds at home. You are heroes. There's special flags and ceremonies and, of course, the bracelets. Almost everyone in the military—and civilians too—wears a bracelet with one of you guy's names on it. I was wearing Captain Chesley's bracelet, but they took it off me when I was captured."

Ceremonies, flags, prayers! I almost had tears in my eyes.

He continued: "My God, sir, us new guys are all just amazed at you all's enthusiasm and sense of humor, and how you've stood up under all this for so long."

I was incredulous. The years of propaganda had gotten to me. Being called a "war criminal," hearing the condemnation of the war, and learning about the strength of the antiwar movement had overshadowed any consideration that we could actually be perceived as heroes back home.

Finally, he said, "It don't matter how people at home feel about the war. At least everyone has been unanimous in their demand for decent treatment for you guys."

We were now preparing our own food in the big circular communal kitchen in the center of the courtyard. The V provided an abundance of canned fish and meat from China and the Soviet Union. There were plenty of potatoes and vegetables, resulting in thick wholesome soup. We received fresh bread daily, half a loaf with each meal, including a "breakfast" of bread and sugar. (We'd receive sugar in bulk, and we would dip our bread into the sugar for a sweet snack.) We boiled our own drinking water, and it was available to make coffee from our packages from home. With few exceptions, we all shared equally the goodies from our packages while they lasted. I must have regained ten pounds during that last month alone. It felt good not to be hungry.

Through much of early '72, we watched the V construct a high radio transmission tower just north of Hoa Lo. We marveled at their ingenuity in constructing this tower section by section, with no heavy crane to lift prefabricated sections into place. Every piece had been hoisted up manually to be bolted and welded into place. When completed, the structure must have hit four hundred feet, towering over the center of Hanoi.

The V were in quite a celebratory mood one day, with upbeat music in the prison yard, and we watched one of their soldiers climb up the nearby tower. Climbing very carefully for about a half hour, he finally reached the top, attached a flag of the DRV—a gold star on a red background—to the tower, surveyed his capital city for a few minutes, waved down to the captured American air pirates in Hoa Lo prison, and then descended as gingerly as he had ascended. He didn't know that he had hung his flag upside down. We all savored the moment, making sure all the Americans in the courtyard saw it.

A few days later, several guards began constructing an elevated stage in the courtyard. We were immediately suspicious, and joked that had this been back in '68 or '69, we would have predicted a gallows was being constructed. Soon, however, we were told that the premier North Vietnamese army entertainment troupe would be putting on a show for us the next night. Indeed, lighting platform, spotlights, and canvas dressing rooms were all being put in place.

Risner recounted his session with Rabbit for us: " 'To show you the goodwill of the people and government of the Democratic Republic of Vietnam, we are providing for you our finest entertainment. There will be dancers and jugglers, and a magician. Our country's top singer, our most famous singer—Trong Vi—will sing for you.' " It was obvious this was their grandaddy effort to kiss us good-bye, to pat us on the back and say let bygones be bygones. No hard feelings, right?

The consensus of the senior officers was clear. After all that had transpired through the years, it would be totally inappropriate for us to attend such a show. Instead we would deprive them of the satisfaction they expected from this magnanimous gesture; it was too little too late. Rabbit seemed genuinely stunned when told no American POWs would attend their show.

The next afternoon during siesta, as many of the others napped, I was standing at the door of the cell block, my hands curled naturally around the worn bars. The preparations for the show that night seemed to be continuing. I was watching sets being stacked in some order as Rabbit and a woman emerged from the group and walked toward me. Rabbit was dressed in his usual khaki, but the woman was dressed in the traditional *au dai,* the high-necked gownlike dress over loose white trousers. Her petite slippers contrasted sharply with the rough rubber tire sandals I had seen on other V women.

Rabbit had a guarded smile on his face as they approached. "Co, this is Trong Vi. You have heard her on the radio."

Indeed, I had heard Trong Vi on the VOV many times. Although never understanding a word she had sung, I had truly admired her voice. It was high and clear and well trained. She was a true artist, and I was struck by how well she looked and moved the part. She was obviously privileged.

Trong Vi's complexion was clear and more fair than most Vietnamese. Her face was delicately sculpted and, except for the muscle definition around her vocal chords, she could have passed for a high-fashion model. Her thick black hair fell to her waist and was brushed to a sheen. She wore some kind of orchidlike flower over one ear. Modest in style though it was, her yellow brocade dress curved sensuously over her body. I was taken aback as she walked without hesitation right up to the other side of the bars, stopped with her face a foot from mine, and looked directly into my eyes with a quizzical little smile on her pink lips.

"Co, Trong Vi and the others do not understand why you refuse to come to their show. They have gone to much trouble. You should not be rude."

I looked back into her black eyes. Her makeup was elegantly soft, and the sweet fragrance of her perfume reminded me how long it had been since I had been so close to a woman. I was suddenly aware that my palms were sweaty on the bars of the cell door and that I had instinctively backed away a few inches. Rabbit appeared amused as I answered: "Tell her that it is nothing personal about her or the other performers. I admire her singing very much, but we simply cannot attend."

Rabbit translated, carelessly I was sure. Her face softened and her smile turned to a puckish little pout. She was accustomed to getting her way.

"Tell her that because you have mistreated us so badly over the years, because you have starved, beaten, and tortured us, we cannot now accept this gesture of good treatment. It is too late to make it up to us."

I had spoken slowly and distinctly, hoping she might understand some English but she only looked to Rabbit. Again he translated loosely, I was sure.

When she turned her face back to mine, her eyebrows were raised and her mouth was in a half smile, half pout. She shrugged her shoulders entreatingly. I shrugged back and shook my head, smiling as kindly as I could. Her eyes saddened and looked away just before she turned. Her hair swished gently from side to side as she walked back toward the makeshift theater in the center of the courtyard.

The show in the courtyard went on as planned that night. A couple dozen guards and prison officials sat enraptured and clapped loudly as Trong Vi, artist that she was, sang her heart out.

A few days later, on the seventh anniversary of my capture, I was told by our turnkey to dress for quiz. There was a small room just off the drive-through opposite the door to the eight cells of Heartbreak Hotel. It had been used for storage, but now as I entered I faced two very young Vietnamese officers sitting across a table.

"Your name is Coffee?" one of them asked.

It was the first time any of them had used my name.

"Yes, Commander Coffee, U.S. Navy." That sounded good.

"Sit down there." He motioned to the stool in front of the table. His companion looked at me as officiously as he knew how.

"How are you?"

"I'm fine. What do you want?"

These guys were so new they didn't even know I was being impertinent.

The first one spoke again. "Today it is our duty to return your belongings."

"What belongings?"

"This."

I swallowed hard, unable to believe my eyes. I reached for the gold wedding band he held between his thumb and forefinger.

"Let me see it, please." My voice was barely a whisper as I took the ring in my hand and examined it. Yes, it was mine. I slipped it onto my finger; a little loose, but definitely my ring. I had never expected to see it again. Suddenly I could again smell the alcohol disinfectant and pus from that gory ring-removal ceremony almost seven years earlier when they thought they had really done me a favor. One of the staff officers there that night had pointed to the wedding ring on my good hand and mumbled something to Rabbit. Then he said, "I think you must give me your other ring now also, and I will keep them both safe for you."

Sarge had grabbed my left wrist with both hands as Rabbit removed my wedding ring as well. God, I hated to see it go. Of course, I valued it even more than the ring with the wings, but I just couldn't muster any further will to resist its removal. Rabbit had then tied the two rings together with a piece of string and handed them to one of the other officers. I had watched as the rings changed hands, the icy blue of the aquamarine refracting a tiny, fiery farewell in spite of the discoloration from the chemicals of the ordeal.

Regaining my composure after the shock of seeing the wedding band again, I now said, "But where is the other ring that was taken from this finger?" I held up the crooked, scarred finger to make my point. "There was another ring tied to this one. Where is it?"

They looked at each other bewildered, and jabbered back and forth intently. Finally, "Well, the other ring must be lost. You should remember it is wartime. Besides, there were floods and many other things. It is many years now."

I knew, of course, he didn't have the slightest knowledge of the naval aviator's ring that had been removed so brutally. These kids were eleven or twelve years old when I first arrived in that entry courtyard, just a few feet away.

Suddenly, in spite of the elation of receiving my ring, I felt very old and weary. Considering how young these kids were when I was shot down made me realize, perhaps for the first time, just how long I had really been here. Seven years today. Seven years! Almost half of my Navy career. In the first seven years of my career I had married, gone through preflight and flight training, made two deployments in Crusaders on the *Saratoga,* fathered four children, flew low-level recce flights over Cuba, and trained dozens of pilots in the Vigilante. What the hell had I done the last seven? During the prime years of my life, I'd sat on my ass in some medieval dungeons, broken my teeth, screwed up my arm, contracted worms and God knows what else, and had gotten *old.* Well, I was almost thirty-nine. We sure as hell better have something to show for it down South.

These two bright, scrubbed faces before me reminded me how much my own children must have grown away from me all these years. I laughed out loud as I realized they had both been staring at me, probably wondering how this decrepit old fart could possibly have flown a hot jet airplane over their country in the first place.

"Is there anything else?" I asked gently.

"No, you may return to your room."

"Right, my room." I chuckled. But as I reached the door I stopped and turned back. "Thank you for returning my wedding ring."

I turned quickly and exited the room. Once outside in the drive-through, I leaned back against the wall beside the door. I took a deep breath and held it but I couldn't keep in the sobs as I stared at the ring again and turned it round and round my finger.

That night I sat up a long time after the last gong. Several others had had their wedding rings returned, so I wasn't the only one in a pensive mood. I had received about a dozen photos of Bea and the children over the past several months. I had them spread on my mat in front of me, glancing at my ring and thinking about going home.

I wondered if the kids would accept me back into the family. What would little Jerry be thinking when we meet for the first time? Kim was a blossoming young lady, a high school freshman. She'd been a skinny-legged little first grader when I left. The older boys looked happy and devilish. What difference had these seven years without their father made in their lives?

Bea! What would our reunion be like? How would she feel in my arms? Had she changed? I smiled as I thought of the POW fact I'd picked up somewhere along the way: "Every seven years, every cell in the body changes, is renewed." Hell, Coffee, you'll be going home to a brand-new woman! A more sobering thought, however, was that the new cells in my own body probably weren't as vital as the ones they'd replaced. Would I be okay for her? Did she still love me? Would we make love? Did she know how much she meant to me all these years?

> Your name is the echo of my heartbeat,
> Your kiss my very breath of life,
> Your face is my sun and my moon and my stars,
> And your precious love my claim to wealth untold.

I fell asleep holding her in my arms.

21
Celebration

Finally we learn that if we are to celebrate, it must be for today alone. This moment—whatever it brings—is the gift. Our celebrations of today create the laugh lines on the face of tomorrow.

Zip-zip! Zip-zip! Zzzzzip!

We were all standing around trying out the zippers on our jackets.

"Goddamn, this is pretty neat! Who invented the zipper anyway?"

"You can be sure it wasn't a V!"

We were like a bunch of little kids in a toy store. Our "going home" clothes had just been issued. We hadn't seen a zipper, buttons, or shoelaces for years. The original khaki prison garb had used buttons, but most of us had gone through them years before. Our subsequent uniforms had been black and then the sickening mauve and red stripes— all with string ties where buttons would have been.

"Come on, Spencer, how many times you gonna lace and unlace those shoes?"

"Hey, man, these shoes are uptown! We're probably modeling the latest in factory fashion from North Korea or some other style setters of the Eastern bloc."

Spence pranced around fully dressed in his new clothes.

"Don't give me any shit, Coffee. I am the Little Black Sambo of Hanoi. I am the grandest tiger in the jungle!"

I'd taught Spence the story of Little Black Sambo when we'd been together at the Zoo years before. We all laughed. Indeed, I think we all felt like the grandest tigers in the jungle.

We had each been issued, to size, underwear, socks, a greenish long-sleeved shirt with buttons, blue cotton trousers, belt, and a gray windbreaker that zipped in front. We all had high-top leather shoes that laced, much like the ones I'd worn self-consciously as a little boy. Each man had also been issued a small black duffel bag. The V had said we could take nothing from the camp, so they must have intended the bags for effect. In spite of the restrictions, most of us would leave with a set of prison clothes, tin cup, and spoon. I would also get my collection of poetry out, dozens of carefully flattened Truong Son wrappers on which I had meticulously printed the many classic poems I had learned. There were many originals by POWs, including a half dozen of my own. I had used impetigo medicine for ink and had sharpened a piece of bamboo for a pen. This collection would be a lifelong treasure for sure.

So far, things had gone smoothly. The senior officer had actually been in touch with U.S. officials to ensure the understanding of how we were to be released. The plan was in accordance with our own internal policy all along: sick and wounded first, then by order of our shootdown.

Our last night in Hoa Lo was one of mixed emotions. On the one hand, the process seemed to be going well, and we were very excited and happy. On the other hand, we were inclined to reserve the expression of that happiness until we were actually airborne over the South China Sea. Our experience with the Communists had taught us that in some ways they were predictable and in other ways capricious. We were still concerned that as our release neared, they would try to capitalize on the momentum of the process to extract further demands, thereby derailing the whole thing. Underlying our excitement was a feeling of anxiety about the more ominous possibilities.

Nevertheless we partied. We used up all the goodies from our packages in a feast of Kool-Aid, marshmallows, and vitamins. We held a joke contest whereby each man told the best joke he'd heard over the years in prison. Of course, I told the wax job joke, but most of the guys had heard it because Tom Storey got so tickled every time *he* told it, he'd already hit almost everyone with it. The jokes were really immaterial, however. We simply laughed at and with each other because everyone was so high.

I didn't sleep much that last night. My mind struggled between anxiety and anticipation. I spent a lot of time just staring up at my mosquito net, pondering it and Old Blue, my threadbare sweatshirt, and my straw mat with the sweat stain outlining my body. I wouldn't miss them, of course, but they had come to represent my way of life here—a sort of weird, foreign lifestyle that in itself was a contradiction.

Military life had taught me to live in increments. Within a given period of time—usually three years at most—I could always anticipate change: sea duty to shore duty, from one location to another, from one squadron to another. Deployment rotation brought change from shore base to aircraft carrier. My optimum career pattern called for change: from one collateral duty to another, from maintenance to personnel, or from training to safety. I had never been stuck with the same commanding officer for more than a year. If I'd ever been dissatisfied, I could always anticipate a change, either in my own status or in my environment. Usually, a change for the better.

Here in prison, the incremental approach to time had been a lifesaver. I had been able to live in six-month bits for seven years, because there was always the chance that within that time frame, political or military developments could have led to my release. It seemed not to matter that anniversary after anniversary had gone without the hoped-for development. I knew that nothing lasts forever, and I had come to realize that even that which seems interminable can at least be perceived differently. Without being able to articulate it, I had become almost subliminally aware that these seven years had been more preparation than ordeal. Somehow I would eventually use my experience to contribute differently, hopefully more significantly, than I would otherwise have done.

Now I realized that I had never really lived here in the prisons of North Vietnam. I had simply been waiting—or, more accurately, processing—there. I had been in a holding pattern because I had maintained faith that my imprisonment was only temporary. And now, it was about to end.

Also on my mind that night was the issue of the whole war and the peace negotiations that had now concluded it. In accordance with the agreements themselves, we had been given copies of the documents that covered all aspects of the accords. I felt gratified that we seemed to have accomplished our objective. During a cease-fire, the most immediate result of the agreements, the North Vietnamese were to withdraw all of their troops from South Vietnam as we withdrew ours. The National Liberation Front, or VC (Vietnamese Communists) as we called them, would observe the cease-fire and enter the democratic political process in South Vietnam.

Best of all, the people of South Vietnam would now have the opportunity to freely determine their own political and economic destiny without a Communist system being imposed by force from the North.

I realized that a "democratic process" in the context of their culture and political tradition would be a far cry from Western standards. It was a beginning, though. It would require patience and understanding on all sides. I felt a sense of pride and accomplishment as well as gratification that my personal sacrifice and Bob Hanson's had in some way helped guarantee South Vietnam that opportunity.

I fell asleep praying, thanking God for my survival and for the promised reunion with my family.

The next morning we were dressed and "packed" by eight. I felt the V, who were even smiling, were genuinely happy for us. They provided a breakfast of fresh hot bread, sugar, some of the malt bars that had become one of our favorites since the food had improved, and hot, strong coffee. A little later we lined up outside cell block seven in a column of two abreast. There would be almost one hundred twenty of us, counting the sick and wounded who were being readied separately.

While we were getting organized, we looked around the courtyard, and there, watching from just above the window ledges of their cell blocks, were our buddies who were to be released in subsequent groups. There were over four hundred of them, many smiling and waving and flashing the ol' thumbs-up, but it was a poignant moment for me. There were many men there whom I dearly loved. We had said our good-byes the previous day, those of us who were leaving, and promised to pass their love on to wives and parents just as soon as we reached the States. But I projected myself into their situation, watching us form up in real clothes to go marching out of this nightmare, leaving them to the iffy specifications of a document signed on the one side by our government that seemed to have fought a two-year war in ten, and on the other side by people who lied, cheated, and reneged. I didn't let myself think about the nervous laughs and preoccupied chatter that would prevail in those cell blocks after the last of our ranks had disappeared through the courtyard gate.

Finally, all was ready. The order was given and we marched out of Camp Unity in military formation, heads held high, as the dream sequence commenced.

Past the foreboding door to Heartbreak Hotel. Past the rose bushes in the main court—now as dry and bare as the morning I had disembarked among them. Through the tunnel at the main gate with the smell of stale piss. On cue the huge metal gate clanged open, calling up the several occasions when a move from another prison had ended with that sound and that smell and the realization: Shit! I'm back at Hoa Lo.

The convoy of several small, rattly buses, each accommodating about twenty of us, wove its way through the morning Hanoi traffic. The sounds were familiar from all the moves back and forth, but now, for the first time, we would see everything; we had no blindfolds. I felt a little weird, like a tourist on a tour bus. The buildings, both business and residential, were even more ramshackle than I had remembered them upon entering the city. I really had to strain to recall my impressions from that morning so long ago.

As usual, the streets were full of people; they were walking, on bicycles, pushing or pulling carts of all shapes and sizes. I had expected to see an air of relief and freshness about these people flowing with the currents on the boulevards and eddying off here and there onto side streets. But they didn't seem particularly relieved. Those who were apparently better informed recognized us as captured American pilots being released, on our way to Gia Lam Airport. Some acknowledged us with stern, thoughtful looks, others with smiles and a wave of the hand. The majority, however, just stared rather passively for a moment, then went on negotiating their way through the crowd. They appeared to be numb, numbed by the war and the constant propaganda harangues; numbed by the recent bombing right here in their capital city; numbed by the years of sacrifice and waiting for good things to happen "after the war." Neither I nor they knew they'd still be at war and things still wouldn't be much better fifteen years after I'd gone home.

The whole time after leaving Hoa Lo, through downtown Hanoi and out through the suburbs and across the Red River on a floating pontoon bridge, I kept thinking, This is it! This is what you've been waiting for. It's happening right now. You're going home, Coffee, you're going home! I thought I was seeing everything in detail, but in reality it was all a blur, a minuscule insignificant part of the overall concept of "going home."

There was the blurred impression of the huge Domier Bridge lying twisted and useless in the swirling waters of the Red River (hence the pontoon bridge). Something that was not a blur, however, as we approached the ramp area of Gia Lam, was the bright, beautiful red, white, and blue flag painted on the tail of the big Air Force C-141 transport plane.

We stopped short of the ramp and entered a one-story building. Between the bus and the building, I looked up to see another C-141 turning on final for landing, and yet a third overhead about to break into the landing pattern. The deep hum of their engines was sweeter than Trong Vi's middle C. We stood mesmerized, necks craning till both aircraft had landed. We found ourselves in a large shabby room that didn't look like it had been on our planned itinerary. The V seemed to be waiting for the last-minute preparations to be made. I had absolutely no idea what to expect, what the process would be, or what kind of official ceremony—if any—might be in the offing. The V gave us more coffee and bread and an orange apiece. By now, though, the butterflies in my stomach were so active, I had no appetite. Come on, let's get on with it! What's the delay? Please God, let it all go as planned.

In actuality the reason for the delay was so the twenty-nine sick and wounded men allowed to leave could be loaded aboard the first plane. These men ranged from guys like Ray Vohden, who had hobbled on his crutch for seven and a half years, to a few of the B-52 crewmen shot down only two months before and in serious condition. Their timing was right, at least. Some were wounded so badly they probably would never have survived if captured three or four years earlier.

Finally, it was our turn. As the release had progressed, filling up the first two of the three planes, Commander Jim Mulligan emerged as the senior officer on our plane. After a V noncom had advised him, he ordered us back onto the buses. It was kind of silly because they just drove us around a corner a hundred yards or so, but what a hundred yards! The waiting C-141 aircraft looked majestic. It gleamed in the morning sun.

I said, "Damn, Sam"—Captain Sam Johnson was the closest Air Force guy—"I never thought I'd call an Air Force plane beautiful, but that one surely is."

The bus stopped on the tarmac just short of a little fenced-off area shaded by a green canvas that flapped casually in the light breeze. A couple of tables had been set up in an L shape, both covered by white cloths. A large crowd of Vietnamese, both military and civilian, stood in a semicircle behind the fenced-off area. I looked for familiar faces from the prison system, but saw none.

On the side of the fenced area next to the aircraft were a couple dozen American military people—air crew and escorts—all in uniforms or flight suits and from various services. They smiled and gave us the thumbs-up signal as we disembarked and lined up again by twos. The V officer behind the closest table was also a stranger. As he called our full names, rank, and service, we moved up in line.

"Commander Gerald L. Coffee, United States Navy." Finally.

I was in a daze, but I thought, that's right, you sonofabitch and don't you ever call me a criminal again.

As I stepped forward, my attention was riveted on the Air Force colonel standing behind the other half of the L table. He was wearing his Air Force blues, wings, ribbons; the first U.S. military uniform I'd seen in years. This guy looked like Colonel Steve Canyon of the comics! He returned my crisp salute.

"Commander Gerald Coffee reporting for duty, sir."

"Welcome back, Jerry."

He shook my hand warmly and firmly with both of his.

Welcome back! I turned toward the aircraft in an emotional daze, tears in my eyes. As I emerged from beneath the canvas shade, an Air Force major in flight suit put his arm around my shoulder.

"Come on, Commander, I'll take you out to the airplane."

Later I couldn't even recall walking the few hundred feet to the tail ramp of the plane. We walked up the ramp, then he turned me over to the care of three Air Force nurses who greeted each of us.

I was overwhelmed. The women were so damn beautiful. Bright, cheerful, smiling. They each gave me a hug, which I returned enthusiastically. Their perfume was heavenly.

The few guys who had preceded me aboard were getting a kick out of watching me with these women. Yes, they were nurses, of course, but they were women first, American women.

I was handed a cup of coffee and a donut and enjoyed watching the others come aboard. We laughed and hooted and hugged each other as each came back and found a seat.

Finally all were aboard and the ramp was raised shut. The nurses checked that we were all strapped in and that we were feeling okay. As the aircraft began to taxi, the laughing and kidding diminished as the anxiety and anticipation set in once more. A moment ago there had been almost boundless joy. Almost! We were still in North Vietnam.

We all seemed to realize simultaneously that what we had all been dreaming of for so many years was about to come true. The end of a long, terrible nightmare, an ordeal that few men know and that, indeed, many had not survived.

The pilot taxied directly from the taxiway onto the runway without holding short, then locked the brakes and jammed his throttles forward. The huge beast rocked and vibrated as the pilot made his final checks of the engine's performance. The roar was horrendous as the brakes were released and we lurched forward on the runway.

At that altitude above sea level and at the existing ambient temperature, I calculated roughly that the C-141 Starlifter would require no more than thirty-five hundred feet of runway to take off—about three-quarters of a mile. It had to be the longest three-quarters of a mile I'd ever traversed. The runway was rough, so we bounced and bumped along, gaining speed slowly. I rocked forward in my seat several times to help the big transport plane along.

The airframe vibrated almost violently as we picked up more and more speed. Soon I felt the nose of the craft tilt upward. The increasing lift of the wings began to lessen the vibration as the last skid and bounce on the runway were left behind.

The wheels clunked loudly into the wheel wells, and the doors closed over them with a hydraulic whine and a loud thump. We were lifting smoothly.

I couldn't believe it.

The pilot's voice came up on the speaker and filled the cabin. It was a strong, sure voice.

"Congratulations, gentlemen. We've just left North Vietnam!"

And then we cheered.

22
Beyond Survival

Is there such a place as home outside of ourselves? Perhaps only in a recollection of the past and a vision of the future. After years of moving toward what I thought was a certain destination, I finally began to see that it was also a new beginning. It is all a process, all a moving toward. Only in fantasy do we think we have arrived.

Although most of that dream flight across the South China Sea was filled with excitement and chatter, I spent at least an hour alone at a small round window in a side access door of the big transport plane. As I gazed out across the horizon, I rested my forehead against the top of the circular frame. The vibration of the four powerful engines and the rushing air coursed down through my body and through my feet to the vibrating deck, completing the mesmerizing loop.

I was aware only that the sky and the sea blended smoothly into one, much as they had on my last fateful flight. Tiny white puffs of cumulus floated separately and serenely below us.

But I was hardly in the present. My thoughts caromed back and forth from the past to the future as I sought comprehension that the nightmare was really over. How had I changed? What would I find when I reached home? All the questions and anxieties and uncertainties of the previous years seemed to be focused in the tiny ten-inch frame through which I was seeing the world anew.

A flight nurse approached.

"Coffee?"

"Yes, Gerald L., 625308, two June, nineteen . . ."

"Sir, I mean would you like some coffee!"

She handed me one of the cups she'd been offering and left me alone again. God, just the taste of hot, black Air Force coffee was heaven.

And heaven was that first deep breath of "free" air as I paused in the open hatch of the aircraft at our destination, Clark Air Force Base in the Philippines. I closed my eyes and sucked it in, an extraordinary sense of relief, strength, and new beginning.

The same colorful, cheering throngs of men, women, and children from the military community there at Clark had greeted the first two aircraft as well. They waved American flags and held up banners: WELCOME HOME! WE LOVE YOU. GOD BLESS. From behind the security lines they called out and applauded wildly as the name of each debarking POW was announced. TV cameras and photographers abounded. We had no idea at that very moment that millions of Americans back home were riveted to their television sets, cheering and weeping as if no distance existed. None of us had anticipated the emotional reception we were receiving right there, let alone nationally.

The senior officer on each of the three aircraft that day was called upon to say a few words on behalf of us all. Commander Jerry Denton, the first man off the first plane and certainly one of the most qualified— he would eventually retire as a Rear Admiral and go on to become a U.S. Senator—stood at the microphone on the red carpet and said it best: "We are honored to have had the opportunity to serve our country under difficult circumstances. We are profoundly grateful to our Commander-in-Chief and to our nation for this day. God bless America."

With the sirens and flashing lights of MP escorts, we were shuttled onto buses from the flight line to the base hospital. The entire route was lined with well-wishers still waving and calling out to us, throwing kisses and sharing our tears of joy and awe. Most of us stuck our heads and arms out the windows, waving back and savoring the wind in our faces like happy dogs.

The hospital wards and hallways were decorated with an array of handmade valentines from the children at the base school. My favorite hung by the door to my room: In bold colored crayon on lined paper and embellished with hearts of all colors was the greeting "I would of give my life for you but I don't think my parents would let me. Happy Valentine's!"

From the moment I took that first step off the airplane, I walked lighter and easier, almost floating across the ground and now down the hallways. The hospital staff had been gearing up for our homecoming for months. Our every wish and need, though simple indeed, seemed to have been anticipated.

Foremost among those needs were the special telephones set up to accommodate our initial calls home. My stomach churned with both trepidation and excitement as I waited the interminable few seconds for Bea to pick up the phone in Sanford, Florida, where she and the children had remained.

"Hello, Babe. It's me. Can you believe it?"

"Hi, Honey. Yes. We watched you on TV when you came off the airplane. I think everybody in America saw you. You look great!"

"I dunno. I'm awfully white and I'm kinda scrawny. But I'm okay. I'm just anxious to get home. Is everyone okay?"

And so it went, oddly routine, with the tentative questions and answers that could go either way. How's your arm, Honey? How are all our folks? Are the kids there? Then the "Hi Daddy's" and "I love you's" and some tears of joy.

Bea sounded great, so natural, her voice exactly as I had remembered it. After I hung up, I paused with my hand still on the phone. How odd: It felt as if I'd just called her from some overnight stopover on a cross-country training flight to tell her I'd been delayed. . . .

Formal debriefings began immediately and focused upon our knowledge of other POWs who were known to have been alive but weren't included on the list released by the Communists. It was essential for our government to press them on every lead we could provide while the releases were in progress. To this day, they still haven't accounted for some men we know to have been alive.

As the debriefings began, I wondered if Tom Storey would finally get to employ his sarcasm of several years earlier as he anticipated filling out his critique sheet: "The exercise was real enough. It just lasted too damn long!"

A task without joy was calling Bob Hanson's wife, Pat, who with no word of hope or encouragement over the past seven years had by now remarried. I also called the families of men with whom I'd become especially close but who were scheduled for later releases. And of course there were daily phone calls to Bea and the kids and a couple to my folks and sister in California.

The reception we had received at planeside was overwhelming but only the beginning. Each returning man was assigned an officer of the same service, a personal assistant who had volunteered for the task of shepherding us through the administrative and medical routines, the debriefings, fittings for uniforms, and overall hospital orientation. The hospital staff had been specially trained to handle whatever peculiar medical or psychological problems we posed. The heavy mesh screens installed over the windows in the homecoming wards made it apparent they were prepared for any extreme—from the paranoid, suicidal zombies they expected to the exuberant, laughing, scratching, wall-banging pussycats they got.

All the things we'd been dreaming about and hoping for and planning for and fantasizing about began to happen. The doctors and nurses and staff were infused by our joy and enthusiasm. Everyone involved was as high as we were.

After the phone calls home and the immediate debriefings, our highest priorities were getting clean and filling up. I'll never forget that first shower: gleaming tile and chrome, lather and rinse, lather and rinse. For a full forty-five minutes I baptized myself in the hot, clear water. Coffee, I said, every once in a while take a cold shower just to remind yourself of the luxury of hot water. Even to this day, I've found that hasn't been necessary.

And the food! The dieticians had prepared bland menus in case we were unable to handle regular food. Those went out the window first thing. While standing in the cafeteria line for our first meal of steak and eggs and cold milk, Ev Alvarez and I found ourselves next to the do-it-yourself ice cream counter. We both polished off double hot-fudge sundaes before the line moved forward.

The four days at Clark included thorough medical and dental exams. New teeth and eyeglasses were provided as needed. With considerable compromise to my aviator's vanity, I put on my first pair of glasses. The sudden realization of what I'd been missing for several years—the detail and clarity—almost knocked me out of the chair. But I still hate to wear 'em.

After probing the stumps of my front teeth with my tongue for seven years, I found my morale boosted into even higher orbit by my beautiful new caps. The dentist had said they'd have time only to fabricate temporary "going home" caps, but they worked around the clock producing the finest permanent caps every subsequent dentist has even seen. The entire dental department was as proud of them as I was.

The guys who were shot down in the later years had told us about miniskirts being in fashion back home, and one of our biggest fears was that we'd get back too late to enjoy them. Luckily, we got in on the tail end of the trend. We hadn't thought too much about how men's fashions might have changed, so that first shopping spree in the base exchange was a real eye-opener. We spent a hilarious evening picking out new outfits. We hooted and slapped our knees as we saw ourselves full-length in polyester bell-bottoms of rust and cranberry, with wide white patent-leather belts with prominent buckles that matched the ones on the shoes. Wide ties and lapels added to the absurdity of it all. I couldn't decide if I looked more like a clown or a Pilgrim, and all of us felt as though we were ready for Halloween.

When I left home in '65, only ne'er-do-wells and hippies had long hair and beards. I would soon have to accept such styles on some of my most respected friends.

If I felt silly in the fashions of the day, that certainly wasn't the case with my new uniforms. Being outfitted with new khakis and blues with wings and ribbons was wonderful. Strange, though, how they all seemed to fit too tightly across the front at first as our chests swelled with pride at being back in the uniforms of our service.

To sleep in a real bed was indescribable. I had huge calluses on my tailbone, on my hips, on the sides of my knees, on my elbows, and on the outsides of my ankles from seven years of sleeping on concrete. The first time I was back in clean, fresh sheets I lay there for an hour, nestling in, turning, rolling to feel the softness on every side of my body. For those four days in the hospital we were surrounded by people who couldn't do enough for us—and we were willing to let them! Especially the nurses. They gave us frequent massages, and being on my stomach in that soft bed with a woman rubbing lotion on my back was unreal.

I shared a room with an Air Force colonel and we were laughing and joking kind of low-key with the nurses while they gave us back rubs. Suddenly, after some silence, the nurse massaging him entreated respectfully, "Colonel, stop that!" More silence. Then again with more emphasis: "Colonel, stop that! I'm not going to rub your back if you don't keep your hands to yourself!" I was afraid he'd ruin it for both of us. He didn't.

Since Bea and the kids had remained in Sanford, Florida, the Navy hospital in Jacksonville, about ninety miles to the north, was designated as my homecoming facility. And during that spring of '73 any military flight, facility, or operation with the code name Homecoming was accorded the highest possible priority. Inbound to the naval air station in Jacksonville, I sat in the jump seat between the pilots of the C-9 as they switched their radio to air traffic control. The copilot turned and handed me the microphone.

"Here you go, Commander. This is your ol' stomping ground. Why don't you check us in? Our ETA is 0410."

My voice wavered just a little as I made my first check-in report in longer than I could remember.

"JAX Center, this is Homecoming three zero inbound. Estimate NAS at one zero past the hour. Over!"

I looked ahead at the familiar sparkling web of sprawling lights that identified the greater Jacksonville area. The clearance came back as crisp and clear as the early morning air: "Roger, Homecoming three zero. You're cleared direct NAS from present position. Descend to and maintain three thousand. JAX weather clear. Altimeter two niner niner one. Report field in sight. Squawk one zero two zero."

I repeated back the brief sequence, after which the controller said, "We understand y'all got Commander Coffee aboard. He's one of ours here, ya know?"

My smile was as broad as the cockpit.

"Right, JAX, that was me just checked us in."

"Well, glory be, Commander. We've missed hearin' your voice up there all these years! Welcome home, sir."

Our senses were like sponges those first days of freedom at Clark. There was so much to see and read and hear and feel and do, and the adrenaline level had been so high that sleep had not come easily. But I'd figured I could catch up on the medivac plane all the way home. As it turned out, in spite of sedation, I stayed awake across the entire Pacific. From Travis Air Force Base in California I called Bea and suggested we not meet at the plane at a cold 4:00 A.M., our scheduled time of arrival.

"Let me just go straight to the hospital and get some sleep, Honey. I'll be in better shape to meet you later in the day."

So she agreed to remain in her accommodations at the Bachelor Officers Quarters and come to the hospital in the early afternoon. And that's the way we did it. Rested and eager, I embraced my sweet Bea as if for the first jelly-kneed time. We chatted about the children and sipped champagne. Then, together on the doorknob outside, we hung the sign lettered by our friends in Sanford: HOMECOMING. DO NOT DISTURB!

Once my general health and state of mind were determined to be "remarkably normal," in-patient responsibilities at the hospital were minimal. Bea and I spent the first ten days together alone—no children, in-laws, or media. At a small quiet resort in Jacksonville Beach we came to know each other again. She shared pictures of the children and told me of their personalities and interests but mostly of how dear and loving I would find them to be. We walked for hours on the shell-strewn beach savoring the blustery winds. To be outdoors again! We talked sadly of grandparents passed on and happily of new nieces and nephews. Our reunion was all I dreamed it would be.

We rendezvoused with the children at a friend's beach house just north of Daytona. My reunion with them, too, was every bit as warm and reassuring as I could have hoped for. With the exception of grandparents and true uncles, all the men in the children's lives who had looked after them were "uncle" somebody: Uncle Gil, Uncle Ron, and so on. After we hugged and kissed and exchanged some welcome-home gifts, routine returned rapidly as seven-year-old Jerry said, "Well, Uncle Daddy's home. Let's go play on the beach!"

Already people were brimming with questions about my experience, and after my first Sunday back at All Souls Church in Sanford, there had been a homecoming reception for me in the parish hall. I was surrounded by the nuns and teachers from the parochial school; there were also friends whom I had known during my initial three years there on shore duty as well as many new friends. Everyone in that hall had embraced and supported my family as their own. The occasion was highly charged, and the words and timbre of my voice reflected my emotion as I responded to the priest's welcome: "I hope you all realize that we are not here just to celebrate *my* survival and return to *my* family. It wasn't just my experience, or Bea's and the children's. It was yours as well. We're celebrating our mutual experience. You have certainly been a part of Bea's daily experience, but you were there with me as well. Each and every day I felt your thoughts and your prayers and the faith that you were keeping in me.

"In fact, faith was really the key to my survival all those years. Faith in myself to simply pursue my duty to the best of my ability and ultimately return home with honor. Faith in my fellow man, starting with all of you here, knowing you would be looking out for my family, and faith in my comrades in those various cells and cell blocks in prison, men upon whom I depended and who in turn depended upon me, sometimes desperately. Faith in my country, its institutions and our national purpose and cause, especially the one in Southeast Asia all those years. And, of course, faith in my God—truly, as all of you know, the foundation for it all.

"This morning I'd just like to thank you so much for your help all those years, for it was our mutual faith and prayers that kept Bea and me going, that gave us the promise of this day.

"In Hanoi we communicated to each other by tapping on the walls between cells. Each night we would sign off with [I tapped on the lectern] GN, good night. GBU, God bless you. And GBA, God bless America. This morning I would say GBUA, for to Bea and me you *are* America."

I soon learned that over the years the media had given Bea fits, starting with the letter "delivered" by Schwinman. Before even contacting her, he had made it public in the defense of David Mitchell, the draft-card burner on trial at the time. The judge had, of course, declared it inadmissible as evidence, but the media had been less discriminating. Before she had even seen it, she was hounded—especially by the Orlando reporters—to confirm its authenticity, to comment on my state of mind, whether her husband was really antiwar. And, when she finally had the letter, "Is that really your husband's handwriting?"

At the official press conference in conjunction with my discharge from the hospital, the first question had been about "the letter" and had my comments reflected my "true feelings"? At that time I was still restricted from saying anything that would jeopardize the release of later increments of POWs: "My wife told you she didn't think the person who wrote that letter was her husband—that I was a loyal, professional naval officer who supported his president and our government. She was absolutely right. The man who wrote that letter was not the man she had known as her husband. At the time he had been reduced to something far less. I have always supported my president and my government's efforts in Vietnam. In fact, my convictions in that respect grew stronger every day that I was a prisoner of war there. At this time I have nothing further to say on that issue."

But the questioning unglued me. How could the poor naive fools attach any credence to anything emanating from a Communist prison? They were so hungry to ferret out a "story," to land a sensational scoop, that they simply ignored that Communists, as we have known them, extort whatever they want by brutal dehumanization and torture. Was all that unforgettable torture for this?

The letter had been only the beginning for Bea. They had pressed her for statements about this or that turn of the war or about statements by our government officials. On several occasions—Christmas or other holidays and when our release was announced—she declined the media request to come into our home "to share the special moments of a POW family" with the public. For this she was berated as insensitive to "the public's right to know."

The ultimate barb was the *Orlando Sentinel*'s headline on the morning following mv return to Jacksonville: "Cold Coffee Returns." The accompanying story was to the effect that Mrs. Coffee had arbitrarily remained in her room at the Bachelor Officers Quarters while her husband returned to a cold and lonely reception of mostly military personnel. Since I had not been interviewed to clarify the situation, the press simply ignored the possibility that we had mutually decided to handle our reunion that way.

The return of the POWs had been perceived as the final chapter of a most painful volume of American history. After years of frustration and disappointment, it was experienced by most as the only positive event concerning Vietnam and it really symbolized the end of our involvement there. The media coverage of our arrival at Clark and of subsequent reunions—proudly uniformed men rushing across the tarmac into the eager arms of awaiting family and loved ones—had been very emotional for most Americans and had magnified the symbolism. We were greeted enthusiastically as heroes. We received an outpouring of letters and phone calls from friends and thousands of people who had worn our POW bracelets. We received offers of new cars, new clothes, and vacation trips for our entire families. We were honored at civic, ceremonial, and sporting events. In my own case, back in Sanford we were honored as Family of the Year. But I knew that had been primarily an expression of the love and high esteem of the local folks for Bea and the inspirational example of strength and patience she had set.

I would soon learn, however, that I had come home far differently than the average Vietnam vet. I was one of relatively few who returned to a national victory celebration. With few exceptions, we had participated in a "cleaner" air war, at least until our capture. The physical brutality and long years of confinement had, of course, taken their toll. But experiences are relative. Early after my return I realized that in some ways my ordeal had been no worse than one intense year in the sinister jungle of South Vietnam, where our men fought an ethereal yet formidable enemy face-to-face, ambush after ambush, with no clear lines of battle and little criteria for victory in a war that would ultimately take the lives of over 58,000 Americans. For an average young GI fresh out of a midwestern high school, it was as devastating as seven years in the Hanoi Hilton had been for me.

I was given convalescent leave to spend time catching up with my family and friends and to adjust to the changes that had taken place both within my family and my country. I felt almost compelled now to seek insight and answers relative to the previous seven years of my life. In the fall of '73, six months after my return and under the Navy's advanced degree program, I enrolled as a graduate student at the University of California at Berkeley to pursue a master's degree in political science. It seemed that all the specific disciplines I had come to especially appreciate in prison—history, international relations, philosophy, politics, even English and psychology—were embodied in political science. I also received two college years of credit, just by examination, for the French I'd learned through the walls in Hanoi. As I have said jokingly many times since my release, I figured if I could survive seven years in a Communist prison, I could survive two years at Berkeley. But I was almost wrong!

The contact with younger students, many of whom had violently opposed the Vietnam war, helped me immeasurably in understanding the division in America over the issue. Aside from my administrative assignment to the Navy ROTC unit, I lived and studied more as a civilian than a naval officer. I learned as much between classes as I did in classes. I began to develop an understanding of the frustration and disillusionment that characterized the average citizen's perception of Vietnam and our involvement there. Initially, when through the course of normal conversation or class discussion my classmates realized I had been a POW for seven years, they were awed and somewhat reluctant to share their honest views about Vietnam. Soon, however, as it became apparent that I was open—almost like a sponge!—to their views and their feelings, we shared openly, usually with mutual respect. I began to temper, if not actually change, some of my own convictions.

Several of my classmates were Vietnam vets who were there for the same reason I was. A few were angry and disillusioned, but most were not. That was before South Vietnam fell to the Communists anyway, in spite of all our effort and sacrifice.

When I completed my master's degree in '75, I was assigned to the Utility Squadron in Hawaii, where I flew jets again and served as executive officer for one year and commanding officer a second. In '77 I was offered the extraordinary opportunity to attend the National Defense University in Washington, D.C. There I furthered my knowledge of international relations, domestic politics, and the economic, historical, and philosophical factors that influence the behavior of nations and hence of national security.

Gradually I began to understand more clearly the many complex factors that caused the divisiveness in our own country about Vietnam. First, there was the very nature of the war itself. It was to a great degree a guerrilla war, with ill-defined concepts of victory. Secondly, there were the seemingly stupid politically motivated tactical restrictions dictated from Washington, many of which resulted in wasteful losses of lives and resources. Prime examples were allowing the VC forces to operate with impunity for many years from their Cambodian bases bordering South Vietnam, and sparing from destruction on the docks of Haiphong Harbor the imported MiGs, rockets, and other munitions that would eventually smash American pilots out of the sky and kill and maim GIs in the jungles of the South.

But it was the adoption of the one-year tour of duty that had the most insidious effect on the feelings of Americans here at home. Families and soldiers were personally involved for what appeared to be a tolerable amount of time. A year's separation—if Johnny comes home—was more of an inconvenience than a real sacrifice. It crippled any sense of commitment or mobilization and undermined the effectiveness of our entire military effort in Southeast Asia. At home, life went on pretty much as usual. In Vietnam, men were sent home at the peak of their combat competence, competence that was frequently eroded anyway by the increasing preoccupation with survival as the tour was coming to a close.

All of this complicated the returning veteran's emotional adjustment. For a year the war had been—and might forever be—the major event in a young man's life, yet no one could understand or seemed to care about what he had just been through. Sis was fretting about her prom dress and Dad was into next weekend's playoff games. How could they understand his feelings when less than two weeks ago he had seen his best friend blown away in a place called Khe Sanh? Or that he felt so relieved to come home alive but so guilty about abandoning the rest of his buddies there when they needed him?

It was all made worse when the version he was seeing on the TV news bore no resemblance to the reality he knew. With so little sense of commitment on the part of the American people, and with so little balance to the media reports, there was a continuing decline in understanding and popular support for the conflict and, worse yet, for each GI's personal sacrifice.

This led to indifference and hostility and much of the difficulty returning vets experienced. Nevertheless, in spite of all this, the vast majority of the millions who served were coming home, putting the experience behind them as well as possible, and getting on with their lives. They pursued education and work, raised families, started businesses, and became stable and productive citizens. They deserve credit not only for putting their combat experiences into perspective but also for overcoming the misrepresentation of Vietnam vets and their difficulties. Even to this day, Hollywood portrays the average GI in Vietnam as a cynical, profane, drugged-out misfit, disrespectful of any authority, with the expedience of survival overwhelming any professional understanding or dedication. There was some of that, of course; our military is a microcosm of society, and there are always those elements of which we are not proud.

But the reality simply wasn't the way it has been portrayed on the screen or the tube. Much of the media coverage would still have us believe that most Vietnam vets are suicidal, alcoholic, wife abusers, or involved in every sniper incident that makes the evening news. Given the nature of many vets' experiences, the vast majority deserve double credit for the incredible emotional and social readjustments they have made.

The most interesting aftermath of the Vietnam war is the emotion and conflict it continues to generate. The Vietnam Veterans Memorial in Washington, D.C., allowed many of the wounds from that national division to begin to be healed. As a nation we have listened to the apology of Jane Fonda for her former activities concerning our involvement yet we continue to be divided as to her intent. Vietnam is a painful chapter in our nation's history that demands resolution before it will finally rest. As a nation and individually, we have sought ways in which to survive the experience and get on with our lives.

One way in which I have done this is through my work. My last Navy assignment was as a public affairs officer on the staff of the Commander in Chief of the Pacific Fleet, on whose behalf I spoke from my experience in the Navy. That was the beginning of my career as a full-time speaker, which I have pursued since my retirement from active duty in 1985. The speech I typically give is an outgrowth of that first sharing with friends in my church upon my return.

As I look at the various positions that have been taken on the Vietnam war, I realize that perhaps many people have not been able to put it to rest because of the depth of the pain beneath whatever rhetoric and rationale we might embrace that has allowed us to handle the trauma and the scars. In my own effort to put it behind me and make up for the lost years, I have had no desire to probe the past—only to share it in a way that is helpful. I have sought more to embrace the future.

The writing of this book has ripped open old wounds and revived sad memories that have tested all over again the lessons for coping that I thought I had learned. They have provided me with a personal clarity regarding the various ways we can handle any situation that defies rational explanation.

Although clarity may provide understanding, it does not guarantee conventional outcomes. Most of us came home ready to live life to its fullest, but we returned to a world of complexity, nuance, and choice, as opposed to the previous years when our duty was clear-cut. The challenges of family and career adjustments, which otherwise may have been routine, were magnified. Lives lived apart so differently for so many years have strained most marriages, many to the breaking point. As one of my comrades put it, "While I was languishing all those years in prison it was like being at idle speed. At the same time my wife was in afterburner; fast pace and high energy, being the best possible mother and father, meeting everyone's expectations. By the time I got out she was ready for idle, but I was immediately into afterburner. The divergence in our pace and priorities was just too great to overcome." Bea and I have not been immune from these pressures which can go deeper than just pace and priority, and we continue to struggle. But whatever happens, through it all, and in spite of the difficulties, as a family we've enjoyed many fulfilling and sometimes idyllic years making up for lost time. Happily, our children, now all grown, I count among my closest friends.

Just as the events of my own life have caused me to reassess the ways in which those years as a POW affected my own dreams, our country, too, is looking anew at how the Vietnam war served our interests and how it did not. I would submit that the issue continues to fester because the final chapter provided by our media does not sit well with most Americans, who at a gut level are uneasy about "the wrong war in the wrong place" and "the first war America ever lost."

The fact is that any war is wrong and is embarrassing to us as citizens of a civilized planet. We have a way to go in our collective journey to enlightenment, but we are moving ahead. I have always measured my own effectiveness as a professional military officer by every day that my country is at peace with honor.

Our country's history is built upon freedom, justice, and human dignity, and fostering those values wherever and whenever it is humanly possible. However inept the succession of South Vietnamese governments might have been, and however inefficiently we might have pursued the war we went to Vietnam at the request of our friends there who were trying to keep from being consumed by Communism.

We did not lose the Vietnam war. We fought to a negotiated agreement, an agreement that the Communists immediately scuttled. That does not change the fact that the tens of thousands of lives lost there and the hundreds of thousands more scarred forever were not in vain. Although we were unable to fulfill our primary mission for the government and people of South Vietnam, millions of people in the other countries of Southeast Asia are thriving in relatively free and democratic societies today because of our ten years of holding action there.

So it wasn't all for naught. Every veteran, every American touched by that noble effort should take pride in the commitment, the effort, and what was accomplished.

Just as the institutions of our society are microcosms of our country, our country is a macrocosm of each individual. It is a reflection of our struggles, our values, our commitments, and our hopes. Our own lives are a continuing journey from which we learn and grow at every bend in the road. As we seek and change, we can simply do our best, sometimes stumbling but always growing and evolving toward the best within us. And so it is with our country. With that as our destination, we can do more than survive. We can go beyond survival to fulfill our vision of a world at peace.

Hickam Air Force Base, Hawaii—November 3, 1988: The huge C-141 Jetstar taxis from the runway complex. It lumbers cautiously toward the ceremonial area in front of base operations. No longer sporting the gull-gray and white paint scheme, this and nearly all the Air Force's planes have been converted to the dusty camouflage pattern that makes even the "heavies" look mean and purposeful. The deep purr of the engines resonates from nearby hangars and from the headquarters building of PACAF, all Air Force units in the Pacific theater.

There is the Commanding General of PACAF himself, along with the Commanding General of the Pacific Army Command, the Commander in Chief of the Pacific Fleet, and Commanding General of Fleet Marine Forces in the Pacific, all with four-star ranks. They stand abreast and erect to honor the approaching aircraft and its cargo: thirty-two Americans who died in Vietnam. Their remains have just been released by the Communist government in Hanoi.

An impeccably creased and polished Marine color guard stands to the flag officers' right, their banners flapping lustily in the moist trades from over the Koolau Mountains. The tarmac is still wet from earlier showers, and heavy laden skies threaten more rain. A troop of ceremonial pallbearers to the left snaps to attention as the big plane pivots around its port landing gear, turns 180 degrees, and bobs to a stop with its starboard side toward the principals and onlookers.

The ceremonial officer in charge nods to the Marine bandmaster, and the band begins to play "The Star-Spangled Banner." The lesser flags of the color guard are dipped, leaving the American flag predominant. The uniformed military personnel salute while I and others present in civilian clothes raise our hands across our heart as the cargo ramp of the plane is lowered.

After a few comments from the Commanding General of PACAF, the offloading of the caskets commences. Although the remains have not yet been positively identified in our forensic lab here in Hawaii, those which are accompanied by dog tags, ID cards, or other hard evidence are announced by name by the officer in charge as the appropriate flag-draped casket is carried down the cargo ramp by pallbearers. As the eighteenth casket emerges, his voice suddenly seems more pertinent: "Lieutenant Commander Robert Taft Hanson, Toledo, Ohio; February 3, 1966."

The pallbearers are smooth and practiced. The casket seems to glide above the glistening puddles that reflect the wind-ruffled flag draped evenly across it. I stare at the casket, but I'm not seeing it. I see only Bob's face—alive and vital, in all the moods of hard work and good times that we had shared during our brief friendship. I am with him again. I am struck by another of life's reminders of the depth of my connection to others. Had Bob survived, the connection would have remained physical, but his presence is nonetheless real. Just as I felt the presence of those at home whose love and prayers sustained me all those years, Bob has returned to remind me that we are all of the same clay and spirit. We are one with each other.

The pallbearers place him down gently next to the others, now lined two abreast before the four senior officers. His sister told me that she had last seen him in December of '65, on his twenty-fourth birthday. He would now have been forty-eight.

Finally, when the last set of remains is in place, salutes and honors are again rendered as the bugler sounds taps as only taps can sound beneath mournful gray skies, some notes lingering in their own echo, some swept away by the wind across the wet ramps and runways and finally out to sea.

Thanks, buddy. Welcome home.

ONE MORE ROLL
Gerald Coffee

We toast our faithful comrades
   Now fallen from the sky
And gently caught by God's own hand
   To be with Him on high.

To dwell among the soaring clouds
   They knew so well before
From dawn patrol and victory roll
   At heaven's very door.

And as we fly among them there
   We're sure to hear their plea—
"Take care, my friend; watch your six,
   And do one more roll . . . just for me."

EPILOGUE
"And Then What Happened?"

When I came home from prison, I thought I was "home free", but I soon found we can get "shot down" more than once in our lives. It's how we bounce back up that counts.

Aiea, Hawaii, September, 2005: Morning coffee always tastes best here on the lanai of my home overlooking Pearl Harbor. Sometimes, as the early sun peeks above the Ko'olau range behind me, a vivid Hawaiian rainbow arches from Ford Island across the shipyard and Hickam Air Force Base all the way to Sand Island beyond the Honolulu Airport. The author of *War and Remembrance*, Herman Wouk, knew this view well, placing Captain Pug Henry's favored Navy pilot son and his new bride on these same heights where mango and avocado trees abound. In those early W.W. II days, verdant waves of sugar cane stretched down the slopes to the edge of the harbor, parting only for the Aiea mill and its surrounding plantation village. But Pug Henry's son was killed in the Battle of Midway, and the mill and the cane are gone now too.

As I look directly to the east across the ravine to Halawa Heights, I see Camp H.M. Smith, headquarters to Commander Pacific Forces, the largest military command in the world. This historical installation use to be identified by a giant white cross illuminated 24/7, erected during the Vietnam War and dedicated as a remembrance of us POWs. Alas, the cross ran afoul of the ACLU, and now in its place is a huge American flag over the smaller black and white POW-MIA flag. They also fly 24/7 and are the first thing I see each morning when my feet hit the deck.

Close aboard Ford Island is the graceful sway of the USS Arizona Memorial, and a mere hundred meters beyond, the Battle Ship USS Missouri on which the Japanese dignitaries signed the surrender documents ending the war; the Alpha and the Omega, so to speak, of that costly conflict.

To the east of the shipyard on Hickam I can almost make out the small monument that marks the revered spot where we POWs first touched American soil as we disembarked from the C-141s that carried us from the Philippines. A wry twist of fate has placed a gas station there now exactly where the plane parked to refuel before continuing on to the Mainland. A mere few hundred meters from there, I can see the VIP ramp in front of Base Ops; the hallowed ground where Bob Hanson and—by now—the remains of scores of America's MIAs have been returned to U.S. soil. This is due to the incredibly challenging and successful work of the highly specialized Joint POW/MIA Accounting Command (JPAC).

Bob would now have been sixty five. Incredible! But equally incredible; that thirty two year old "Red Hot" who zigged when he should have zagged over Vinh City, North Vietnam is now over seventy!

In the spring of 1977, as my one year tour as Commanding Officer of Fleet Composite Squadron ONE (VC-1) at Naval Air Station Barbers Point in Hawaii was nearing an end, I had mixed emotions. My command tour of the Navy's oldest fighter squadron, flying the A-4 Skyhawk had been all any Naval Officer in command could have hoped for; a terrific airplane to fly, loyal and talented troops to lead, and a real-world mission that made a difference. But when I received word my next assignment would be a year's tour at the National Defense University in Washington D.C., or the National War College (NWC), as it was more commonly called, I was thrilled! NWC was a joint college of senior military officers and government managers from all departments, from State to Energy to CIA. The course dealt with all aspects of national defense, and assignment there usually meant you were viewed as a "comer" in your respective service or department.

But I knew a family move to D.C. would almost ensure subsequent orders to the Pentagon. Kim was at the University of Hawaii, Steve and Dave were in High School, and Jerry was comfortable in the elementary school on base. And we all loved Hawaii, and felt we had found a home. So we held a family meeting and decided that they would stay and I would go. It was worth a short family separation—a ten month "school year"— to almost ensure orders back to Hawaii. I would return for the holidays and Bea would visit me in the fall and spring. And that's what we did. The boys joined me for NWC graduation and my official promotion to Captain, then we hit the road together; first to their "home town" of Sanford Florida, diagonally across the USA for white water rafting in Idaho, then to family and friends in California.

Even though Bea had joined me in D.C. as planned and I was home for Thanksgiving and Christmas, the separation was difficult and there developed an emotional separation between us disproportionate to the physical distance. Indeed, it seemed to be a turning point in our marriage. In retrospect, the dynamics of that long seven year separation were beginning to exact its toll.

I was still searching for the purpose of my long incarceration and still dedicated to my Navy career. I had taken myself out of the running for Admiral because all the qualifying assignments for Flag rank would have required more sea duty, longer and more frequent separations from my family. After my return to Hawaii, I served the next three years on the staff of the Commander of the Pacific Fleet as the Air Operations Officer, a job that dealt with real-world issues, required dedication and leadership and sometimes long hours. If I could no longer be flying airplanes off carrier decks, it was a great job.

While still on active duty I had been accepting more speaking engagements; the military, school, church and civic club circuit was increasingly punctuated by corporate groups and trade and professional associations. Given the positive feedback I was receiving, I was led to recall the moment in prison when I realized there must be some purpose to what I was enduring. Now, it was falling into place. The light bulb clicked on; "this is what I'm supposed to be doing! This is the purpose of my ordeal."

Upon retirement from active duty in August of '85, my speaking career took off and we built a beach-front home at Ma'ili on the western shore of Oahu. Morning swims were the norm and the wide steps off our lanai were perfect for watching sunsets. It was an idyllic setting for enjoying one another, our kids, our friends, and our dogs, and for both Kim's and Jerry's weddings overlooking the sandy beach. Bea and I had every reason to be happy, grateful, and optimistic about our future. But all was not perfect in Paradise. Although our marriage had survived tremendous upheaval and trauma, the disparity between our emerging paces and priorities was widening

In early '91 my dad died of emphysema, and Kim's husband, Pete, died of leukemia only a few days after their daughter, Amy, was born. And Bea and I separated. It was hardly conceivable that my marriage of 32 years had survived seven years of uncertainty and separation, but now couldn't survive our being together. Friends were incredulous, and the prospect of disappointing everyone weighed me down. Just as it had been in Hanoi, the guilt and second guessing nearly consumed me, but I sought and found perspective.

The inner conflict, the insomnia, the anxiety attacks, and the sadness for my dad and for Pete took their toll. Though otherwise physically fit, and with virtually none of the usual risk factors, angina attacks while jogging revealed coronary artery disease (I've learned that this is a condition associated with the stress and deprivation of the POW experience). During my prep for the angioplasty the jovial nurse said "I know this is kinda uncomfortable, dearie, but it's better than the 'Black and Decker' through the sternum!" During the procedure the cardiologist was too aggressive, and induced a cardiac arrest. He instantly restored my heart beat with electric shock, but left no alternative to double bypass surgery. I got the "Black and Decker" anyway!

Because I was in good physical shape going in, my recovery was rapid and within three weeks I was traveling and speaking again. This made it easier to conceal a "broken" heart, as Bea and I were divorced in early '92. Years later I would realize that in spite of the odds against it, we had managed to hold our family together another 12 years after my release, affording countless rich experiences and happy memories.

When trying to provide comfort and perspective to friends going through similar travails, I remind them that feeling terrible is normal and to give themselves some slack, that divorce can really be tough, and that mine—to me—was almost worse than seven years in Hanoi. That's perspective!

My speaking program evolves directly from my POW experience and has just been an elaboration of the comments I had made at that welcome home reception in the All Souls parish hall in Sanford right after my return. I always say it wasn't just my experience but our collective experience in that "you (the audience) were there with me every day, sustaining me with your prayers and your love, and your faith in me." I emphasized that "faith" had been the key to my survival; faith in myself, faith in one another, faith in America, and faith in God. I explain with examples how those aspects of faith had sustained me during the prison experience, had continued to sustain me since returning home, but even more importantly, how they can work for any of us even without going through such a horrendous experience. I emphasize that there is really nothing extraordinary about me, and I point out that "I am from you! We are all the same clay and spirit, and we all draw our strengths from the same source. What I say is in all of us!" I plant the seed of belief in each person's mind that had it somehow been them in my rubber-tire sandals all those years, with the same training and orientation going in, they too would have gone "beyond survived" for the same reasons I did, and probably say and feel the same things. Since my message draws from a Vietnam era experience I thought it would surely have a "shelf life", but instead it has proven timeless and seemingly universal in application.

In "reaffirming the invincibility of the human spirit", which is the core theme of my presentation, I frequently speak to young technology engineers, software designers, and sales and marketing professionals who weren't even born when I was shot down, but their positive feedback and enthusiasm are sometimes the most fervent. There is such a dirth of positive messages in our daily environment, so much fear mongering, so much politicization and polarization of every issue, it's no surprise that people respond positively to a message of human goodness and strength, loyalty, patriotism, and faith. This is especially true since the heinous Islamic Fundamentalist's attacks on September 11th, 2001, which crushed out or incinerated nearly 3000 innocent lives. Since then, understandably, we have lived with an underlying, pervasive sense of uncertainty and fear. Faith is the opposite of fear, so it's no wonder people respond to a positive message about faith in their own possibilities. From Singapore to Johannesburg to Anchorage to Rio, to the schools, churches, civic clubs and military units of Hawaii, I have spoken, and will continue to speak so long as people seek faith over fear.

During my studies at NWC, by the luck of the alphabet I was assigned to the same study group as Lieutenant Colonel John Ditto, probably the sharpest Marine I had ever known and possibly even destined for Commandant of the Corps. Early on we developed a warm friendship based upon mutual professional respect and admiration, and a common enthusiasm for sports. Because I was a "geographical bachelor"—anyone attending the University without their spouse, and their were several—John and his wife, Susan, frequently invited me to join them for dinner and weekend outings with their children, Joy (6) and Kyle (2). This afforded a happy respite from my BOQ room at Andrews Air Force Base. John and Susan were Texans and they both exuded that "Texas friendly" charm. When Bea was in town the four of us sampled some of the District's finest eateries together.

After NWC I returned to Hawaii, and John had his squadron command and was in line to take over a Marine Air Group at Cherry Point, N.C. In late January of 1982 I received a call that John had been killed in the crash of a Harrier jet, and Susan had asked that I be an honorary pallbearer at his memorial service in San Antonio, Texas. Of course I could, and I was. It was a sad but fateful reunion.

Susan and her children spent two years in Dallas and then moved to Hawaii where she had many friends from the Vietnam days when she had met John there for his R&R trips from South East Asia. Sometimes she would stay on, modeling and teaching modeling at the same agency and school she ended up buying upon her return. She met and married another Marine Officer, Major Randy Page, hence the founding of "Susan Page Modeling School and Agency", which became Hawaii's premiere enterprise of it's kind. We stayed in touch over the years, crossed paths socially, and sometimes grabbed a lunch carved out of busy schedules. She and the kids thrived in Hawaii.

In the summer of '94, after being out of touch for a year or so, I called her for lunch, but she was leaving for the mainland on a business trip that evening and needed a ride to the airport. Her plane's departure was delayed which gave us some time to catch up. By then I had been single for two years, and her marriage had ended as well. I agreed to pick her up at the airport upon her return. I did, and the rest—so to speak—is history.

We have been together now for eleven years, and were married in 2002. Our friendship and history going back so far has made our union seem totally natural, and the blending of our respective families and friends has enriched each of our lives tremendously. Together we have fixed up this modest, plantation style cottage, adding some lanais to take advantage of the spectacular view; "the house that love built", because it has truly been a labor of love.

We are blessed most of all by our six children and seven grand children. My daughter Kim, the little first grader I left in 1965, never tried to replace Pete, and is a great Mom to her blossoming 16 year old daughter. She is a talented artist. and very active in the local arts community having founded an Art Center and gallery in Honolulu's blossoming Chinatown. Stephen teaches at a Hawaiian Charter School on the Big Island of Hawaii. He and his wife, Sandy, have two boys, four and two, both lovable little rascals. David and his wife, Sabine, both teach in elementary schools in Northern California, and have two of the world's sweetest little girls, five and three. Jerry Jr. ("Well let's hit the beach, Uncle Daddy's home!") practices Behavioral Medicine in Honolulu and his wife, Allana (Dr. Coffee), has a PhD in Psychology. They have creative, curious seven-year-old twin boys. Susan's Joy graduated from Vanderbilt University and worked on Capitol Hill for several years before joining the private sector as Director of Legislative Affairs for the American Public Power Association. Kyle graduated from California State University Chico, and is now a Marine Captain flying F/A-18s out of the MCAS Iwakuni, Japan; the same base his dad flew from on two tours and where Kyle himself went to Kindergarten. He served a combat tour in Iraq last year. Kyle is his father's son, and having known him and Joy since they were so young, it's been easy to love them as my own.

Susan and I remain committed to serving our community and our country. With Susan having had a Marine father, two Marine husbands before me, and now a Marine son, I sometimes wonder how I—a Navy guy—slipped in under her radar. We both write weekly columns for MidWeek newspaper which serves over 270,000 households on Oahu. We are active in military and service organizations, and Susan just returned from a church mission in Africa.

Bea continues to live on the beach at Ma'ili and stays close with the kids and grandkids.

I am committed like never before to the cause of patriotism and Judeo/Christian values, because they are the values upon which our beautiful country was founded and have allowed it to thrive for the past 230 years. They are simply the values that work. We hear so much about "diversity" nowadays, and it is important to honor and respect every person's ethnic and cultural heritage. But our strength lies not in diversity. Our strength lies in "UNITY" (Remember "Unity over Self"?). E Pluribus Unum!—From many, one!"

I am dedicated to victory in America's war against Radical Islamic Fundamentalism. Not only is the survival of America at stake, but also the survival of Western civilization as we know it. Every suicide murderer, every improvised explosive device (IED) that explodes, every drive by shooting in Iraq or Afghanistan is directed not at Iraqis, Afghans, or U.S. troops—although they are the ones who die, of course—but directed at you and me, the American people. It is us the terrorists want to intimidate, cause us to lose faith in our cause, to demand the premature withdrawal of troops from those countries which only now are beginning to taste the fruits of democracy, and freedom from systemic terror. Iraq has been carelessly compared to the "quagmire" of Vietnam. With the anti-war movement gaining more visibility and polls showing lessening support for the war, the only—I say ONLY—valid comparison to Vietnam is that the enemy could defeat our will, and like in Vietnam, win the war "in the streets of America". We must not allow that to happen! Unlike Vietnam or Korea, our war against the evil of fanatical Islamic fundamentalism is not an elective war. It is a war thrust upon us; an essential war that MUST be won.

****

In his book, *Happiness is a Serious Problem*, talk show host and author, Dennis Prager, says "Happiness is directly proportional to gratitude." I agree. And that makes me one of the happiest people I know. I recall having said to myself many times in the prisons of North Vietnam, "Hang on, Babe, there's gonna be better times." But, honestly, I had no idea just how much better they would be!

GB/GBA!